D0554023

HARD PLACES

The American Land and Life Series

Edited by Wayne Franklin

Hard Places

READING THE LANDSCAPE

OF AMERICA'S HISTORIC

MINING DISTRICTS

RICHARD V. FRANCAVIGLIA

Foreword by Wayne Franklin

University of Iowa Press Iowa City

University of Iowa Press, Iowa City 52242

Printed in the United States of America
First edition, 1991

Library of Congress Cataloging-in-
Publication Data
Francaviglia, Richard V.
    Hard places: reading the landscape of
America's historic mining districts/by
Richard V. Francaviglia; foreword by
Wayne Franklin.—1st ed.
        p.   cm.—(American land and life
series)
    Includes bibliographical records and
index.
    ISBN 0-87745-337-3 (cloth: alk. paper)
    1. Mines and mineral resources—
United States—History. 2. Mineral
industries—Environmental aspects—
United States—History. 3. Human
ecology—United States—History.
I. Title. II. Series.
TN23.F73   1991   91-16616
333.76′5′0973—dc20   CIP

Generally, to the people who have had the energy to create America's mining landscape, the enthusiasm to interpret it, and the vision to preserve the best of it; specifically, to Jim Strider of the Ohio Historical Society, who provided encouragement and support; and especially to my wife Ellen, daughter Heather, and son Damien, who never complained when I vanished into America's mining landscapes for weeks at a time or sat in front of the word processor for hours on end, in order to tell this story.

CONTENTS

ACKNOWLEDGMENTS

Many kind people generously provided material and information, and without them this book could not have been written. The list includes miners and mining engineers, professors, mining museum administrators, historic preservationists, staff members of government agencies, and local historians, among them Steve Gordon, Ray Luce, Jeff Brown, Franco Ruffini, Mary Anne Peters, Glenn Harper, and Elizabeth Reeb of the Ohio Historical Society; Harry Metz and Ed Lehner of Bisbee, Arizona; Linda Carrico of the U.S. Bureau of Mines; Donald Hardesty and Earl Kersten, Jr., of the University of Nevada at Reno; Tom King, preservation consultant in Washington, D.C.; David Nystuen, Dennis Gimmestad, and Homer Hruby of the Minnesota Historical Society; Ronald Reno and Mona Reno of Silver City, Nevada; Mary Ann Landis of the Eckley Miner's Village in Pennsylvania; Shaune Skinner of Columbus, Ohio; Barry Price of Fresno, California; Jane Jenness and Joe McGregor of the United States Geological Survey; Carolyn Torma and Paul Putz of the South Dakota Historical Preservation Agency; Tom Green and Merle Wells of the Idaho Historical Society; Dale Martin and Fred Quivik of the Klepetko (Montana) section of the Society for Industrial Archaeology; Kent Powell and Phil Notarianni of the Utah Historical Society; John Reps of Cornell University; Michael Hansen of the Ohio Geological Survey; Marjorie Tibbetts of the Orton Hall Geology Library at the Ohio State University; historian David Myrick of Santa Barbara, California; Pat Cummins, Bill Lawson, and the able staff of the Mahoning Valley Historical Society; the good volunteers of the Lincoln County Historical Society in Pioche, Nevada, and the World Museum of Mining in Butte, Montana; Larry Tanner and Tom Vaughan of the Bisbee Mining and Historical Museum in Bisbee, Arizona; Julia Costello and Judith Cunningham, mining history consultants in Mokelumne Hill, California; the National Park Service's Paul Gleeson (Anchorage) and Robert Spude (Denver); Professor Duane Smith of Durango, Colorado; Patrick Andrus at the National Register of Historic Places; Warren Wittry of the Missouri Mines State Historic Site; David Gradwohl of the Iowa State University; Pat Nolan and the able staff of the Hagley Museum and Library in Wilmington, Delaware; Robbyn Jackson and Eric DeLony of the Historic American Engineering Record: Ivan Tribe of Rio Grande College; William Edwards and Mack Gillenwater of Marshall University; Sherry Kilgore of the Tennessee Historical Commission; Professor John Webb of SUNY-Albany; Professor Arnie Alanen of the University of Wisconsin at Madison; Paul Wannarka of the Tower-Soudan historic mine in Minnesota; Ed Nelson and the fine staff of Iron World at Chisholm, Minnesota; Sheppard Black of the Ohio University Library at Athens; and fellow landscape geographer and friend Gary Peterson of Bountiful, Utah. Dr. Margaret King at the University of Maryland, Baltimore, suggested the American Land and Life Series as the appropriate place for the ideas in *Hard Places*. In subtitling this book *Reading the Landscape* . . . I acknowledge ecologist May Watts' seminal work of the same title.

FOREWORD by Wayne Franklin

That stone lieth there yet, and much burnt slag nigh.
—Egil's Saga

In this fascinating excavation of America's mining landscapes as cultural and historical resources, Richard Francaviglia shows
us how to read the massive physical evidence that mineral extraction
has left all across the land. More than anything else, his book reveals
the order in the disorderly landscapes of Hibbing or Bisbee, the coal
towns of Pennsylvania or the gold towns of California. These are places
that have a distinct and distinctive history. And they reveal, if we look
aright, the causes that have brought them into being and the technical
and social processes that have given them their shape. The rubbish
that clutters the ground and even the very holes that penetrate it become, under Francaviglia's gaze, an impressive historical text.

The resulting insight gives a new clarity to the settings within
which the almost mythic events of American mining took place. In
reading the physical and social remains of this industry, we thus are
led to recall more elusive remains. These include the stories that miners, especially those seeking precious metals, have always told or have
had told about them. Like all toilers in elemental scenes—the sailor is
another—miners enjoy an almost primitive communion with the durable things of the world. We finger their stories as if they were gold
coins.

Some are tales of enormous finds and great, sudden riches. But mining is richest of all in a kind of narrative slag that clutters its old
haunts. Particularly when the minerals sought after are precious, it is
not so much the durability or desirability of gold or silver that creates

the value of ores; it is instead the enormous waste of labor and resources and lives that gives the ores their worth. They are valuable
because it costs so much to find them and haul them out. Hence for
every single tale of success the memory of the culture is filled with
hundreds of tragic or tragicomic stories of failure.

The very earliest voyagers to the New World brought with them the
"mineral men" whose job it was to locate and prove and bring back the
promising ores of future wealth. Most of them, alas, were masters of
golden tongues more than of metallurgy. In the far North, Martin Frobisher, thinking that samples taken home earlier had yielded good
gold, loaded more than a thousand tons of worthless rock onto his ships
in the late 1570s. Pointlessly refined at great cost in England, it ultimately was used to pave roads there. (Frobisher should have listened
to the writer who chronicled his second voyage. Speaking of the na-
tives of the regions they visited, that man wrote with considerable
irony that "their riches are not gold, silver or precious drapery, but
their said tents and boats, made of the skins of red deer and seal skins;
also dogs like unto wolves.")

The absurdity of importing American rock for paving English roads,
or looking for European-style riches where Europeans could see only
poverty, suggests a larger absurdity in the lore of mining. Nor was
that theme symptomatic merely of the early centuries. A few tales
culled from the most recent of North America's big "rushes," in the
Klondike, may help to underscore the madness almost endemic to it.

Not a hundred years ago, in July 1897, a filthy ship called the *Excelsior* flung ashore at San Francisco a former YMCA instructor named
Thomas Lippy who carried in his grip two hundred pounds of gold that
neither physical fitness not clean living but simple luck had let him
find. Two days later the *Portland*, a ship once seized by the government of Haiti for running ammunition to rebels there, and then by the
United States for smuggling opium and illegal Chinese immigrants,
docked in Seattle with two tons of the same bright hope aboard.

Times were tough in Seattle and indeed the nation then, and word
spread quickly about the strike in the Klondike. Individually and in
groups, people quickly began to fall into the absurd patterns that mineral wealth has often stimulated. The mayor of Seattle, W. D. Wood,
was in San Francisco when the *Excelsior* docked and immediately
wired his resignation to the city council back home: "I resign. Stop.

Klondike. Stop." It was his plan to charter a ship with money taken in from would-be miners, then use the surplus to buy cheap supplies that he later would be able to sell (to those same men, of course) at vastly inflated prices once the ship with its cargo and captive passengers and ex-mayor arrived in the North. Wood's first mistake was buying so many supplies that the *Humboldt* was too cramped to allow his passengers any space for their own gear. Only when they threatened to lynch him even before the ship left San Francisco did he reconsider.

That did not end the *Humboldt's* troubles. When it reached the clapboard illusion called St. Michael's, on the Yukon delta, it found no dock to unload its goods on. As if in exasperation, it simply shuddered to a halt. The ex-mayor put his passengers to work building a new vessel that with a touch of nostalgia he dubbed the *Seattle Number One*. But soon the men nicknamed it the *Mukluk*: for it had the shape of a shapeless Eskimo boot and Seattle lay too far behind them now, for the ex-mayor's simple magic words to work here.

Ahead of them lay the Yukon. It led back through vast, cold spaces to no source known to these European interlopers. They were intent on doing what their kind have always done with these places so far from home—reduce them to coin of the old realm by seeking out the portable commodities their eyes can detect as they miss all the strange, silent beauty around them. Almost as soon as the *Mukluk* plashed down into the Yukon, the river froze against its stammering bow. So the Klondike was lost to the miners, who were anything but miners yet, for 1897 at least. And these men, icebound as none of them had dreamed of being while the vision of gold warmed their minds in San Francisco, once more turned against their captain. At first, it was a matter of names again. A shantytown called Woodworth, after Captain Wood and Captain Worth (commander of another iced-in vessel), had sprung up around the two sad hulks. The men called it Suckerville instead. And soon their wit had a sharper, more dangerous edge. As their own supplies ran low, Wood began to sell them his (which, of course, their money had paid for once already), and at prices that further chilled the shivering miners. With a kind of verbal justice, they once more talked of mutiny until he agreed to sell them all they needed at—for he still remained mayor of a city afloat—yes, *Seattle* prices.

With the spring and the crushing thaw of the Yukon River, the miners turned once more toward their increasingly loathed goal. They reached Dawson City 314 days after they had left San Francisco. Any of them that had the wherewithal quickly turned around and booked passage home; the rest lingered on, too poor and too wearied by hope to turn back. But eventually they gave up, too; none of them ever made a strike. Ex-captain or ex-mayor or whatever he was, Wood himself already had slipped away from Suckerville and walked back alone to St. Michaels in the frigid winter. One may fancy this as a kind of justice. He was not to be Klondike-rich either.

Thomas Lippy, who started it all, *did* make a fortune. He dug two million dollars' worth out of his claim on Eldorado Creek before releasing it for cash in 1903. He and his wife, Salome, sailed around the world, then went to a high house in Seattle, where sunshine played on the muraled ceiling of the ballroom through ornate stained-glass windows. He was generous, probably too generous, with his many relatives—and with many charities, including the YMCA, the Methodist Church, the Anti-Saloon League, the General Hospital, even the pompous-sounding Fund for Seattle's First Swimming Pool. He also held many honorific positions, including the presidency of both the YMCA and the hospital, and at one point was the Pacific Northwest's senior golf champion. But Lippy's money was being spent unwisely in these years. First came the crash of 1929, and then his death in 1931. His widow, who inherited nothing from him, lived on $50.00 per month through the 1930s; their home finally housed the followers of Father Divine.

All in all, some 100,000 men set out on the trail to Dawson City. Maybe a third of them reached their destination, and only half of that group actually looked for gold. Perhaps 4,000 found some, but only 300 of them ever became rich. Twenty of those fortunate souls were lucky enough to die rich. It was the labor of all the luckless ones that bought them prosperity; it was the failures of so many that paid for the few successes. With other minerals, the results were not often so dramatic. But the extremes of the Klondike expressed well the mine-madness (as the eighteenth-century Virginian William Byrd II termed it) that afflicted the European imagination as it sought to comprehend—and thus control and exploit—the potential resources of the continent.

These are a few of the other tailings that mining has left on the landscape of America. They share with those so well studied by Richard Francaviglia an oddly compelling beauty beneath their repulsive surfaces. In human terms, as in the landscape, we have scattered much ruin to mark our values in this New World.

INTRODUCTION

Across the country, mining has left its legacy on the land-scape. Wherever miners worked and ores were processed, one can see the results of their labor: mining communities huddle amid barren piles of waste rock, and mountains of tailings and slag are left in the wake of historic milling and smelting activity. Even places that were mined a century ago often show the results today, whether or not many of the more ephemeral traces of man's activities, such as buildings, remain. Mining, in fact, creates its own distinctive topography that may last for thousands of years.

Mining landscapes may not be especially pretty to look at. Nevertheless, in the course of extensive travel around the United States over the last thirty years, I began to see that these mining landscapes had a story to tell that is every bit as interesting as the story of those beautiful places featured on calendars—perhaps even more interesting. *Hard Places* is based on the premise that there is as much meaning and value in places that we are not supposed to revere as there is in those that are venerated. Mining has been one of the most important occupations in shaping the character of the United States; its greatest monument, the cultural landscape it has created, remains underappreciated. This book attempts to correct that oversight.

I must, from the outset, admit my fascination with the landscapes of our mining areas. The more one comes to know them, the more they seem to possess a kind of repellent beauty. Words like "stark," "austere," "wasted," and "forlorn" are often used to describe them. Ironically, the same words were used to describe the desert regions a century ago, yet the desert has become one of our more appreciated landscapes today. In retrospect, it is no surprise that my first interest in the landscape of mining country developed in the deserts of California and Nevada; over the years, it has extended to mining country everywhere, including the forested hollows of Ohio's bituminous coal country, the rugged ore dumps hidden among clusters of birch and pine trees in Michigan's Upper Peninsula, and some of the grandest manmade topography on earth—the blood-red tablelike escarpments of Minnesota's Iron Ranges. In all these mining landscapes, one can catch glimpses of the desert created by industry.

Over the years, I have searched out these landscapes, directing my travels and vacations into all the major mining districts of America. As a historical geographer, I found myself with a collection of several thousand color slides and photographs, a file cabinet full of historic reports, and notebooks filled with anecdotes of old-time miners. As a college professor, I have often used mining landscapes to illustrate various themes in historical geography, including ethnicity and landscape change. As a professional planner and historic preservationist, I found myself with the challenging task of advising decision-makers and the public about preserving historic mining landscapes. Above all, I found myself with an untold story to tell about the landscapes of mining country, and how they have evolved.

There is a process to reading the landscape, and it begins with observation. This first step, seeing the landscape, is often followed by an appreciation of its content. Only after putting what we see in context can we make effective decisions about what—if anything—is worth saving. Those of us who are involved with the interpretation and preservation of mining landscapes know that it is difficult work, for most people have been conditioned to avoid thinking about, much less preserving, places that are unattractive, unpleasant, or controversial.

Hard Places assumes that much of the mining landscape has been created by the application of technology to solving the problem of extracting minerals from the environment. Historians of the mining industry tell us that there are several types of mining: placer, underground hard rock, surface or open pit, and (more recently) various types of leaching operations. Each has a different, and equally important, impact on the landscape. This book also assumes that there are messages hidden in the landscape; these go beyond technology to include some of our deepest cultural values.

One of them involves the most profound distinction in human culture: gender. In this book, the term "man" (as in manmade landscape) refers to humankind, but it necessarily also refers to the works of males. As we shall see, the primary shaping of the mining landscape is a manifestation of male identity. Mining has traditionally been "man's work," and no amount of neutralized language can—or should—conceal that fact. *Hard Places* speaks of inherent conflicts in values, and the terms "man" and "nature" are as fundamentally different as male and female.

Some readers may question the scope of this interdisciplinary book: why so many types or techniques of mining are discussed; why so many minerals (metal ores and coal mining) are considered; why such a long period is covered; and why so many mining locations are described.

Hard Places recognizes that various types of mining have differing visible impacts on the look of the landscape, that all types of mining are interrelated, that mining may affect any particular area over a rather long period, and that all mining areas are interconnected (that is, parts of a larger sociotechnical system). The definition of "historic" is adopted from the historic preservation community, which normally sets a fifty-year limit: that now includes landscapes created before World War II. As an overview of the mining industry and its visible impact on places, this book emphasizes commonalities and similarities. Just as miners and speculators often drifted from one type of mining (and mining location) to another, I shall show the visible interconnections among all of America's major mining districts in as comprehensive a manner as possible. *Hard Places*, therefore, is not meant to be a definitive study of any particular mining district, but is intended to serve as an introduction to the rich and complicated subject of mining landscapes and how to understand them better.

The full story of mining's legacy on the landscape will be told only when the visual tapestry of each mining district is documented, a task begun only in the last twenty years by historical geographers, historical archaeologists, and historic preservationists—most of whom know little about each other's interesting work. Their particularistic studies, and the works of many local historians, greatly helped in writing this book, for it is through the efforts of local historians that those processes that led to the shaping of the landscape were recorded. My personal library contains about two hundred relatively obscure books and reports written by local historians in the mining districts that I have visited over the last three decades. Some are cited in the notes and listed in the bibliography.

By visiting all of America's major mining districts over the last thirty years, I have come to appreciate their complexity and their individual uniqueness, while being impressed with their striking similarities. Mining country bears a certain brand, or visual identity, and that is what *Hard Places* is about.

This book also strives to address and correct several misconceptions about mining country, among them the popular notion that all of our important historic mining areas are "western," that is, located west of the Rocky Mountains; the idea that mining areas are new (or young) and had short histories that ended when the boom went bust; and the naive notion that historic mining landscapes are not threatened by development.

Addressing such popular misconceptions led to the structure of this book. Each chapter treats a major area.

1. Identification: what are the visual clues that tell us that an area has been mined, and how do we read the landscape to find them?

2. Interpretation: what major processes or forces have shaped the landscape of mining areas?

3. Perception: what do mining landscapes mean to us as Americans? Answering this question sheds light on why mining landscapes are surprisingly long-lived and have become part of the iconography of our popular culture.

It is hoped that *Hard Places* will help provide a framework that will enable all students, professional and amateur alike, to see, understand, and critically evaluate the American landscape.

1

READING THE LANDSCAPE

LANDSCAPE AND IDENTITY

*If any of my readers have a lingering romance about a mining
country, or the "golden sands" of California, they should travel
through the "southern mining counties." Mining, at the best, is a
sort of devil's or ghoul's work, on a landscape. . . . The gay wild
flowers of California are dug up as if with fresh-made graves; the
rounded outline of hills is broken with heaps of dirt, . . . the
whole landscape is a picture of roughness, waste, and desolation.*
—*Charles L. Brace*, The New West

By the time these words were written in 1869, mining had
transformed landscapes from Georgia to California. Its distinctive visual signature was usually described by Victorian era travelers and
writers as a necessary outcome of civilization. In the next half century,
the impact of mining would become even more profound, and the interpretation of its landscapes more polarized: mining country would be
described on the one hand as mephitic and infernal, and on the other
as prosperous and productive.

As we join the countless interpreters—among them novelists, miners, and mining engineers—who have described the visual character
of mining country, we, too, shall find fascinating visual contrasts: what
seem to be temporary, flimsy shacks lean in the shadows of nearly
indestructible industrial artifacts such as huge skeletal headframes
and concrete ore bins; rugged piles of fractured rock and colorful waste
dumps are scattered amidst serene natural beauty; and everywhere
our eyes are drawn both to details—such as the wheels of an abandoned mine car or a cluster of wildflowers—and to the mega-scale features such as tailings ponds and towering ore dumps.

Our impressions and interpretations of what we see in today's mining landscapes are aided by early written descriptions, historical maps,

and vintage photographs that show just how change has occurred. By comparing them to what we see today, we learn that change is one of the constants of mining landscapes. Few places provide better laboratories to study the ongoing effects of society on nature, and vice versa, than our mining districts.

A look at the distribution of historic mining areas (fig. 1) shows that mining is a very widespread activity in the United States. Moreover, certain regions are characterized by very specific types of mining—for example, iron mining in the Iron Ranges of the upper Midwest and lead-zinc mining in the Tri-State mining area. Mining is a rather localized activity in some places, while in others it may affect very large regions. In all of these places, mining has had a profound effect on the economy, environment, and people: landscape is the visual legacy of this relationship.

In mining country, aggressive industrial forces have been unleashed on the land, but not without very high costs. Nature has responded to man's hasty intrusion by annihilating miners, either individually or in groups of several hundred at a time, through falling rock, fires, and explosions underground. On the surface, torrents of water and debris have swept over settlements downstream in areas ravaged by mining activity. The costs of mining and settling such places are measured in terms of both human life and dollars. The statues, markers, and monuments to lost miners are one of first indicators we have that man and nature, as well as labor and management, have traditionally been adversaries in mining country (fig. 2).

These are hard places—where making a living is tough work, where mining interests continually struggle to outwit both nature and the economy, and where miners are constantly transforming the earth, from bedrock to boulders, from rubble to dust. In mining districts, nature and man seem to stand in stark contrast to each other as gaunt headframes, dusty tipples, huge waste dumps, and flimsy boom towns struggle against relentless erosion, sliding earth, fires, and floods.

For more than 150 years, the landscape of mining country has been described in terms of more familiar—or softer—landscapes. Two of the most common are the agrarian countryside and the pristine wilderness. In comparison to greener or less industrialized places, which we like to think show a kind of harmony, mining landscapes are viewed as industrial and exploitative. We see machinery as having invaded the garden, as Leo Marx describes it.[1] In a culture that has yet to develop an aesthetic appreciation for industry, such comparisons lead to the inevitable juxtaposition of positive and negative metaphors and images. Landscape becomes the battleground on which comparisons are drawn.

Viewed in these terms, one of the greatest visual contrasts in our culture occurs as one crosses the line from agriculture to mining: if one were to drive from, say, the fertile, verdant, orderly Mormon villages in the West into the nearby smelter smoke–filled canyons where copper mining towns are crammed onto the hillsides in seeming disarray, the dichotomy would become apparent. The West has a way of juxtaposing contrasts, one of the greatest being found in Lincoln County, Nevada, where only about a dozen miles separate the flat, bucolic checkerboard order of Panaca, a Mormon farm village, from seemingly chaotic, densely settled Pioche, a silver mining town perched in a canyon/hillside setting.

In reality, much the same mining-agrarian contrast can be found in other parts of the country: mining seems to occupy marginal, often hidden, locations. Eastern Ohio comes to mind. Here, in contrast to the open agrarian cornbelt countryside of trim farmhouses and huge barns that most people associate with Ohio, we find coal mining communities packed into deep hollows barely wide enough for a row of miners' houses and a railroad siding. On a regional scale, mineral resources do not seem to coexist with large-scale agriculture, the ultimate example being found at the northern margins of the Midwest, where some of the world's richest copper and iron mining deposits are hidden at the edge of the seemingly endless woods that mark the northern edge of the cornbelt.

What appears to be a pattern of mining resources being tucked away from productive farmland is partly a result of history as well as geography: in Iowa, Illinois, and Indiana, coal mining may have once thrived in what appears to be forest and farmland today. We can see this if we look more closely at the landscape for the telltale signs of mining. Reclamation efforts have, in some places, replaced mining landscapes with prosperous crop and grazing land; in the heyday of mining, one would have found gritty, dusty coal mining towns where the banging of conveyors and machinery was almost constant.

When compared with the rolling farmland or wilderness so preva-

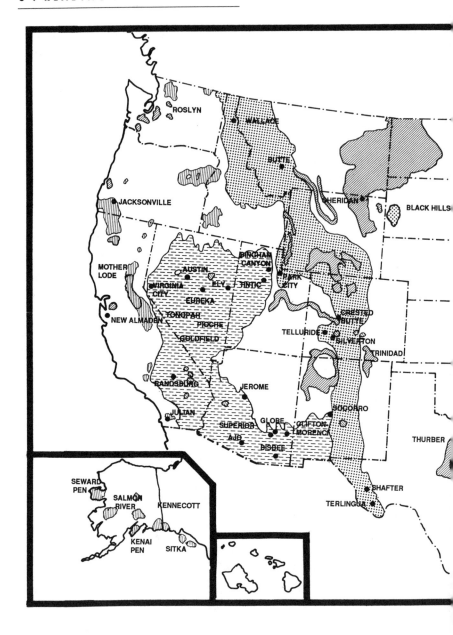

1. A map of the United States showing historic mining areas reveals how widespread, and diverse, a legacy mining has left over the last 150 years. Map by the author.

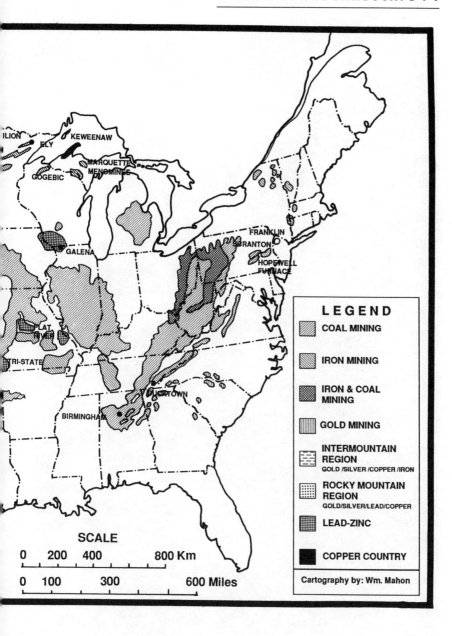

LEGEND

COAL MINING

IRON MINING

IRON & COAL MINING

GOLD MINING

INTERMOUNTAIN REGION
GOLD /SILVER /COPPER /IRON

ROCKY MOUNTAIN REGION
GOLD/SILVER/LEAD/COPPER

LEAD-ZINC

COPPER COUNTRY

Cartography by: Wm. Mahon

SCALE

| 0 | 200 | 400 | 800 Km |

| 0 | 100 | 300 | 600 Miles |

ILION
ELY
KEWEENAW
MARQUETTE
MENOMINEE
GOGEBIC
GALENA
FRANKLIN
SCRANTON
HOPEWELL FURNACE
FLAT RIVER
TRI-STATE
DUCKTOWN
BIRMINGHAM

2. Adversaries: a statue of a miner commemorating a mine disaster near Wallace, Idaho, symbolizes man's struggle with nature in mining country. 1983 photo by the author.

lent in our imagery of scenery, mining country does not fare well. Many observers are likely to characterize mining country as a ruined, hellish wasteland, but we must remember that such was not always the case: to Americans in the late nineteenth century, mining activities symbolized progress and man's domination over nature.[2] We had a lot of unsettled country that still challenged us, so most Americans accepted mining landscapes as inevitable. Today the barren landscapes around the copper smelter town of Ducktown, Tennessee, and the huge gob piles that stand like purplish slate-gray ranges in the valleys of coal country from Wyoming to West Virginia are often contrasted unfavorably with their nearby natural settings; yet they, like all landscapes, are neither good nor bad, but simply historical artifacts and symbols.

Mining has created some of America's most distinctive—and interesting—landscapes. To understand and appreciate them, we can put ourselves in the position of a traveler who notices that something peculiar happens to the look of the land as he or she approaches a mining district. Very likely, the landscape begins to take on a more heavily used look as the signs of mining become visible: abandoned mine workings and tailings may veneer or deeply scar a landscape that usually has a more barren or worn look than the surrounding countryside (fig. 3). The density of structures increases, and unfamiliar types of buildings and structures may appear. Company houses often dot the landscape or cluster in small settlements interconnected by roads and frequently paralleled by railroads whose roadbeds are stained in the exotic rainbow hues of mineral oxides or smelter slag. Very close to these settlements—usually in the immediate background—stand impressive mine buildings, headframes, and ore bins.

This is mining country, where the repetition of standardized architectural and engineering features contrasts with the natural setting, where the works of man are strewn in the form of surreal topography and the sculptural, rusting ruins of machinery, and where social class and status are imprinted in the ethnic and visual geography. Industry forms the backdrop for all human activities: machinery and buildings designed to extract, process, and ship mineral wealth stand shoulder to shoulder with small mining communities.

Some of these communities have peculiar names proclaiming their functions (Smelterville), their social position (Jiggerville), or their ar-

3. Mining results in distinctive landscapes. Communities often cluster near the mines, which are marked by large conical ore dumps, as seen in this view overlooking Tonopah, Nevada. 1989 photo by the author.

chitectural quality (Tintown). Some commemorate the men who located or founded them (Warren, Wallace) or the geological factors that led to their creation (Galena, Rhyolite, Telluride, Leadville). Some are named for other fabled places of mineral riches, such as the ancient Arabian gold mines at Ophir mentioned in the Bible. Others, especially those created by large companies as part of a system of mining communities, may have far more mundane designations by numbers, such as the Berwind Coal Company's towns numbered 1 through 40 in southwestern Pennsylvania.

Although we tend to think of individual towns when mining areas are mentioned, these towns exist in the context of mining districts that may cover dozens or even hundreds of square miles. Mining districts are created when and where sufficient prospecting and mining activity has occurred to warrant the establishment of specific laws and agreements governing the mining of ores and the designation of claims. Thus, the establishment of a mining district occurs at the end of a period of pioneering and marks the beginning of serious colonization or settlement. The ultimate shape of a mining district is determined by the distribution and character of its ores and by the attitudes and backgrounds of the miners who initially develop and settle the place. The district is a kind of political-geographic reality that defines all economic and social activity.

Mining districts, therefore, provide a context or larger setting for individual towns with which they are popularly identified: for example, the Comstock District's Virginia City, the Warren Mining District's Bisbee, the Bullfrog District's Rhyolite. These mining towns are part of a larger tapestry of everyday working industrial landscapes—the actual fabric of mining districts.

READING THE LANDSCAPE

In this book, "landscape" refers to an image of a place based on its visual characteristics. The term "scenery" is similar, but usually has pleasant bucolic connotations at odds with the terms that many observers and travelers use to describe mining landscapes: "ugly," "abysmal," and "revolting." Mining landscapes may be ugly to some (conservationists or romanticists, perhaps) or beautiful to others (mining engineers or some artists, perhaps), but that is beside the point. For most people who live in them, these landscapes have simply become part of the visual framework of ordinary everyday life.

We now know that many factors—not the least of which are education and income—help determine how people interpret the landscape. Therefore, categorizing mining landscapes as "wasted" involves a kind of elitism that prevents us from understanding what such places really mean to the people who create and inhabit them. So, rather than place value judgments on the mining landscape, I shall simply describe it and at times compare it to the landscapes of the surrounding countryside. Doing so will serve two purposes. First, it can help us determine what is distinctive about the landscapes of mining districts; second, it may help us to see these landscapes in a new light—as creations that reveal deep-seated cultural attitudes toward land and life.

A number of observers have a disdain for mining towns because such places seem temporary, ephemeral, or artificial. However, even though many mining towns developed rapidly, they have rich histories that reveal much about the tenacity and faith of their residents. The typical mature mining district may now be more than a century old—these places are often truly historic. Their landscapes frequently reveal interesting change and offer a rich legacy of architectural design. Thus, historic preservation has become an important factor in the landscape we see today. We can call upon the hands-on methodology of historic preservationists—and their experience in the interpretation of historic sites and structures, their evaluation of such properties (often through the National Register process), and their expertise in the treatment or stabilization of historic properties—to help us read the landscape of historic mining districts.

The historic mining landscape consists of many visual elements—among them the natural and manmade topography, vegetation, structures and buildings of several major types (commercial, residential, institutional, and industrial), the way they are situated with regard to each other, the street pattern, the transportation lines, and the property parcels. Mining-related activities often concentrate many features into a relatively small space, and reading their landscapes usually requires that we consider the architecture of a particular building or structure in the context of other buildings and features. The most applicable methodologies for studying this type of landscape, therefore, are those derived from urban design and landscape architecture.

One of the earliest and most effective methodologies for reading the landscape of communities was developed by Kevin Lynch, who coined the term "image of the city."[3] The "imageability" of places was determined by looking at five rather simple aspects of the landscape.

1. Paths—the channels along which people move: these may be streets, railways, or sidewalks.

2. Edges—the boundaries that separate two different environments, such as walls, creeks, and escarpments.

3. Districts—medium to large sections of a community, such as neighborhoods, that have some common identifying character.

4. Nodes—strategic points into which the viewer can enter, such as a major street intersection.

5. Landmarks—visually prominent forms in the landscape, such as monuments and objects, that are external to (not entered by) the viewer. Their scale may vary from a miner's statue to a large mountain.

These five elements must be considered as a pattern if we are to make sense out of the typical urban landscape. A landmark, for example, can only be interpreted in light of its relationship to the paths from which it is seen or the district in which it is found. Thus, reading the landscape is very kinetic: it accounts for the necessary motion that is involved as we experience places by moving through them, as workers, shoppers, or travelers. Throughout this book I shall use terms derived from Lynch and others to help decipher the complex landscapes of mining districts.

Mining landscapes are visually complex. In fact, there may be too much information in any one vista for the viewer to comprehend without being confused, unless he or she is selective. Therefore, it is advisable visually to diagram the scenes we see.[4] Diagraming can involve actually making quick sketches, but it also refers to abstracting what one sees. For example, instead of being captivated by the wealth of details such as the architectural trim of buildings, which is a common tendency, we might simply first observe the overall shape and size of buildings and structures. Are they rectangular or square? Are they all of the same shape, or is there variety? This naturally leads to comparisons: are these the same size and shape as buildings we have seen in other places? If not, how do they differ? Omitting certain visual information can help us see basic patterns and relationships. Simplifying or abstracting what we look at may, paradoxically, help us better understand the complexity of what we see.

Architectural historians Frances Downing and Thomas Hubka invite us to "diagram" historic scenes in order to understand them. They remind us that diagraming a scene involves abstraction and visualization (in which ideas are distilled and given visual form) and intensification (which isolates a particular visual characteristic or set of visual characteristics). It permits us to reduce information to a manageable form. Step back, for example, and observe only how a mining community sits with regard to its surroundings, forgetting about its individual buildings: is it in a valley or on a hillside?

The visual character of any particular mining district is determined by many factors, all of which can be fitted into three fundamental categories.

1. Site: the configuration of the natural or manmade topography and vegetation.

2. Layout: the way in which the streets are laid out and property parcels are arranged.

3. Architecture: the design of the buildings, structures, and objects.

SITE

The lay of the land and the quality of its vegetation set the scene, for it is these factors that we tend to notice first. Is the site flat or mountainous? Forested or desert? These seemingly natural factors help to determine the shape of the settlement and activities and are also important because they are in turn shaped by the aggressive actions of miners. Few places have been so extensively—some say brutally—modified by human activity. The site may be terraced or otherwise excavated to make room for human activities such as housing and mining.

A look at the sites of several mining districts helps to illustrate this interrelationship between site and the character of place. Perhaps the setting of Tonopah, Nevada, will seem familiar, for it is similar to many hard rock mining areas throughout the intermountain West. Tonopah, located in western Nevada, was the site of an early twentieth century silver mining boom that gave renewed life to the economy of the state. A mining engineer looking for work in 1905 tells us that "Tonopah was a busy place, mines going full blast and street crowded with people."[5] Although it is much quieter today, Tonopah is still an important place, for it is the county seat of Nye County and the largest community on the long, lonely highway between Las Vegas and the Reno–Carson City area. A panorama of the town (see fig. 3) reveals a rugged, mountainous site with very sparse vegetation, mostly widely spaced desert shrubs such as sagebrush and creosote bushes.

Looking more closely, we see that the town itself is located at the break in slope where steep, knoblike mountains rise from the desert floor. It is best to read this landscape, and the landscape of any mining area, with a United States Geological Survey (USGS) topographic map in hand, for this can help us interpret relationships that the eye alone might miss (fig. 4). These topo maps provide a way of determining the relief and show all the major settlement features in relationship to it.

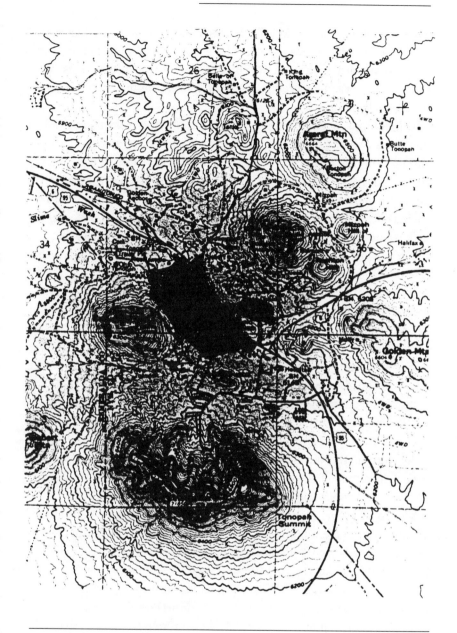

4. *The 1982 USGS topographic map of Tonopah, Nevada, shows that all features in the mining district are developed with regard to the topography and the location of ore bodies; note that the mines are located on the hillsides, while the downtown commercial area is located on gently sloping land between the rugged hills.*

The map reproduced here tells us much about the historic landscape, for it shows older mines and railroad grades which date to the town's boom years in the first decade of the twentieth century. This topographic map was prepared in 1982 and shows the important features in today's landscape.

In reading topographic maps, we see that three colors are used to document the site itself: all land relief features are shown in *brown* through the use of contour lines (which connect points of equal elevation above sea level, just as the ring in a bathtub shows water level above the bottom of the tub); blue, which shows all hydrologic features such as streams and lakes; and green, which shows all wooded areas and certain growth such as scrub forests and orchards; areas that are not green are meadows, grass, desert, or cleared land. The landscape around Tonopah shows as desert.

By consulting the photographs and the topographic map of Tonopah, we see that several prominent mountains, including Mount Oddie, Ararat Mountain, and Mount Butler rise abruptly to reach elevations of about 7,000 feet. These mountains almost surround the community, which is actually situated in a pass or flat just a little over 6,000 feet above sea level. Visually, these mountains are the prominent reference point for all activity. Situated at approximately middle distance, they are landmark features that frame the viewer's perspective. In Tonopah, as in many western mining towns, much of the commercial area is located on the lower slopes, the residences are scattered on the lower elevations of the mountains, and most of the mines are located on the steep slopes above town.

The topographic map reveals a tremendous amount of information about the settlement patterns. Black is used to depict all features such as buildings and most political boundaries, red for roads and certain lesser land boundaries, pink for all urban areas, and purple for all revisions done since the last map edition. This last category means that topographic maps can help us find new or altered areas quickly, a great help in an active mining district. They also remind us how active man is here, for the brown contour lines are often altered as mining shapes the landscape, as shown on the topographic maps.

Looking at the cultural features on the Tonopah map, we see that mining activities are closely related to the topography. The town is almost surrounded by mines that are situated on the hillsides above the town. The railroad (which shows either as a stylized railroad track symbol or as a dotted line where only the abandoned grade remains) follows the contour lines as closely as possible in order to reduce the gradients while reaching the mines. The topographic map shows the abandoned railway line entering Tonopah from the northwest; this railroad, the Tonopah & Goldfield, was abandoned in 1947, but its roadbed still shows on the map and in the landscape. Like most historic mining towns, Tonopah is a place where heavy work was done. Looking at the topographic map, we see that man's activities are carefully designed to overcome, or at least take advantage of, gravity.

So far, I have described how Tonopah fits into the natural topography. Looking a bit more closely at the map, however, one can see the hachure marks (short, closely spaced parallel lines) that indicate another type of topography—the manmade ore dumps and tailings that are so characteristic of mining country. The dumps below the Ohio Tonopah mine on the north slope of Brougher Mountain are a good example, clearly shown on the topographic map. Mine dumps are usually located very close to the mines, which are shown as small square symbols with white square centers. The mine dumps consist of material that has been removed from the underground workings of the mines. Material on these dumps may be waste rock of no value at the time it was mined or lower-grade material that was stockpiled in hopes of rising prices.

In the Tonopah mining area, the mining claims show as a complicated pattern of properties that adjoin each other in the most highly mineralized area (fig. 5). The silver mines in the Tonopah district are of the deep shaft type. Their mine tunnels may be framed or supported by stout wooden mine timbers, called stulls, although many hard rock metals mines require little support if the rock into which they are dug is solid enough. Once underground we would find ourselves in another world, a stygian labyrinth of shafts and tunnels that connect the underground workings with the working face of the mine.

There are three main types of underground mines: drift mines enter the ground horizontally (often from a hillside opening; in slope mines the tunnel descends at a pronounced angle; and shaft mines are often vertical, or nearly so, requiring the use of lifts. The type of mining access technique depends on the geology and the position of the ore body with regard to the surface. Christopher Davies describes these

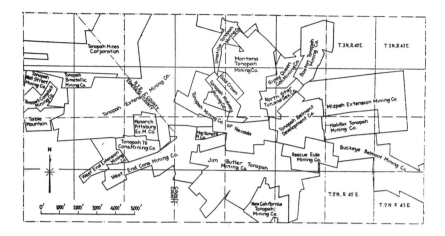

5. *The typical mining district is a crazy patchwork of mining claims that have complicated irregular boundaries, as this 1924 map of Tonopah, Nevada, shows. From H. D. Budelman, reprinted in Carpenter, Elliott, and Sawyer 1953.*

"bible black" shafts and tunnels as "Dark Inner Landscapes" whose "underground horizons are traversed with alacrity, if not without pain, by miners as if walking the streets of a familiar village."[6]

Miners themselves are ambivalent about this dangerous but embracing subterranean world. More than a century ago, a mining engineer asked: "Can poetry be associated with the deep pits and long underground galleries in which the never ending rows of timbers look like processions of ghosts and the masses of fungus remind you of strange monsters without form, yet of most fantastic shape, as seen in the dim light of the lamps which gleam like stars in the heads of the miners? The answer is yes."[7]

As we shall see, the underground world of paths and nodes—tunnels and galleries—serves to separate mining populations by class and gender. For every feature we see above ground in the landscape of light, there is an arcane, almost mythical world beneath the surface that was only revealed to the public by vivid descriptions and somber candle-lighted (or lamp-lighted) photographs. The layout of underground pathways is dependent on the geological structure and prevailing methods of ore extraction. A diagram of the underground workings (fig. 6) simultaneously documents the operation and awes the unini-

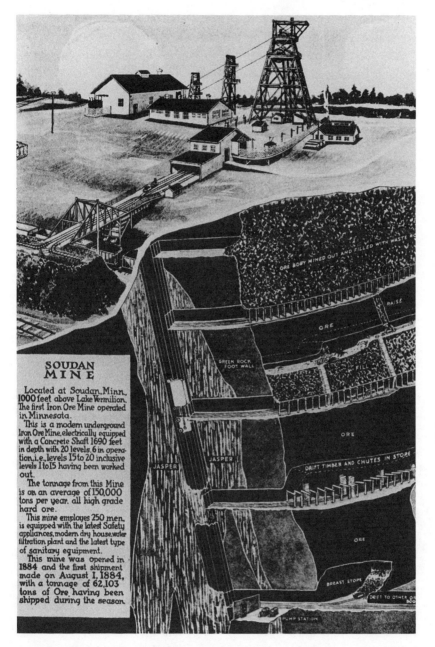

SOUDAN MINE

Located at Soudan, Minn. 1000 feet above Lake Vermilion. The first Iron Ore Mine operated in Minnesota.

This is a modern underground Iron Ore Mine, electrically equipped with a Concrete Shaft 1690 feet in depth with 20 levels, 6 in operation, i.e. levels 15 to 20 inclusive levels 1 to 15 having been worked out.

The tonnage from this Mine is on an average of 150,000 tons per year, all high grade hard ore.

This mine employes 250 men, is equipped with the latest Safety appliances, modern dry house, water filtration plant and the latest type of sanitary equipment.

This mine was opened in 1884 and the first shipment made on August 1, 1884, with a tonnage of 62,103 tons of Ore having been shipped during the season.

6. The underground workings of the Tower-Soudan mine, in Minnesota's Vermilion Range, are reached by a nearly vertical descent. The State Historical Society operates it as a site that helps interpret the varied iron mining history of the region. Minnesota Historical Society.

tiated, for the typical mine is a three-dimensional system resembling several street maps placed on top of one another.

Mrs. Hugh Brown has described the three-dimensional models that geologists made of the Tonopah mines:

> On thin glass slides, some of which hung vertically in slender grooves while others lay horizontally on tiny cleats, all the workings of the mine were traced to scale in colored inks. When you stood in front of the model and looked into its serried sections, you seemed to be looking into the earth with a magic eye. Here the shaft dropped down from level to level through ore and country rock; here were "drifts" and "stopes" and "crosscuts" with every foot of ore blocked out; and here you traced the meandering vein, noted where it petered out or widened into richness unimagined as it continued into regions still unexplored.[8]

This description reveals that the mental map of the miner and mining engineer must be translated or demystified to be comprehended by the public. The mine model's being so enthusiastically described by a woman is ironic, since women usually were not permitted to enter many mines, lest they bring about calamity, according to the superstitious male miners who dominated underground in most, if not all, mining districts.

Actually, most residents in mining districts never see the underground world of the miner, which is usually reached by what Davies calls the umbilical link—the connection between mine workings and the mine head at the surface. Depending on the kind of underground mine, miners may enter through a portal much like the entrance to a tunnel or by descending a vertical (or steeply inclined) mine shaft in a cagelike elevator suspended from a cable in order to reach the deeper horizontal tunnels or stopes, along which ore cars are trundled to the working face. It is often a damp, poorly illuminated world consisting of tunnels that run horizontally at different levels, perhaps 100 feet apart vertically, so that the levels may be numbered the 2,300 level, the 2,400 level, and so on, indicating that they are 2,300 feet and 2,400 feet below the mine opening, respectively.

It is the underground world we most associate with the term "mining"; but, beginning in the early years of this century, another type of mining became common as large earth-moving machinery became

7. *1958 USGS topographic map of Bisbee and the Warren Mining District,*
Arizona, reveals the location and layout of all communities, including the
original town of Bisbee, and the early twentieth century satellite community
of Warren.

*8. Mining creates some of the most spectacular topography on earth.
Arizona's Lavender Pit is an excavation more than 500 feet deep and about a
mile in width; like other open pit mines, it is characterized by a series of
benches or terraces, each about 50 feet high. 1981 photo by the author.*

available. This is open pit or surface mining, which often removes huge
amounts of overburden to expose and then remove the entire ore body.
Open pit mines are among the most spectacular manmade features on
earth. They may be more than 1,000 feet deep and several miles
across, their shape and size being dependent on the configuration of
the ore body that was extracted.

The topographic map of Bisbee, Arizona (fig. 7), provides a good
example of an open pit mine—the Lavender Pit, which resulted from
the removal of Sacramento Hill, a remnant of which can be seen at the
northern edge of the pit. Like most large open pit mines, the Lavender Pit consists of a deep, scooped out depression surrounded by a series of benches about 50 feet high, a classic landscape of subtraction
(fig. 8). Railway lines or roads run along these benches, permitting the
removal of ore and waste rock. A sign at a view point near the brink
of the pit proclaims that "a total of 380 million tons of material was
removed from the Lavender Pit. This total includes 94 million pounds
of copper ore, 111 million tons of leach material, and 175 million tons

9. The development of an open pit mine creates huge features of accretion because overburden must be dumped nearby. Here we see the remains of the historic (1902) community of South Bisbee, Arizona, completely surrounded by overburden and mine dumps. 1990 photo by Damien Francaviglia.

of waste rock—roughly 3 tons of waste and leach material for every ton of ore."[9]

All of this material had to be put somewhere. The topographic map shows three major areas of deposition or accretion typical of open pit metals (especially copper) mining: the overburden or waste rock consists of coarse material blasted away from the barren (nonmineralized) zone above the ore body in boulder-size fragments; most of it was hauled to the west edge of the pit and dumped in a huge ridge that completely surrounded the old mining community of South Bisbee (fig. 9). Second, the material to be leached or piled up so that water could be passed through it to remove further concentrations of copper was configured into a huge leach dump. This is located to the east of Bakerville. Called Leach Dump No. 7, it is an impressive topographic feature consisting of a rather heterogeneous mixture of rubble and coarse, shattered porphyry (fig. 10). At the top of leach dumps one finds shallow ponds or cells into which acidic water is pumped. By percolating through the leach dump, this water becomes rich in cop-

10. *Originally built in an idyllic setting, the early twentieth century mansion of a copper company president is now dwarfed by Leach Dump No. 7, one of the most impressive topographic features in Arizona's Warren Mining District. 1990 photo by Damien Francaviglia.*

per, which is then precipitated or deposited in metallic form on scrap iron.

Third, we find another very impressive accretionary topographic feature on the Bisbee map—the tailings pond located south and west of Black Gap on the Espinal Plain. Here tail water (a mixture of pulverized, slimy, nonmetallic wastes from which virtually all metals have been removed) is piped from the copper concentrator and dumped into huge ponds to evaporate. These tailings dams consist of terraces about 20 feet high: each successive terrace indicates the front of an earlier dam. In the arid and semiarid West, these tailings features are often seen for miles. Their light-colored, symmetrical terraces are a distinctive feature found in the West from Montana to Arizona (fig. 11).

In the Tri-State lead and zinc mining area, one finds huge piles of chat (the sandy wastes from the concentrating process) that tower above the landscape. These are local landmarks, and their steep-sided conical shape is diagnostic of the region. Though usually off-limits to most activity, it is not unusual to see them serving a recreational pur-

11. *Tailings ponds or tailings dams are a distinctive topographic feature in the semiarid western United States. They result when tail water is impounded to evaporate after the concentration process, leaving white terraced topography. 1981 aerial photo by the author.*

12. A chat pile looms above the surrounding countryside near Bonne Terre, Missouri. These piles are the sandy wastes from the lead and zinc mining process. They are slowly disappearing as the chat is used for other purposes, such as construction, but in the meantime they serve as a recreation spot for dune buggy/ATV operators: note the tire tracks. 1989 photo by the author.

13. Piles of waste slate and other rock separated from coal are locally called gob piles or culm banks. They form an impressive, austere backdrop for the company mining town of Revloc, Pennsylvania. 1989 photo by the author.

14. The smelting process also creates distinctive topography. This jet-black hill of slag stands near Montana's Anaconda smelter. 1989 photo by the author.

pose as the drivers of dune buggies and All Terrain Vehicles (ATVs) tackle their steep slopes (fig. 12). In coal mining areas, one finds characteristic gob piles or culm banks that loom behind communities, creating localized topography that helps to define the geography of any particular district (fig. 13). These consist of the slate and other waste rock that is separated from the coal and piled onto the land.

In most metals mining districts, one finds another very important manmade topographic feature—the slag piles or slag heaps that result when ores are smelted. In many cases, they outlast the smelters themselves and remain as dark, steep-sided hills or tablelands. Sometimes deeply eroded, these vitrified, cindery wastelands are common at smelter sites. Slag is usually deposited as molten dross or waste from the smelter and can be identified by its glassy consistency, which testifies to the high temperatures involved in its creation. In some places, such as Anaconda (Montana), Clifton (Arizona), and Eureka (Nevada), slag dumps are prominent landscape features (fig. 14).

A look at the topographic map legend shows several categories of mining-related topographic features—some of the most important in-

National Mapping Program

Topographic Map Symbols

National Large Scale Series

Provisional edition maps ————————————————
New or replacement standard edition maps ————————
Standard edition maps ————————————

SURFACE FEATURES

Levee . . . .

Sand or mud area, dunes, or shifting sand . . . . . .

Intricate surface area . . . .

Gravel beach or glacial moraine . . . .

Tailings pond . . . .

MINES AND CAVES

Quarry or open pit mine . . . .

Gravel, sand, clay, or borrow pit . . . .

Mine tunnel or cave entrance . . . .

Prospect; mine shaft . . . .

Mine dump . . . .

Tailings . . . .

15. The symbols used to identify features associated with mining include mine openings as well as manmade topographic features such as tailings and ore dumps. USGS.

dicators of mining at a particular location (fig. 15). The first four categories are subtractive, that is, they depict areas from which ore and other materials have been removed. The crossed picks, once the standard symbol for any kind of mine, are used by the USGS to show a quarry or open pit. These features are usually excavated into bedrock. The crossed shovels are used to depict features where man has removed gravel, clay, or other unconsolidated materials. These are usually not ores, but are either aggregate materials used for construction and building trades or fluxes, such as limestone, that may be used in the smelting process. Mine shafts and prospects, which usually have distinct openings, are shown as small crosses or half-shaded squares.

Accretionary features are also indicated on the maps. Mine dumps are shown using the distinctive brown hachure marks, while tailings are shown on the standard edition maps by beige, tightly hachured, scabby symbols, and on new or replacement maps by finely dotted beige symbols. On provisional maps, which do not yet show the symbols, "mine dump" or "tailings" is written in. Where tailings are impounded behind tailings dams, as in Bisbee, the USGS maps show them in a beige horizontal pattern on standard and new edition maps, while designating them as a "tailings pond" on provisional maps under the "surface features" category.

Site, then, is one of the fundamental aspects used in reading the landscape. The natural topography can be classified into several basic categories (flat-open, flat-dissected, hilly, mountainous, etc.), and the manmade topographic features (such as open pit mines, ore dumps, or slag piles) can be described in terms of the types of processes that created them (extractive or accretionary) and their overall form or morphology (conical, tabular, irregular). Some of the more spectacular features may be incised hundreds of feet into the landscape or tower hundreds of feet above it to form landmarks. Each of these topographic features in a mining district is the result of specific processes; they do not result by accident and are surely one of the most distinctive aspects of the site—the topographic framework in which all activity is developed.

Similarly, the vegetation of the site can be documented through mapping; vegetation cover can be plotted on a density continuum (barren, sparse, scattered, grassy-shrubbed, scattered trees, forested) or in a mosaic of plant communities by percentages of species (e.g., sagebrush-pinyon pine or birch-alder-maple). The distribution of vegetation, when correlated with specific topographic features, can help to reveal interrelationships. This is especially important in mineralized areas where the underlying bedrock geology may exercise strong control over the types of vegetation found on various sites.

The distribution of vegetation in mining areas is further complicated by mining activities, for a close look at the site may reveal that certain plants have an affinity for—or are at least able to tolerate—the manmade topographic features: the birch trees that grow on the huge culm piles of slate and waste rock in Pennsylvania's anthracite region and the yuccas that grow on smelter slag in the southwestern copper mining areas are examples of such adaptations.

LAYOUT

In mining districts, the distribution of towns, the pattern of roads and streets, and the layout of property parcels within those towns further define the character of place: are the communities clustered, scattered, or located in any particular pattern? Are these communities laid out in regular, geometric patterns or helter-skelter—or do we find a number of different patterns in a mining district? And what about the individual property parcels? Are they large or small, geometric or irregular? As we look at landscapes, we see that such abstract spatial arrangements are revealed by features such as fence lines, roads and streets, sidewalks, and electric/telephone lines.

Two examples will suffice to show how the layout of a mining town influences the look of the landscape and the feel of the place. These two are selected from Arizona's Warren Mining District, where we were introduced to aspects of the mining-related topography. Looking at the settlements of this mining district, we find about a dozen communities, including "Old" Bisbee. In this, the oldest settlement in the district, we find very little or no regularity to the street pattern, which consists of two main roads—Tombstone Canyon and Brewery Gulch—that parallel the twisting course of two streams. The town's center is situated at the confluence of these two streambeds. The side streets follow con-

16. *The topographic setting and layout of a mining town help determine its character: Bisbee, Arizona, is crammed into a canyon setting and is characterized by small, uneven lots. This view of B Hill is framed by curving Main Street. 1990 photo by Damien Francaviglia.*

tour lines where possible, and small, irregularly shaped property lots dot the hillsides. Except for a couple of very small parks, there is virtually no open space in downtown Bisbee. The community has a crowded, urban feeling (fig. 16).

The town of Warren, on the other hand, has a geometric layout: the community is laid out in a fan-shaped pattern, down the center of which we find a large open space called the Vista Park (fig. 17). The property parcels are much larger than those in Bisbee. In contrast to Bisbee, Warren feels more orderly and serene. This is intensified by the prevalence of large trees and well-watered lawns in Warren, but it is also a result of the lower density of buildings. As we shall see, the feeling of a mining town relates to whether or not it was deliberately laid out, and how and by whom it was developed.

Mack Gillenwater, a student of mining towns in West Virginia's Pocahontas Coal Field, has found four major layouts: grid, linear, converging, and fragmented.[10] This general typology could easily be adapted to other mining districts. We should first ask ourselves whether a town

17. In contrast to the stereotyped hard rock mining community, the site and plan of Warren, Arizona, give the town a spacious feeling; this view of Vista Park shows that the feeling is accentuated by shade trees. 1980 photo by the author.

is developed more or less evenly around its commercial core (centripetally nucleated); is strung out along a line such as a canyon or railroad (linear); is developed along a series of intersecting routes much like a starfish (convergent); or has developed as a series of smaller nodes that are rather scattered (fragmented).

The character of a mining district is determined by the layout of the towns within it and their spatial relationship to each other. Thus, we can say that the communities of the Warren Mining District are roughly distributed in a Y-shaped pattern from Bisbee on the north, to Warren on the southeast, to Don Luis on the southwest. This district has a convergent urban morphology. Moreover, the district's individual towns are located in diverse geographic settings—some in canyons, others in open locations at the upper reaches of broad alluvial fans—and are themselves diverse, no two towns being laid out exactly alike. Thus, the layout of the district is characterized by diversity; a variety of townsites with individual identities are interconnected by main roads that weave around the prominent features of the natural and manmade topography.

ARCHITECTURE

Architects use the term "built environment" to refer to the buildings, structures, and other constructed objects in the landscape. As in studying other urban communities, we need to consider the design or style of an individual building as well as its relationship to other buildings in order to understand the architectural character of mining towns. We may be tempted to consider the form or shape of a building or structure first, but the function that it serves is equally important. One should first ask the question: what happens in this building? What purpose(s) does this building serve? By doing so, we soon realize that there are two basic architectural forms in the landscape: those that house people and their varied interpersonal activities such as shopping and worship—these are called buildings; and those that people use only for the processing or storage of commodities, for example, a conveyor or headframe—these are called structures and are among the most interesting, but poorly understood, features in the landscape.

COMMERCIAL ARCHITECTURE

Because so much of the character of mining towns is dependent on the business buildings downtown, the commercial core is a good place to start looking at architecture. In a mining town, as in all towns, main street serves both as a functional marketplace and as a stage setting for the drama of everyday life. This drama is likely to be very cosmopolitan and very intense, especially in a booming mining town. It is on main street that we can learn much about the development of the mining district, for it may be home to dozens of competing businesses or dominated by the single store of a large company.

Students of western town design have noted that the main streets

18. Mining town main street: is mining town commercial architecture more ornate than that of nearby agricultural towns? Here at Shawnee, Ohio, we see a row of false-fronted buildings with elaborate overhanging porches, a design characteristic of coal mining towns in the Hocking Coal District that boomed between 1880 and 1920. 1989 photo by the author.

of mining towns differ from those of agricultural towns. Historical/geographical studies of the main streets of small towns in northeastern Oregon by Barbara Bailey, and more general regional observations of western mining town commercial districts by Randall Rohe, reaffirm that specialty stores and saloons are more common in mining towns.[11] Historian Duane Smith describes the profusion of signs and the generally thriving activity that characterize mining communities in the Rocky Mountains.[12] In southeastern Ohio, the coal mining towns of the Hocking Coal District are differentiated from other types of towns by the presence of distinctive overhanging porches along main street that were "well adapted to the dense settlement and intense social environment of mining communities" (fig. 18).[13] The construction of these elaborate porches coincided with the boom period of mineral production in the region, the 1880s to the 1920s.

A visual/architectural intensity is evident along the main streets of many historic mining towns—especially those boom towns that were

19. Building form is related to function. Prostitution was common in mining towns, especially those that were not under the control of a single company. Here we see a row of cribs in the former red light district of Butte, Montana. 1989 photo by the author.

developed by speculators—and this helps contribute to the urban feeling that is often portrayed by novelists. Mining town commercial districts also differ from those in nonmining towns in another important way: they are usually larger than those in agricultural towns or nonmining towns of comparable size because the population of single males actively engaged in extractive industries is more dependent on others for the provision of basic goods and services.

Thus, the commercial district of a mining town would offer a wide range of services. Depending on its isolation, its stage of development, and the views of the authorities, it might also have a red light district. Although prostitution was a fairly common activity in many American communities, mining towns are often notorious for their houses or cribs. As we look at the streetscapes of places like Butte, Bisbee, and Tonopah, we can see a distinctive architecture: buildings whose facades are arranged into a series of narrow bays, each of which has a doorway to the outside (fig. 19). These cribs were the rooms out of which prostitutes operated. They do not appear on most historic walking tour maps (though there are exceptions, such as Tonopah in Nevada, a state that still permits prostitution in some places). One can determine their location by clues in today's landscape, by looking at police records that list the addresses of apprehended prostitutes (changes in town politics often centered on "cleaning up" vice), or by discussions with local historians and old-timers. Often, the signs of prostitution are difficult to find in today's landscape, for buildings associated with vice are tempting targets for those who hope to clean up the town. Therefore, the clues may be almost archaeological; in Bisbee's Brewery Gulch, for example, the only remains of the cribs are rows of closely spaced steps leading to vacant, weed-grown lots. The same may be true of saloons, breweries, and other seamy buildings. What we see in the landscape is always the result of prevailing social values.

What we see is also affected by the ways we are taught to observe. In looking at the main street of a mining town, for example, we may be tempted to focus on what merchants tell us we should look at: the facade. This, the most enticing part of the building, is meant to attract the attention of the passerby, but should not distract us from asking several important questions about the rest of the building. What is the overall shape of the building? What is it made out of (and is the material used on the facade the same as on the rest of the building)? What type of roof does the building have? How is the building situated with regard to its neighbors? And last, what is its architectural style?

Most of the buildings we see on the main street of a mining town (or, for that matter, any historic American town) are what Richard Longstreth has called the one-part or the two-part "commercial block."[14] In reading the architecture of main street, however, we want to be certain not to focus on individual building style to the point where we lose sight of the character of the streetscape itself. That character is determined by the ways in which the buildings relate to each other as well as by their individual morphology.

For our purposes, most commercial architecture can be classified by looking at six aspects of its design.

1. How it sits with regard to the street or sidewalk: assuming that most buildings are rectangular, is its streetscape elevation—its facade—the shortest or longest dimension of the building (that is, is the

building's facade wide or narrow)? Is the building front flush with the sidewalk or set back from it?

2. The number of stories or floors: this may be determined by looking at window openings or doors and outside staircases.

3. The shape of its facade when viewed from the street or sidewalk: is it wider than it is tall, roughly square, or taller than wide?

4. The relationship between solids and voids: is the facade at street level mostly window, mostly wall, or about half and half? Is the upper level mostly wall or does it have windows? And what about the rest of the building? Do its side and rear elevations have windows and doors?

5. The building materials: what material is the facade made of, and is it the same as the rest of the building? Materials may vary; wood may consist of log, clapboard, board and batten, or finished novelty siding. Masonry may be brick, stone, or even adobe. Metal may be solid cast iron or galvanized metal sheathing over other materials. Look closely, for what might appear to be one material, such as stone, may really be another, perhaps cast iron or even wood pretending to be stone. (Note: a magnet is one of the handiest research tools to have along when looking at historic buildings.)

6. The architectural detailing of the building, sometimes called its style: the building may feature trim of a fairly identifiable style (Greek Revival, Gothic, Italianate, and Romanesque are common) or a complex combination of stylistic details that may best be called eclectic.

Using this six-part system, we can easily classify buildings visually. We may say, for example, that a building on main street is deep (that is, narrow in width), two stories, has a tall facade made of stone, has numerous window openings, and has Greek Revival trim. Another building may be wider than it is deep, be two stories tall, have a wide facade, be of wooden frame construction, have many window openings, and have Victorian trim.

Students of main street architecture realize that the type of storefront on a particular building is one of its diagnostic stylistic features. Does it have large glass windows? Is it ornate or simple? Does it have a porch, balcony, or awning? Other features, such as signs, are extremely important. Is the sign that advertises what is available inside placed on the windows or painted or mounted on the facade? Do signs project out over the sidewalk from the building facade? And what does that sign advertise, a product or a service?

Looking at main street as a system of visual signals and clues is an exciting kind of detective work. Some buildings might actually bear a date, either on a cornerstone or, more typically, toward the upper cornice or roof line of the facade. Lacking these dates, we may search city or courthouse records that reveal when a building was built. This, however, will not tell us anything about the stylistic storefront remodelings that may have reshaped the look of main street. It is here that a knowledge of architectural style is indispensable, for architectural styles are among the better clues to when a particular building was built. For example, are the buildings along the street mostly late Victorian in style, that is, from 1875 to 1890? Are they mostly early twentieth century styles, such as the popular Chicago style that seemed to sweep the country from about 1905 to 1920? Or is main street a mixture of styles? If one style does dominate, this may tell us that construction occurred in a short period, perhaps as a result of a boom in building or as the aftermath of rapid rebuilding following a disastrous fire.

Fire hazards are calculated by insurance companies to determine categories of risk. They use building density, siting, materials, and other factors to determine the insurance rates for various buildings. Needless to say, a row of contiguous wooden buildings is more prone to destruction by fire than a group of freestanding masonry buildings. In this regard, fire insurance maps can help in our architectural detective work, for we also want similar information. Sanborn Fire Insurance Maps are among the most helpful; available for most communities, they can reveal much about the way mining towns are developed. In a color-coded montage, they depict building shape and dimensions and show the building materials of all major structural elements, including walls, roofs, and porches. They are especially good in helping us read the landscape of built-up areas, for they show us which walls are common and which are independent of other buildings—conditions that we are not always able to see in closely packed downtown commercial areas. Thus, the Sanborn maps that once helped agents determine insurance rates can now help us to interpret the historic landscape of mining towns more effectively. They also help us understand the way speculators and town developers put mining towns together,

20. *The company store was often situated in a prominent position. This one at Arno, Virginia, had a standard false front and faced the company houses at a jog in the main road. Westmoreland Collection, Hagley Museum and Library.*

for they treat all types of buildings and structures, including industrial and residential.

So far, we have discussed the commercial architecture of towns that were developed by entrepreneurs and speculators. Many mining towns, however, were under the control of a single mining company, which might forbid certain types of buildings such as saloons or houses of prostitution and prohibit any retail commercial buildings other than its own company store. Typically, the company store was a rather large building that housed many different departments; it was, in effect, a large general store. Some, especially those in larger communities, occupied an entire city block. The company store was often situated in a prominent location, perhaps at a main intersection like the Northwestern Improvement Company Store in the coal mining town of Roslyn, Washington, or at a place where a road or street jogged and the store could face oncoming traffic, as in Arno, a small mining town in the coal fields of western Virginia (fig. 20).

The architecture of company stores varied: some were ornate, some simple, depending on the philosophy and finances of the company. A few mining companies appear to have deliberately selected distinctive architectural styles different from the mainstream standardized commercial architecture being built across the country. The majority, however, did not. In most large mining districts where the presence of the company was strong, such as the Sunday Creek Coal Company in Ohio's Hocking Coal District, one could find a company store in each small community. These might be numbered: Company Store No. 14, No. 15, and so forth. They might all be similar in architecture, or they might be quite different from one another. Overall, mining company commercial architecture was not radically different from the commercial architecture erected in other towns.

Although there appears to be no specific commercial architectural style that sets mining towns off from other kinds of towns, the actual placement of buildings in the context of property lots and peculiar topographic situations is often distinctive. Because the main street of a mining town frequently runs along a contour or parallels a streambed, property parcels may slope steeply up and down on either side of the thoroughfare. The rear portions of commercial buildings are often either built into the hillside or, on the downhill slope, stand on substantial foundations. This helps further to accentuate the dense, urban quality of the building pattern in many mining towns.

Despite much study of their economic histories, we know rather little about the historic architectural design and development of our mining towns. Several questions remain unanswered. For their size, are mining town commercial streetscapes more elaborate or ornate than other towns? Certain types of brickwork and corbeling, as well as ornate porches and balconies, appear to be more common in mining towns. In many areas of the West, iron window shutters appear to be more common in mining towns than elsewhere. If they are, could this have resulted from an increased concern about threats of fire and theft?

INSTITUTIONAL ARCHITECTURE

The location and design of institutional buildings (such as town halls, miners' unions, schools, and churches) say much about the organization of public or social space in mining towns. The density of construction, competition for commercial space, paucity of flat space on which to build, and emphasis on intense indoor social activities such as drinking, gambling, and carousing may result in relatively little open space being set aside for parks and squares, especially in those mining towns that developed in the nineteenth century. Just as

21. *Space restrictions, especially in nineteenth-century boom towns, often resulted in little open public space. Here, in Eureka, Nevada, the historic Victorian (Italianate) Eureka County Courthouse occupies a building lot right on Main Street. 1989 photo by the author.*

the commercial architecture of mining towns may be cramped or compressed into the business district, institutional architecture often tends to be sited and constructed on small lots: in numerous mining towns, setbacks and side lots/yards are scarce; churches and civic buildings are often located on main street or very close to it. In other words, as a rule, mining towns seem to be more compressed than non-mining towns.

This compression may lead to the elaborate detailing of their facades, so that formal, originally cubic building designs are transformed into fronts or silhouettes; the Storey County Courthouse in Virginia City, Nevada, provides a good example, as do the beautiful courthouses at Pioche and Eureka (fig. 21); their hillside/main street locations and small lots have rendered them more like elaborate Victorian Italianate storefront buildings than their counterparts in courthouse square towns, designed with a great deal more deliberation, symmetry, and centrality.

Ideally, institutional buildings are designed as freestanding struc-

22. *Miners' union halls and other lodge buildings were common along main street in mining towns. Shawnee, Ohio, a coal mining town noted for its union activity, had several during its heyday. This one, which served as the Knights of Labor Hall and the local opera house, was built in 1881. 1990 photo by the author.*

tures; when situated in hyperurbanized settings what they lose in visibility is countered by visual tension: their scale now commands less of our attention than their placement very close to other buildings. This juxtaposition may accentuate their formal architectural styling, for their form and detailing may differ from those of adjacent buildings. In mining towns, this positioning may seem irregular, even serendipitous, to those more familiar with agrarian or commercial communities. The topography may accentuate the dense spacing of institutional buildings on small lots in mining communities. The spires of churches and the towers of schools become strong landmarks when the community is viewed from hilly vantage points, while the same buildings may be far less visible and impressive when viewed from below. Any particular view may yield a different perspective, but the overall image of the city is a composite based on combining many individual views.

Mining communities may have a rather large number of union buildings or lodge halls, a testimony to the cosmopolitan but clannish populations of relatively young working males. These buildings, such as the Pythian Castle in Bisbee, Arizona, and the Knights of Labor Hall in Shawnee, Ohio, often contained large meeting rooms in their upper stories (fig. 22). They were usually constructed in high styles typical of the architecture of the period. Town halls, opera houses, and fire stations were also likely to be impressive storefront-style buildings with towers or cupolas. Being rather prosperous, truly cosmopolitan, and fairly civic minded, mining towns abounded in impressive institutional buildings. Generally, mining communities are richer than surrounding nonmining towns in buildings that reveal cultural diversity: church architecture alone is often a good clue to their ethnic and social diversity. These diverse institutional buildings are architectural ingredients that give the cultural landscape of mature historic mining towns such an urban character.

RESIDENTIAL ARCHITECTURE

Residential architecture is one of the most interesting and diagnostic—and poorly studied—features of mining towns. As we study mining towns, we immediately become aware of two fundamen-

23. *Company housing is one of the distinctive traits of mining landscapes. This long structure at Eureka townsite number 40 (near Windber, Pennsylvania) houses six mining families under one roof, a classic example of attached housing. Since being sold by the company some years ago, each of the miners' houses under this one roof now receives separate maintenance. 1989 photo by the author.*

tally different types of housing: individual homes (cabins, cottages, and houses) and attached housing (duplexes, fourplexes, etc.), consisting of more than one housing unit under one roof.

Although more detailed studies are needed, it does appear that housing can be used to distinguish mining towns from other towns. Looking at southwestern Pennsylvania's bituminous coal country, for example, we can immediately tell we are in a coal town, where we are likely to find attached housing: rows of fourplex and sixplex attached houses line the streets in towns like Windber and Berwind (fig. 23). By contrast, most of the housing in nonmining towns in this area consists of single family dwellings.

This type of pattern—housing differences between mining and nonmining communities—appears to be common throughout the country. Ironically, few regional studies have compared mining towns and nonmining towns; the reason, it would appear, is that mining community housing is so different from its counterpart in other communities—and

24. Many miners lived in small detached houses called miners' cabins, especially in the western mining towns like Goldfield, Nevada. 1989 photo by the author.

mining towns so different from their surroundings—that researchers have avoided making such "obvious" comparisons. We now know that we have missed opportunities to interpret the landscape by making these assumptions, for much historic mining town residential architecture has been lost in the last thirty years. An inherently rural or agrarian bias in architectural studies has kept us from giving mining communities the study they deserve.

As we look at the architecture of mining towns, then, we find some types of housing that are either rare or nonexistent in nonmining towns. The closest kin to mining towns are other industrial communities, such as railroad towns and factory towns, both of which face the same task of housing workers. This generalization does not mean that mining-related housing is the same throughout the country, but that it is usually quite different from housing found in nonmining communities within any particular region.

The western hard rock mining districts provide a case in point. Their residential architecture is diagnostic: we can usually tell when we are in a mining town by looking at the housing alone. What may appear,

25. *The T-cottage, so named because of the shape of its floor plan, was a common form of detached housing in mining towns, especially those in the Midwest and Far West. This T-cottage is located in Bisbee, Arizona. 1982 photo by the author.*

at first glance, to be a rather confusing hodgepodge collection of structures normally, upon closer examination, turns out to have a great deal of order in space and time. To see the housing we must separate it into several categories based on the simple overall form of the building, including its roofline.

In a detailed study of residential architecture in Park City, Utah, for example, Deborah Lyn Randall has found that the majority of the historic housing stock could be classified into three main types: the rectangular miner's cabin (fig. 24), the T-plan cottage (fig. 25), and the pyramidal (roofed) cottage (fig. 26). [15] These housing types are found widely throughout the West and parts of the Midwest. Although these house types may be found in many types of communities, they are especially common in mining towns—so common that a concentration of them indicates mining. Historic photographs of Bisbee, Arizona, show relatively limited architectural diversity; the bulk of the housing can be classified into four major types: the rectangular miner's cabin, the T-plan cottage, the pyramidal roofed cottage, and the linear-connected rectangular cabin, which is really a type of attached hous-

*26. The pyramidal cottage, so named for the shape of its roof, was also
common in mining towns of the South, Midwest, and Far West. This cottage
is located in Eureka, Nevada. 1989 photo by the author.*

ing. Because there was relatively little new construction after about
1915, these houses today give "Old" Bisbee its historic mining town
character. Places like Tonopah, Bisbee, and Park City witnessed a
good deal of speculation in housing, which is typical where there is a
diversity of mine ownership.

In company towns, however, we encounter a very different architectural complexion. Here we find rows of standardized housing that may
be devoid of high-style detailing. They may be single family homes or
attached houses. All are usually painted in the same color scheme.
Their maintenance, too, is liable to vary little from dwelling to dwelling. Despite what we hear about the monotony of company housing,
however, the variations are impressive when considered over the
United States as a whole. The uniformity is place-specific, for where
we would normally expect to see some variation in a row of houses, we
encounter little or none (fig. 27).

About the only generalization we can make concerning company
housing is that it is usually standardized in any particular location and
is not highly ornamented. It varies from small cottages to the largest

27. Company housing is distinguished by simple architectural styling, little variation from house to house, and identical maintenance: this ca. 1920s view at Roda, Virginia, says company town better than a sign. Westmoreland Collection, Hagley Museum and Library.

and longest attached row houses found in mining communities. Although there is no single company house style, even speculators who built "pattern-book" or catalog homes in mining towns across the country provided more variety than company architects, who stressed severe uniformity in both style and maintenance. We shall discuss company houses in the section that treats homogenization, but it is important to read the landscape with an eye toward uniqueness and uniformity. What patterns are consistently repeated? How much individuality do we see in the residential landscape? If we see little variety, we are likely to be in a company town.

INDUSTRIAL ARCHITECTURE

The industrial architecture directly associated with the actual business of mining, milling, and smelting ores gives strong visual definition to the mining landscape. The headframes, ore bins, concentrators, and smelters form the backdrop for all settlement and transportation patterns and are among the strongest visual signatures of mining district landscapes. These are liable to be the largest structures with the boldest profiles and the oddest angles (fig. 28). Unlike the other architectural features, they are the legacy of mining and industrial engineers, and their form follows function so closely that

28. Mining-related structures are usually the largest and most visually interesting of the buildings and structures in a mining district. This historic (1907) view of the Federal Lead Company Federal Mill No. 3 in Flat River, Missouri, shows the complex of mill buildings required to reduce and process ores. Missouri Mines State Historic Site photograph.

they are best described in terms of the technical engineering processes that capitalize on the force of gravity, minimize energy expended, and reduce the distance traveled in the reduction of ores to metals.

Headframes mark the location of mines (fig. 29). These gallowslike structures are topped by sheave wheels, and they serve to hoist men, equipment, and ore from the mines. Like other features associated with mining, the earlier they are, the more likely they are to exhibit vernacular forms and to be constructed of wood rather than metal. The headframe marks the top of a mine shaft; its cable, which runs over the top of the sheave wheel, is powered by an engine in the hoist house. Hoist houses are typically rectangular, often sheathed in board and batten siding, though double-board siding was more common after about 1895, and corrugated galvanized iron siding had become common in mining districts by about 1900.

Where deep mining is practiced in coal mining country, one is liable to find an impressive array of structures. The main mine building itself may be most conspicuous. It may cover the headframe and include hoisting mechanisms and sometimes the powerhouse, which is usually identified by its smokestack(s). Quite often, however, the powerhouse is separate and constructed of masonry. At the mine complex, one finds

29. The headframe symbolizes the "umbilical connection" between the surface and the underground world of the miner. Most, like this steel headframe at Butte, Montana, are found at the top of steeply inclined or vertical mineshafts. 1989 photo by the author.

other buildings, such as storage sheds and shower/bath facilities, which were required after about the turn of the century. Buildings associated with ventilating the mine are often located at some distance from the main mine buildings. These usually contain electric blowers or fans that assure the safety of miners by regulating the flow of air and removing any dangerous gases. In many mining areas, one also finds pumphouses to remove water from the mines.

At most coal mines, one usually finds a large structure associated with the washing, sorting, and loading of coal. This is often a huge, rambling structure that spans several railroad tracks and may be called a breaker in the anthracite coal country of Pennsylvania or a tipple in most bituminous coal mining areas (fig. 30). Here coal is sorted into various sizes, such as lump, stoker, nut, and egg. Much of the slack or finer coal is separated at this point, and the boney or slate and other useless rock is separated to be dumped in the culm or gob piles. In reading the landscape of the coal country of Athens County, Ohio, Eugene Palka describes the layout of a more or less typical coal

30. A tipple or breaker is the structure at which coal is sorted and loaded into railroad cars or trucks. This tipple stood at Imboden, Virginia, straddling a stream and the railroad tracks as it stretched completely across the narrow valley. Westmoreland Collection, Hagley Museum and Library.

mining complex, the Sunday Creek mine at Millfield probably serving as an example (fig. 31). [16]

In virtually all metals mining districts, one is likely to find a mill or concentrator in addition to the main mining buildings. The milling-concentrating process increases the concentration of metals by removing waste rock. By doing so, the ore is transformed into a higher-grade (hence more valuable) commodity that can bear the cost of transportation to the smelter; as a textbook on ore dressing put it, "it is cheaper to transport a few tons of concentrate than several hundred tons of ore." [17] A number of techniques have been used to crush ores to finer sizes for ease in separating out metals, and these have left a legacy of industrial features in the landscape. [18] Stamp mills are among the most distinctive features associated with hard rock metals mining; they crush ore to the consistency of sand under a series of metal weights driven by camshafts. [19] The size of a mill is determined by the number of such stamping mechanisms or stamps.

The typical stamp mill in western mining districts is constructed on a sloping (as opposed to flat) site wherever possible. The mill has several levels, each of which is set on a stone foundation. As we read the landscape of mining areas, we can readily recognize a mill by its long, sloping roofline and stepped foundation (fig. 32). The roofline, which sometimes has a number of small gabled windows or skylights, follows the same downhill gradient as the entire building: gravity favors a mill building constructed on sloping land. Like other mining-related indus-

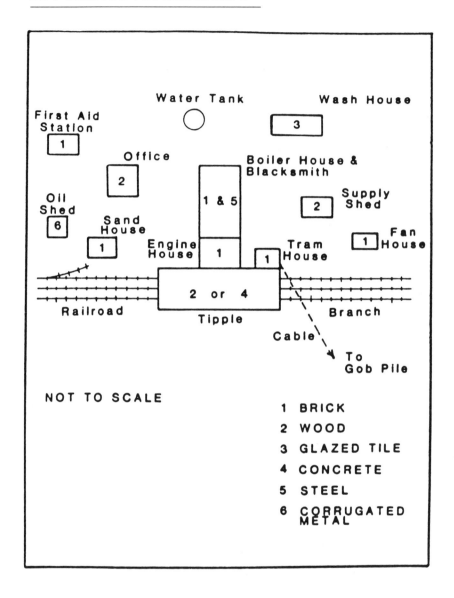

31. *The layout of a coal mining facility in Athens County, Ohio, shows the distribution of existing buildings and structures and their relationship to the railroad sidings that ran under the tipple: large-scale mining and railroads are inseparable. After Palka 1986.*

32. Concentration of metals ores usually required stamp milling and preparation in solutions and took advantage of gravity in the movement of processed ores. This stamp mill at Austin, Nevada, shows the distinctive sloping profile and terraced site. 1989 photo by the author.

trial buildings and structures, mills of this type usually have board and batten siding if constructed between about 1870 and 1890; double siding is common in the later nineteenth century, and corrugated metal siding becomes common around 1900. Mining engineers advised that wooden mill buildings, as well as other mining structures, be painted with "red mineral paint." This helped preserve the wood and also aided in fireproofing.[20]

Depending on the types of processes used, one also finds large vats or tanks associated with milling operations. The earliest of these tend to be wooden with metal hoops; metal tanks are common after the turn of the century. One needs to understand the processes used in a particular operation to determine the purposes served by the features at the site. Were the vats used as part of the thickening process or as part of the chemical process (such as chloridination or cyanidation)? Typically, mills and concentrators are associated with pipe systems that convey liquified ore solutions to different stages in the process and tailings to the tailings ponds.

33. Smelters are usually large and have prominent smokestacks designed to disseminate noxious fumes and smoke as far away from settled areas as possible. Utah's Magna smelter has become a regional landmark. 1991 photo © Gary Peterson.

In the larger metals mining districts, at the end of the ore reduction process stands the smelter (fig. 33). This is usually one of the largest buildings in the district, its roof surmounted by a tall stack (or stacks), out of which poured sulfurous clouds of smoke. Miners and residents could read the economic health of the district by the condition of these smoky, metallic banners that wafted across the landscape. The smelter complex was usually several buildings. Many had clerestoried or monitored roofs to let in light and dissipate heat. All had piles of dark-colored, vitreous or sintery volcaniclike slag nearby; those marking the location of the long-vanished Richmond and Eureka smelters at Eureka, Nevada, are vivid reminders of the community's boom days and stand as landmarks at the entrances to this historic mining community.

As we explore mining districts, we may find other features that are located at some distance from the mines themselves, but were an essential part of the process of mineral production. Charcoal ovens supplied charcoal to early smelters and furnaces, but were usually replaced by coke ovens in the later nineteenth century. Coke ovens were

34. The sight of coke ovens in full operation was unforgettable. Such beehive ovens were found where coking coal was available. In this historic (ca. 1920) photograph, we see dozens in western Virginia producing coke for the mills and furnaces. Westmoreland Collection, Hagley Museum and Library.

designed to turn coking-grade coals into coke—a porous, dark gray high-grade fuel needed for the smelters and furnaces. Their distinctive architecture usually consisted of rows of twenty or more individual chambers lining railway sidings, each chamber having an arched opening that could be bricked up when the coke was being prepared (fig. 34). These are called beehive coke ovens. Thousands of them were in operation at the turn of the century in areas where coking coal was mined—including West Virginia, New Mexico, Colorado, and Pennsylvania; some remained in operation into the 1950s. Today the ruins of coke ovens often remain as silent testimony to the era when mining was in its heyday.

Interconnecting all these features is another industrial feature: the railroad. A look at the landscape reveals a maze of trackage that connects mine to mills, concentrators to waste dumps, and coke ovens to smelters. Until just a few years ago, the typical mining district was a veritable museum of railroad-related features, from trestles and culverts to buildings and structures such as sheds and roundhouses. Today, however, many of these are vanishing as railroads seek to avoid tax liabilities and demolish vacant properties. Their abandoned grades often remain in the landscape until vegetation conceals or erosion removes them.

Many of the more prosperous mining districts had another type of rail line that linked the communities to each other—the electric streetcars and interurbans that threaded their way through the district and left, here and there, a few remains such as old carbarns and power stations that have somehow escaped the bulldozer. The presence of such streetcar and interurban lines can often be detected on older USGS topographic maps; the series done around 1910 is especially helpful.

In addition to railroad lines, we may find inclines (or their remains) in some mining districts. Whereas the gradients of normal railroad do not exceed about 4 or 5 percent for steam-powered and diesel-powered lines on secondary trackage and 9 percent in some electric traction lines, inclines are very steep, 20 percent to 40 percent grades being common. Inclines depend on cables, as opposed to wheel on rail adhesion, to haul their specially designed ore cars. Inclines usually appear as steep, straight lines on hillsides, and they serve to convey ore by gravity from the mine to tipple or ore bins in the valley below. In areas where the inclines have been removed, their location can often be seen as a scar up the hillside.

In many mining districts, materials are also moved by water; in these areas, flumes may be an important feature in the landscape. Flumes are open structures through which tail water carries the wastes from the concentrating process to the tailings dumps or tailings ponds. They usually maintain a gently sloping gradient, less than 4 percent, through the use of cuts and trestles. In some mining districts, one can still find wooden flumes built forty or more years ago in daily operation. Pipes or slurry pipelines may serve much the same purpose in some areas; a few are also of wooden construction, being put together much like wooden barrels, but most of these have been replaced by metal piping.

Where the topography is especially rugged, we may find aerial tramways.[21] These distinctive features consist of a continuous cable suspended by towers or pylons (fig. 35). Ore buckets are moved along this cable in a seemingly endless procession from mine head to ore bin or concentrator. Tramways may remain in operation today, but often we find only their remnants, such as occasional towers, that may be traced across the landscape. In a few places, the entire tramway may

35. *Aerial tramway at Pioche, Nevada, was constructed to haul ore from mines to distant ore bins and milling facilities. Abandoned, its buckets swing in the wind as it stands near the town cemetery. 1989 photo by the author.*

stand abandoned but intact, its rusting ore buckets swaying silently in the wind.

OTHER ARCHITECTURAL FEATURES

No discussion of the cultural landscape of mining towns would be complete without a look at their cemeteries. In mining towns, the location of graves and the design (and setting) of tombstones reveal much about ethnic and economic segregation, the acceptance of high styles, and the persistence of vernacular traditions. Most cemeteries are located at the edge of town and are very likely to be a microcosm of the nearby urban environment. In common with the funerary art/ design of all cemeteries, the markers in mining town cemeteries vary through time and reflect cultural values and social status.[22] This may account for the wide variation in tombstone design (quality, material) and the intense partitioning of graves and plots—through elaborate wooden and iron fencing—in the cemeteries of many mining communities. A few headstones or grave markers may contain information about the miner's occupation, but most markers are fairly standard designs common in other cemeteries.

The cemetery remains one of the most intriguing aspects of the mining landscape, for from its serene vantage point we may look back and see the rest of the mining district as an island of buildings, structures, and forms that permitted its occupants to extract wealth quickly from the earth, and each other, and then move on.

CONCLUSION

In this chapter, the basic elements that characterize the landscape of a particular mining district have been outlined. Certain features—such as the housing stock, waste dumps, and engineering features—are often diagnostic: they can be used as indicators that mining has occurred at that particular location. Combined, these features are so apparent that they can be used to distinguish mining communities from other communities. Some features, such as the head-frame, indicate mining even though their function is poorly understood by the public. In this sense, certain landscape features are almost as symbolic as the standard miner's symbol—the crossed pick and shovel.

Students of mining district landscapes are fortunate that such good imagery is available. They can thank the thousands of professional photographers who recorded street scenes and mining activities, many of which wound up as postcards. These, better than almost any other record, help us to read historic landscapes, for they can easily be compared to the same scenes that we see today. These comparisons help us understand the prodigious building feats accomplished by the developers of mining districts, and how much their work has been changed by time, man, and the elements in the intervening years.

Also of great aid in reading the landscape are the maps and reports created by the mining companies and government agencies. The best single source of historic reports for entire mining districts is the United States Geological Survey: virtually every major mining district has been the subject of at least one definitive report that treats the geological structure and the development of mines. These reports were done by economic geologists when the districts were in production, describing current conditions in, say, 1898 or 1913.

These USGS reports are usually well illustrated and well written and often describe the mining and treatment of ores. In so doing, they may make reference to mining and milling techniques, transportation systems, housing, and conditions in the community. They often contain panorama photographs that indicate various mines and geological formations and provide a benchmark of sorts against which change can be measured.

Academic studies of mining districts are also useful. Those involving landscape architecture and historical geography methodology are among the most valuable for students of the landscape to consult. Most of them remain unpublished. The pioneering landscape study of the Pocahontas Coal Field of southern West Virginia by Mack Gillenwater—a native of the region—may serve as a model.[23] The author carefully analyzes the morphology of the communities and describes their architecture, concluding with the hope that researchers will use a similar methodology to study other mining areas. Comparable studies of American mining districts are needed in order for us to understand their relationship to other mining districts and to the settlement and architectural patterns of the regions in which they occur.

Even those mining landscapes abandoned long ago, where all buildings and structures have vanished, can be read by historical archaeologists. At sites of former mining communities, such as Aurora (Nevada), Santoy (Ohio), and Buxton (Iowa), where virtually nothing remains above ground, the artifacts, old foundations, mine wastes, and changes in gradients can be used to reconstruct the past mining landscapes. According to archaeologist Donald Hardesty, "mining sites are geographical clusters of house sites, trash dumps, privies, roads, millsites, and mines organized into feature systems," a feature system being defined as "a group of archaeologically visible features and objects that is the product of a specific human activity."[24] Mining sites are distinctive in that they exhibit cyclical occupation and abandonment; unlike most archaeological sites, they are more likely to show horizontal than vertical stratigraphy—that is, have components that are separated horizontally (geographically), rather than vertically (chronologically). As we shall see, mining tends severely to alter the landscape in episodic waves; therefore, many mining sites show what archaeologists call mutilation, meaning that their surviving remnants are discontinuous. In many cases, mining sites have an underground structure that offers certain fragmentary clues as to what happened to the ore body.

Two historical archaeologists, David Gradwohl and Nancy Osborn, conducted extensive field research at the site of a long-vanished coal mining town, Buxton, Iowa, and wrote a book about their search entitled *Exploring Buried Buxton*. When they first found the Buxton townsite in 1980, it was little more than a few forlorn ruins in an otherwise rural countryside of pastures and cornfields. Armed with historical information, they set about to find the lost town's features. Much of the place had begun to vanish almost sixty years before they began their research; Buxton was founded in 1900 but was abandoned during the 1920s. "Standing in the middle of a patently featureless pasture, holding a panoramic view of Buxton as photographed in 1907 in one hand and in the other hand a town plat map drawn up in 1919," they began to ask several questions, the first of which was: "Where is Main Street?"[25] With the help of their students, they used a wide range of clues—including artifacts—to reconstruct Buxton's commercial and residential districts. The process shed much light on the vanished coal mining community and its social life.

Like other ventures in reading the landscape, historical documentation is used wherever possible to supplement the archaeological record. Yet the tangible evidence may speak for itself when it conflicts with the written word, for it is the actual record of what people actually did, as opposed to what they said, or thought, they were doing at the time.

Historical and archaeological studies are important, for they show us how past activities have shaped the landscapes we observe today. We are often astounded by the degree of change: entire earlier mining communities may have disappeared and new settlements may have appeared almost overnight. As we shall see, mining landscapes have often changed dramatically over the years. In order to understand these changes, and interpret why mining country looks different than non-mining country, we need to identify the processes that shape the landscape of our American mining districts.

2

INTERPRETING

THE

LANDSCAPE

THE ART AND SCIENCE OF INTERPRETATION

*The traces of [underground] mining are not so pretty. . . . All
the work goes on below the surface. But what we see is still bad
enough—a desolate landscape of shafts and mine dumps, tailing
ponds and railroad tracks.*
—Spiro Kostof, America by Design

We know that mining districts have a distinctive look. Although no two mining districts are identical, the site, layout, and architecture may be similar enough from place to place to imply interconnections. The headframes and ore dumps we see in virtually all mining landscapes are not random features; they tell us a great deal about an aggressive system of winning metals and materials from the earth that originated in Europe and transformed the New World. The housing styles we see tell us much about the control of power and the persistence of community in rapidly settled places where minerals are exploited. The very locations that these communities occupy say as much about decision-making as they do about environment. When we find three towns in three states—Colorado, Utah, and Nevada—named Eureka and all of them look similar, we have to ask ourselves why.

The name "Eureka" is appropriate, for it implies discovery. In the case of three silver/gold mining towns in canyon settings, almost 500 miles apart, it means "I have found it"—a cry of triumph. It also implies cultural diffusion, for the name is said to have originated with the adoption of the exclamation as California's motto in 1850 and spread from the Golden State. For those wanting to discover the reasons why places have certain visual and cultural characteristics, the discovery comes through interpretation, a word with three separate meanings—one scientific, one artistic, and one somewhere in between.

Interpretation can be the act of explaining the meaning of something (elucidating), of construing something in the light of individual belief, or of representing something by means of art. Interpreting a landscape may at first appear to be a scientific endeavor, and it is to some extent, for it involves a search for truth based on rational abstraction. However, since the interpreter cannot be separated from the subject, in this case the landscape, our objectivity is partial at best. This is so because landscape—a multifaceted, three-dimensional tapestry— helps shape our identity before we learn the power of deduction. If, as David Lowenthal and Hugh Prince claim, "landscapes are created by landscape tastes,"[1] then we are interpreting both a work of utility and a work of art.

Interpreting landscape is akin to art history, and perhaps art criticism, for landscapes can only be analyzed in terms of the social forces and aesthetic preferences that created them. We interpret landscapes because we are intrinsically interested in their form as well as their content. Thus, we call upon two rich traditions, the artistic and the scientific, that are artificially separated in our culture. Furthermore, when we set out to interpret a particular landscape, or group of landscapes, we become artists ourselves in that we create something, either verbal or diagrammatic, by abstracting the essence of the real world.

Mining itself, that most businesslike of earth-altering professions, has an aesthetic component. In describing the surface mining of the porphyry copper ore deposits in the West and the iron mines of Minnesota's Mesabi Range, the president of the Homestake Mining Company wrote: "Even from an aesthetic standpoint, the result is not distasteful, for the terraced walls resulting from the removal of ore in successive benches have a peculiar beauty of their own. Indeed, the great man-made pit at Bingham Canyon excites high admiration, as do many other similar workings on somewhat smaller scale."[2]

The creators of mining landscapes have provided us settings that are difficult to view with neutrality, for these landscapes appeal and repel simultaneously. The fact that we judge landscapes aesthetically and moralistically makes their interpretation all the more interesting.

Mining landscapes are the legacy of several processes. These may vary from place to place, but overall they explain the distinctive look of mining country.

ISOLATION

*Men put an end to darkness, and search out to the farthest bound
the ore in gloom and deep darkness. They open shafts in a valley
away from where men live; they are forgotten by travelers, they
hang afar from men, they swing to and fro.*
—Job 28:3–4

So reads a part of an ancient, and perennially beautiful, description of mining. Miners toil far from civilization, forgotten by those who benefit from the minerals and metals they mine. In his classic seventeenth-century *De re metallica*, Georgius Agricola continues the biblical analogy when he describes miners toiling in "mountains otherwise unproductive" and "valleys invested in gloom."[3] Historically, miners have been separated from population centers, and our American mining districts are part of this timeless tradition.

In his thought-provoking 1987–1988 television series called *America by Design*, architect Spiro Kostof set out to describe the forces that shape the American countryside. Naturally, he was fascinated by mining's role in the process. As he looked at the relationship between features in the countryside, he underscored the physical remoteness of mining: "Mining camps established themselves in these far-flung frontier regions before there were any settlements, railroad lines, or good roads. Leadville, Colorado; Helena, Montana; Deadwood, South Dakota; Central City, Colorado—these were isolated islands of people surrounded by wilderness."[4]

Kostof's description provides a distant view into mining country from the outside perspective (civilization). Consider the same concept—isolation—looking the other way, that is, outward from the isolated center of a mining town:

Our house was well up on the side of a mountain, and directly opposite was another mountain. Between them, in the canyon and climbing both sides, lay the little rough-board town. Snuggled in and among the shacks and dwarfing them were mine shafts with hoists and ore dumps. West of town the desert stretched for miles to the horizon, which was edged with the snowcapped Sierra Nevada. In the opposite direction, to the east, a curving scratch indicated a road winding up the draw and disappearing over the edge of the hill.[5]

So wrote Mrs. Hugh Brown of her recollections of the panorama of Tonopah, Nevada, in 1904. Like many other mining communities, Tonopah was located in the middle of nowhere. Travelers to this mining district, and many others, often described arduous journeys that took days in dusty/muddy bone-jarring stagecoaches or hour after hour in rattling trains that rolled along tracks cut through the wilderness to reach booming mining camps from Cantil (California) to Calumet (Michigan).

The term "isolated" is derived through French from *insula*, the Latin word for island. It describes well both the physical remoteness of many mining districts and their differences from the surrounding countryside. Isolation—the quality of being set apart from others—is an important distinguishing characteristic of mining districts: when they are located fairly close to other types of land use, they maintain a distinctly different identity due to their exploitative economy and the composition of their population. Their rapid growth and wealth may affect the surrounding countryside by creating a demand for materials and services such as wood, charcoal, and farm produce. Mining tends to take more resources from the surrounding countryside than it gives, although it can offer employment for those who provide goods and services to the mining district.

In areas where mining districts are located in farming country, such as the Old Lead Belt of eastern Missouri and the lead-zinc mining area of southern Wisconsin, for example, farmers found seasonal (winter) work in the mines. In some coal mining areas especially, where mining jobs were more plentiful in the winter when the demand for coal was highest, miners might use the summer to advantage in farming and other pursuits, as was the case in the coal fields near Sheridan, Wyoming.[6] In Minnesota, where Finns served as miners, they returned to the rural countryside after the mines closed. The same types of conditions prevailed in the lead mining areas of southern Wisconsin. More often, however, there is little opportunity in the surrounding countryside because mining communities are located in marginal areas where agriculture is rather limited. The surrounding land might be ranched or logged or might serve no other economic purpose at all.

When the term "isolation" is used to describe a condition of mining districts, it should not be confused with provincialism. Mining towns are not deliberately located away from the corrupting influences of civilization as are, say, certain utopian communities. In the nineteenth century, many utopian leaders sought to locate their self-contained agrarian communities at some distance from the mainstream population—the Mormons in the western United States being a good example.[7] In a number of these utopian communities, mining of precious metals was forbidden or discouraged, lest it corrupt the population. These utopian communities are distinctly, and ethically, different from the typical mining boom town.

Mining towns would be considered "cumulative" communities, as historian Page Smith uses the term to differentiate communities based on economic trade and intercourse from "covenanted" communities developed through a pact with God.[8] In the case of mining towns, the isolation is both unintentional and ironic, for they are often the most cosmopolitan of our communities, bringing a great deal of sophistication to a region. We might say that mining communities represent urbanization in the absence of nearby cities. They may be islands in an unpopulated or lightly populated hinterland, and they are culturally different from the surrounding countryside.

The physical isolation of mining districts is not confined to their historic periods. Even today, they are among the most remote of America's industrial/urban communities. This isolation is underscored by an anecdote. Some years ago, while serving as the director of the Mining and Historical Museum in Bisbee, Arizona, I set out to define the problems faced by America's mining museums. One condition shared by virtually all of them was a lack of visibility—they were not very well known because they were off the beaten track, a direct result of the isolated location of most of America's great mining districts. Butte, Eureka, and Tonopah may be synonymous with rich mineral enterprises, but they are located in the interstices of road maps and the nether geography of the American psyche (fig. 36). Bisbee had company in its loneliness.

This is ironic, because many remote mining communities were very

36. Isolated—and proud of it. This scene at the entrance to Eureka, Nevada, says much about the physical isolation of mining communities. 1989 photo by the author.

important during the periods in which they flowered: Bisbee, for example, was the largest city in Arizona for several years in the early twentieth century. Butte was the undisputed seat of political power in Montana for years. Fabled Virginia City controlled the destiny of Nevada for the better part of a generation. But no matter how historic or how interesting they may be, one normally does not travel through mining communities—except on vacation—for most are located hundreds of miles from large cities, off the beaten path (the interstate highways). This means that our exposure to these gritty, industrial workplaces usually occurs in the context of recreation or leisure.

The distribution of mineral wealth often put mining communities in rugged, marginal areas that required much effort to reach and called for the investment of large amounts of capital in the development of transportation systems before they could become productive. Generally, mineralization is associated with mountain building or at any rate geological activity or strong structural control—the very locations that are not likely to spawn cities. It is this factor that further acts to differentiate mining districts from other places, for their landscapes are developed in physical isolation from other urban places. This isolation, which is often reinforced by the seeming inhospitableness of their surroundings, makes a strong impression on the traveler—and on residents of mining districts.

Even in the earliest years of our nation's mineral development, copper and lead production were located some distance from urban centers such as Philadelphia and New York, in hilly, remote places like Phoenixville (Pennsylvania), and Franklin Furnace (New Jersey). Today these places are located about an hour or two from the metropolitan areas, but two hundred years ago they were reachable only after several days of rough travel. With the move west, Americans discovered greater and greater mineral treasures at greater and greater distances from urban centers.

By the 1880s, minerals were being mined in places so remote that the average American had almost no firsthand knowledge about them. William Ralston Balch, for example, tried to improve popular understanding of the developing mining regions of the West:

> Colorado and the mining states to many an Eastern man who obtains his impression from nowhere particularly, are not much more than a succession of huge, deserted brickyards. The very name of the State conjures up forsaken mining camps, ragged ravines, and barren mountains, rocks, plains and precipices that go to make up a very uninviting view, and yet if you question him as to the source of his impressions he can give none.[9]

This, it must be remembered, was written in the time when mountains were considered foreboding and unattractive; only the two occupations of "hunting or prospecting for ledges . . . will make unscientific men climb high mountains."[10] At that time—before rugged scenery came to be considered sublime—mining towns were seen as places where heroic men attempted to wrest mineral riches from nature for the benefit of civilization. It required Herculean efforts to reach, much less settle, these places, which seemed to be dwarfed, at least at first, by powerful, sometimes stupendous, settings.

The scenery that often overpowered these communities may have seemed so limitless that indiscriminate dumping of waste and extensive alteration of the land were considered inconsequential, if not actually an improvement. Located far from the truly desirable places to live, the finer towns and cities, the shapers of mining district landscapes probably felt little need for visual pretense around the workplace. Because they were temporary and sequestered from view, these late nineteenth-century mining landscapes came to exemplify the other side of gentility; thus, isolation probably contributed to a kind of desolation.

Because they were so aggressively developed, mining districts often overcame—or at least mitigated—their physical isolation at an early stage. Typically, a mining district came into being as several mines developed in close proximity in a rather remote area. These mines first produced high-grade ore—a grade high enough to be transported long distances. In the case of copper ores, these might be rich oxides and even native copper, the bulk of ore reaching as high as 50 or 60 percent copper. Horses and mules often were used to haul these rich ores out of the district to more distant smelters.

Primitive roads soon connected the district with the outside world. Although much of the traffic consisted of mineral products, stage lines also were formed to haul passengers. Historic photographs and records frequently reveal these roads to be graded by the mineral producers, and many were toll roads developed by private individuals. These roads were often deeply rutted and extremely hazardous. The heavy loads carried by ore wagons, which might haul upward of three tons each, called for wide steel tires to be fitted to the wheels and teams of several horses or mules. It has been noted that the production of mines frequently suffered because transportation systems of this type were so slow and expensive that they could not keep up with the production of ores, which then had to be stockpiled. In a few places, notably the northeastern United States, canals were constructed to export mineral products; they served well, but were subject to delays caused by low water and freezes in winter.

Railroads provided the answer to overcoming isolation. In many mining districts, an internal system of railroads developed before the district was connected to the outside world by rail. Animal power was usually used on the early railroads, which were constructed to haul ore and waste rock out of—and equipment into—the mines themselves. The rails were usually spaced only a foot or two apart (that is, to light narrow gauge standards), and their cars could haul up to a ton of material. Large stables often existed to house large numbers of horses and mules. In some cases, these animals were kept underground for years, rarely or never seeing the light of day.

But animal power was subject to diseases such as the great epizootic outbreaks and expensive, requiring care and feeding. The steam locomotive proved much more predictable and economical in moving large quantities of mineral products. Within a matter of months or years, depending on the abilities of the mine owners or the acumen of railroad developers, most mining districts were connected to the outside world by the iron horse.

The railroads constructed to get mineral products to more distant urban markets underscore the isolation of mining districts. In fact, it can be argued that most of the major coal and metals mining districts could never have developed without their railways, many of which were constructed by the same outside investors who capitalized the mines. The relationship between mining and railroading is intimate and is seen everywhere in the landscape.

The picture of mineral products being conveyed out of a mining district by rail captured the imagination of nineteenth-century writers, who often saw the railroad as a method of improving upon the natural order. An 1854 description of the Schuylkill River valley in the anthracite region of northeastern Pennsylvania conveys something of the energy and synergism of the mining-railroad link: "On the one side we have the Norristown Railroad and the Schuylkill Canal, and on the other the Reading Railroad, over which are seen passing an almost endless procession of black coal-trains, and as they wind around the projecting knolls, and intervening valleys, a great rumbling noise is heard, amidst the shrill whistle of the locomotive . . ."[11]

The railroad led to the end of the canal system, of course, and assured the flow of mineral products to markets. This traveler's guide describes the coal-hauling Reading Railroad and its relationship to nature as follows: "One hundred miles in length, sloping gracefully from the coal-beds to the river Delaware—is not that a beautiful idea to contemplate? Nature has had a hand in it, and enterprising man has improved what she carefully prepared. She made the route, and raised the coal-beds to their present height with the express purpose, no doubt, of rendering them available to our wants. For this, all thanks!"[12]

By the time the mining frontier reached the interior of the Far West, this relationship with nature had to be reassessed, for nature had thrown precipitous mountain ranges and vast deserts in the path of progress. With the completion of the transcontinental railroad in 1869 (which was built to connect gold-rich California with the rest of the country), the West had been breached, and the mineral riches from the hinterlands—from Nevada's silver to Wyoming's coal—could be tapped.[13] Within a few decades after the completion of the transcontinental railroad, the West was laced with a complex web of standard and narrow gauge rail lines, most of which were constructed to haul mineral wealth out of the region. Some of America's most spectacular railroad lines, such as the Denver & Rio Grande lines in Colorado, were built to connect mining districts with the outside world.

Most of these mineral-hauling railroads have now been abandoned, but the fact that they were built in the first place is testimony to the richness of the mines and the aggressiveness and tenacity of their promoters. In the early years of this century, the 1,000-mile long El Paso and Southwestern was constructed by Phelps Dodge copper interests to avoid dependence on the Southern Pacific, essentially duplicating the route of that earlier railroad.[14] Equally impressive was the ambitious Tonopah and Tidewater Railroad that connected Nevada's booming early twentieth century gold and silver mining area with the outside world.[15]

Most of the mineral-hauling railroads were constructed from 1870 to 1910; some, like Michigan's Mineral Range, Pennsylvania's East Broad Top Railroad, and the Black Hills lines in and around Lead and Deadwood, South Dakota, were narrow gauge connectors. Most, however, were standard gauge, with rails spaced 4 feet, 8 1/2 inches apart. All helped define the regional character of the mining districts they served. They were the lifeline of the mining district, extending the influence of mining country into the outside world: their trains might rumble hundreds of miles from the mines in strings of several dozen, perhaps a hundred, heavily loaded cars. The eleven iron-hauling railroads of the Lake Superior region featured "some of heaviest, hardest railroading in the world."[16]

But even the enterprising financiers of the ambitious railway development projects that connected mining country with the outside world must have had second thoughts as scenery dwarfed their projects: classic among these was Darius Mills, who, upon touring the recently com-

37. *For the first half of the twentieth century, most coal reached market in two-bay hopper cars about 32 feet in length. Here, in a photo from about the 1920s, long lines of hopper cars stand at an Appalachian coal tipple in western Virginia along the Interstate Railroad. Today the two-bay hopper has essentially vanished from the American railroad scene. Westmoreland Collection, Hagley Museum and Library.*

pleted Carson and Colorado Railroad in eastern California and western Nevada, is reported to have remarked to his associates: "Gentlemen, either we built this line 300 miles too long, or 300 years too soon."[17] Like many mining railroads, this line was constructed through remote country in anticipation that mineral development would be sustained and that new riches would lead to increased revenues. Without question, the most isolated and most scenic railroads in the United States were those built to serve mining districts. Each of these railroads, such as the Denver & Rio Grande, Carson and Colorado, White Pass and Yukon, and Nevada Northern, attained its own corporate/visual identity.

Railroad equipment and the associated architecture of railroad lines helped to define the visual character of mining country. In the Great Lakes iron mining region, for example, the 24-foot, drop bottom ore car became standard; as it evolved from wood to steel construction, it came to define the railroading of the area for more than eighty years, for it was designed to accommodate the 12-foot pocket spacing of the gravity type ore docks and the 12- or 24-foot hatch spacing of the Great Lakes ore-carrying vessels.[18] These were a distinctive feature of the Iron Ranges of Minnesota and Michigan. The two-bay, 32-foot-long hopper or coal car became a standard of the industry from about 1900 to 1950 and was as much a part of the coal mining landscape as the tipple (fig. 37).

Although ore and coal cars are usually of the open top hopper or gondola type, mineral concentrates were often shipped out in boxcars adapted for the purpose. Companies produced standard cars, but these were frequently adapted to handle different types of ores in particular districts. To avoid per diem costs as much as possible, railroads that served the mines often owned large fleets of cars. Mineral district railroading featured fairly uniform trains—for example, solid trains of hopper cars. These were often painted in rather dull colors reminiscent of the loads they carried, such as black coal hopper cars or mineral red iron ore cars.

The railroad that connected the isolated town of Birora in Phil Stong's regional novel *The Iron Mountain* offered service in "dingy coaches" that passed through nearby tracks occupied by a few hundred 50-ton gondolas.[19] Ore hauling cars are usually short (due to the heavy loads they carry), simply painted (for ease of maintenance), and rather monotonous in appearance. Early twentieth-century historian Ralph D. Williams describes the rail-hauled Lake Superior iron ore traffic as "this toil of Titan, this transfer of red, brown, blue, and purple earth from the Lake Superior mines to the hungry and roaring furnaces of the Ohio and Pennsylvania Valleys," in long trains "day and night, month after month, all the year round, along the up-grade from Cleveland, giant locomotives at front and rear, pulling, pushing, puffing . . ."[20]

The inseparable relationship between mining and railroads has another, often overlooked, corollary: upon the completion of the railroad, building materials, supplies, and architectural components could be shipped in as readily as mineral products could be shipped out, thus signaling the end to the pioneer phase and accelerating the exchange of products and information to temper the isolation. Railroads helped connect mining communities to the rest of the country, a condition that hastened their adoption of nationwide trends and styles.

Although railroads continue to haul substantial mineral tonnage today, trucks have replaced them in many mining areas. What the railroad was to most nineteenth-century mining districts—a lifeline to the outside world—the highway has become today. Mining companies aggressively lobbied for highway improvements in many areas; some initiated early paved road construction themselves to facilitate the shipment of mineral products. It should come as no surprise, for example, that the first concrete road in Arizona was constructed between Bisbee and Douglas in the early twentieth century, thus in effect connecting the mines with the smelters. Much of this road later became upgraded as U.S. Highway 80, but a few abandoned sections of this historic concrete road can still be seen just east of Bisbee, where they parallel the new highway.

Typically, a two-lane blacktop state or federal highway now connects a mining district with the outside world. It is on this path that most travelers enter the district today. As in many other places in America, the services that were once confined to the downtown area may have relocated out along the main roads. Nearly universal automobile ownership has led to the development of peripheral services, including an occasional shopping center along the highway. Most mining towns, however, are not large enough or prosperous enough to have enclosed shopping malls, and the downtown areas of the major communities in the district (such as East Main Street in the Old Lead Belt town of Flat River, Missouri) may remain surprisingly active in the 1990s.

The persistence of historic commercial businesses in mining communities may be a function of isolation, for the nearest large service centers are often many miles away. Even though many of these communities may have far fewer residents than they did in, say, 1915, they still remain important service centers for the surrounding areas because they are the only settlements of any consequence. In many of our larger historic mining towns, the commercial core has persisted even though it may not be particularly prosperous. Eureka (Nevada), Calumet (Michigan), and Wallace (Idaho) come to mind. However, these commercial cores may persist at the expense of the smaller towns in a mining district, whose commercial enterprises may close as neighborhood populations drop below the threshold required for survival.

But the isolation persists despite the initial development of railways and the later upgrading of roads and highways. The silver mining town of Austin, Nevada, is perched in a canyon in the isolated Toiyabe Range, a location described as "dead center in the American West" or, more specifically, "set square in the center of the state, and almost as far from the interstate highway network as it is possible to be . . ."[21] Similarly, residents of the Houghton-Hancock area, nexus of Michigan's copper country, are fond of the anecdote that their community and its university have the distinction of being among the most remote in the United States. They remark that the nearest four-way stoplight is 95 miles distant and that the nearest interstate highway is 150 miles away! As one resident put it, "If you are here, you must have wanted to get here pretty badly."

NUCLEATION

If, as we have seen, mining districts often developed in isolated settings, their settlements did not usually spread out very far from the mineralized areas. In fact, many were concentrated close to the mines—a condition that has fascinated observers for more than a century. Travelers often describe a surprising degree of crowding in the midst of wide open spaces. This description of the development of Rand Camp (later Randsburg) in California's Mojave Desert is typical:

> Here were the usual ingredients of a mine camp. Men continued to flow in, too busy searching for a fortune to care or even think about how the town should build. Streets just happened where it was most convenient, where wagons had already cut a path, or where buildings happened to cluster to shelter each other from the wind. Tents and eventually wood structures followed the curve of wagon ruts, and thus many stood at odd angles to each other. For convenience and companionship, shelters were pushed close together, and later, store buildings were built so near each other that they appeared to be attached. In spite of a whole mountain and miles of desert, the camp huddled in one small draw that led up to the mine diggings.[22]

The descriptive phrase "thrown together" is often heard in discussions about mining towns. This refers not only to the hastily constructed architecture of boom towns, but also to the way in which the place is settled. Writers tell us that buildings huddle as if seeking protection from the elements. Things are concentrated or clustered, and there is a sense of togetherness. In the case of mining communities, growth may be explosive, but it is rarely very scattered; rather, human activities cluster, and the resulting landscape is concentrated in a relatively small area.

Much has been written about the seemingly chaotic development of mining towns—a chaos that is intensified by the close proximity of building activity. In many interpretations, mining is considered more important than formalized town development. In this scenario, the resulting fever of mining claim development leads to a lack of regularity and to an intense clustering of activities close to the mines.

A familiar situation is described in Bisbee, Arizona, which, "like many other mining camps, did not develop as a consciously planned company town . . . Private saloons, stores, lumberyards, and other businesses found their way into town. The layout . . . could hardly be well planned, for its location in a narrow canyon compelled those who built houses to locate them wherever convenience dictated." [23]

According to many interpreters, mining boom towns develop rather organically, in seeming disregard for surface property rights. These descriptions often emphasize a kind of fundamental cooperation on the site. Mrs. Hugh Brown describes the relationship in Tonopah this way:

When I got down into the town, I would see that ages of cloud bursts running down the canyon had levelled off a perfect townsite. The outcroppings where the original discovery had been made were midway up the side of the mountain opposite. All the location claims had been laid out there, but tents "set" better on the level, so the first settlers naturally had put up their tents on the floor of the canyon. As cabins replaced tents, footpaths followed the land level and became streets. [24]

In Tonopah, the topography of the site—a swale or flat between prominent mountains—helped create a nucleus for all activity. Nucleation is the process by which things develop around a nucleus, which the dictionary defines as "a central point, group, or mass about which gathering, concentration, or accretion takes place." The point at which nucleation takes place in a mining area is, of course, the earliest developed mines. It is near this point that the first commercial development usually occurs.

The settlement patterns and resulting landscape of mining country are closely tied to the geology of an area; where and how a town develops depends on what miners know about the quality and shape of the ore body underground. The social and political institutions of the miners and speculators who flock to an area may vary, but town building and mine development go hand in hand because there is a good deal of money to be made from both. As we read the landscapes of mining districts, we see that activities are concentrated in specific places. The result may look haphazard, but it is far from it. The typical mining town is the results of hundreds, perhaps thousands, of individual decisions and mutual agreements between property owners. In company towns, fewer people make these decisions.

Nucleation had serious consequences. Much has been written about the epidemics that swept through mining camps. Crowded accommodations, poor diets, and inadequate health care probably took more lives than mining accidents. Diseases were common in the nineteenth-century mining towns, and even the twentieth-century mining boom in Tonopah brought with it an epidemic of pneumonia that claimed fifty lives the first winter. The typical mining boom town had poor sanitation facilities; in many communities sewage flowed in open ditches; where outhouses and privies were present, they often fouled the ground waters or surface waters or both. In the mid to late nineteenth century, Americans tended to dump all wastes in watercourses, nearly oblivious to the consequences. Given their population densities, mining towns were among the most polluted of our industrialized communities.

Nucleation brought with it the scourge of all mining towns: fire. The densely spaced buildings, many of which were constructed of wood, were easy prey. The sites of many mining communities often exacerbated the situation. Many were located in semiarid hilly or canyon settings that permitted winds to sweep fire from building to building with amazing rapidity. It is a rare mining town indeed, such as Virginia City, Montana, that did not experience a devastating fire during its history. The list of mining towns that suffered disastrous fires is almost endless, including Roslyn (Washington), Goldfield (Nevada), Bodie (California), and Bisbee (Arizona). We need to ask ourselves what effect these fires had on the landscape.

We now know that a disaster simply reinforces—in fact, accelerates—the trends that were underway before that disaster occurred.[25] Thus, if a mining town suffers a fire during a boom period, it will continue to grow rapidly after the ashes cool. This means that its architectural character will be modernized almost overnight, for the fire will be viewed as an opportunity to rebuild in more current style. When the 1908 fire swept through a row of twenty-year-old commercial buildings

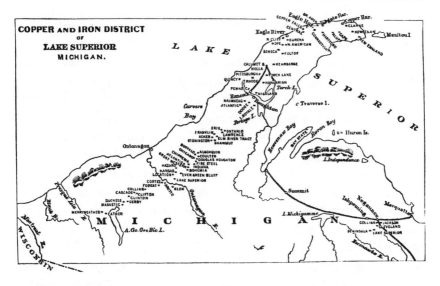

38. *Mining towns are not randomly distributed but are located at places where ore deposits are close to the surface. In the case of the Keweenaw Peninsula of Michigan's copper country, town distribution follows the copper-bearing basalt-conglomerate, and iron mines cluster near Negaunee and Ishpeming, as shown on this map. From Balch 1882.*

along Bisbee's Upper Main Street, the new streetscape that rose from the ashes possessed a kind of architectural homogeneity, in an early twentieth century style. And, of course, brick and stone were selected for new construction because masonry was considered more fireproof.

So far we have discussed the nucleation or concentration of building activities that occurs (and has consequences) in a particular mining town. Nucleation, however, can also be seen in the district as a whole, where the distribution of towns follows certain patterns. A look at the map of any mining district reveals a distinctive distribution of communities whose individual locations are determined by the presence of mines or facilities associated with ore processing. The distribution is rarely if ever random: rather, most mining districts have an overall grain or texture of urbanization that closely follows the ore bodies and topography.

Consider, for example, the distribution of communities on the Keweenaw Peninsula of Michigan: the mining towns such as Ameek and Calumet extend in a nearly straight line defining the surface exposure of copper-rich conglomerates and basalt flows (fig. 38). Likewise, the communities of Minnesota's Iron Ranges follow the trend of the ore bodies, resembling so many beads on a chain. The historic mining districts of Nevada bear a close relationship to the state's corrugated basin and range topography, with the mines being found in the faulted, uplifted mountain range blocks that rise like islands from the desert valleys (fig. 39). It is the nucleation of towns in proximity to mineralization—and, in rugged areas, the need to accommodate topography— that leads to settlements being concentrated at very specific points. In some mining communities, the scarcity of level land often encourages development on steep hillsides, and very high densities may result.

The Iron Ranges of Minnesota provide a textbook example of town nucleation. Here in the Great Lakes mining areas, a location refers to a small residential community fairly close to a mine. In studying the distribution and character of Iron Range locations, historical geographer/landscape architect Arnold Alanen has described three major types: unplatted or squatters' locations, company locations, and model locations. Squatters' locations developed haphazardly; Alanen quotes one observer as saying they appeared to have been "poured out of something into a heap." These locations resemble helter-skelter squalid boom towns in that there are few improvements and houses are placed at angles to one another. The company location was "laid out by mining engineers in regular, grid-like patterns" and often contained "well-built housing units that were similar in form, appearance, color, and dimension." The model location was similar, but might have better housing and amenities, including a park, improved utility systems, and perhaps even a tennis court.[26]

As we compare these range locations with mining towns nationwide, we see some parallels. Generally, the physical improvement of mining towns occurs through time: the earliest are often the most primitive or at least are the most lacking in order. Their nucleation is a result of expediency, and there is little thought of amenities or permanence. They may be designed, or rather developed, around a feature such as a gulch, creek, or early trail rather than being oriented to the compass. There is evidence that the regularized platting of mining towns occurs in a second, more formalized phase characterized by the regularization of internal space in the entire mining district. This, as we shall see, coincides with the consolidation and heavy capitalization of the mines, that is, strong control by powerful companies.

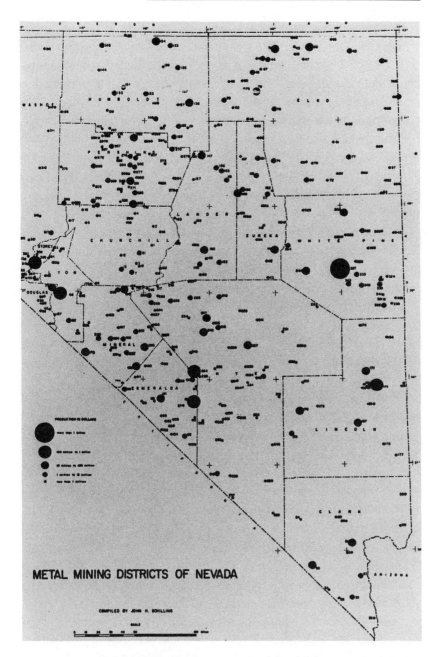

METAL MINING DISTRICTS OF NEVADA

39. *A map of mining districts in Nevada shows a very different spatial distribution: each is located with regard to mineralized, uplifted mountain blocks that stand like so many islands above the surrounding desert valleys. After Schilling 1976; also in Hardesty 1988.*

By carefully comparing the layout or street plan of mining towns, we see that they are highly variable in design: some have no particular order, while some are platted in grids from the outset; still others become more regularized with the passage of time, being replatted as more formal organizations and institutional structures develop to set things right. Some mining communities, perhaps the most distinctive, beautifully and defiantly reflect their topographic settings in tortuous canyons and steep hillsides. Urban planning historian John Reps has shown that many mining communities developed with a surprisingly high degree of regularization, platted in the checkerboard grid patterns common in America during much of the nineteenth and early twentieth century.[27] This, of course, reveals that there was much planning in addition to much speculation going on at the time of their initial development. Nevertheless, other researchers have noted that mining communities tend to develop in linear (as opposed to square) patterns; in studying the street and road patterns of smaller mining communities on the Nevada frontier, Donald Hardesty concludes that "it is clear that the grid pattern was not all that common. Many small settlements are linear strips along roads or convenience clusters around mills and mines."[28]

In addition to the factor of time, size may be a determinant in the shape or layout of mining communities; perhaps the smaller communities were likely to be developed with less need for, or sense of, regularized order. And then there is the factor of topography: in a number of cases, we find that community layout bears a fairly strong relationship to topographic setting, with towns on relatively level sites (such as Tombstone and Leadville) being platted in the most desirable familiar checkerboard patterns, while places in decidedly recalcitrant topographic settings, such as Bisbee and Central City, are the most likely to show few or no traces of a grid.

Certainly the stereotypical or popularized mining community is a place where the topographic setting controls street and land division patterns. Its crooked, winding, narrow main street, irregular, postage stamp–size lots, and maze of narrow side streets tackling the steep hillsides impart a sense of mystique and beauty that early speculators probably never anticipated. These places are common and memorable enough to form an archetype. In reality, however, they represent a minority of mining town layouts. Overall, the majority of mining town plats, about 70 percent, exhibit varying degrees of rectangularity in their layout, an indication of the need for order and ease in surveying property lines. But this pattern varies according to time settled, the degree of centralized planning versus speculative development, and regional conditions.

In whatever type of plat, mining towns often tend to be densely settled—actually crowded—places. The character of the entire mining district, however, is determined by the shape of individual communities and their relationship to each other, and, furthermore, by the three-dimensional objects or landmarks that are found in each scene. Towns are developed in the context of artifacts—many of which are architectural. The layout of streets helps to determine the view we get of objects and topography. Towns laid out in regularized grid patterns are likely to be more open than places that have streets that intersect at odd angles. Our views are liable to be more restricted in mining communities that exhibit little formal planning, a factor that adds an element of intrigue and then surprise as familiar features such as headframes, mine buildings, and ore dumps are framed or targeted by our lines of view. Such large objects in the landscape, regardless of plat type, help accentuate the feeling of nucleation, for they define the horizon line and create a feeling of clustering, if not compression, of activities: in mining country, the evidence of mining activity pervades every scene, reinforcing the dominance of a single industry in the life of the settlement and its residents.

DIFFERENTIATION

Surely there is a mine for silver,
and a place for gold which they refine.
Iron is taken out of the earth,
and copper is smelted from the ore.
—Job 28:1–2

This quotation reveals an age-old fact about the mining industry—it has two faces: acquisition and production. Very few metals are found in the native or pure state. Most are combined with other undesirable minerals or rock, called gangue, or are found in states where the metal is combined with another element, such as sulfur or oxygen. It is the role of the industry to separate them and to provide as nearly pure a product as possible. This means that a mining district often has at least two tasks to perform, mining and smelting, and that two primordial elements of nature—earth and fire—interact here.

Smelting, the use of heat to separate metals from their ores, may require the intermediate treatment of ores before they get to the furnace. This often includes milling (the physical crushing of the ore) and concentration (the use of liquid systems to separate ores from the gangue physically or chemically). Smelting may also involve the addition of other materials (fluxes), such as limestone or charcoal, that must be mined or produced. After smelting, the metal may require further treatment, which is called refining. All of these processes may be carried out at some distance from the mines; but, ideally, the closer the better in that transportation costs are reduced. All of the industrial processes associated with the mining industry are interconnected, requiring large amounts of energy, labor, and two other primordial elements: air and water.

The typical mature metals mining district unites or integrates a series of separate activities, such as mine workings, ore crushers, and furnaces. Each of these activities may spawn separate communities of workers, and each community may develop its own character or identity. This process actually begins in the first mining community settled. This nucleus tends to grow into an urban hub for the district. It does so by becoming internally more complicated, in terms of both its services and its built environment. Mining historian David Wolff describes the process in the Black Hills gold mining town of Deadwood:

> As mining processes became more sophisticated, so did Deadwood. It evolved into a mining hub, providing necessities for the miners and mining companies of the area. Beginning as a town mainly inhabited by miners, it became a business center that catered to the mining men. The census of 1880 indicated that of the nearly four thousand residents, only twenty-nine percent classified themselves as miners.[29]

Diversification is the process by which variation develops: when things diversify, their variety increases. Because mining camps attract

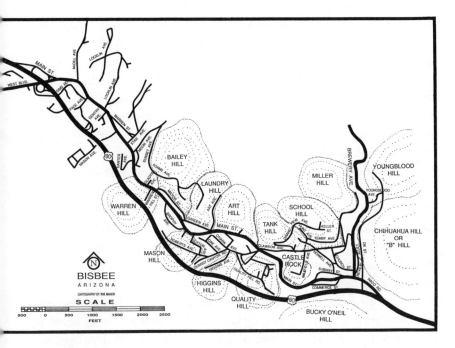

40. Map showing the hills of Bisbee—a vernacular interpretation of the social geography of the community in relation to the topography. Map by the author based on research done in 1982.

a large number of unrelated people, social diversification may occur very quickly and be long lasting. Shortly after its founding, Bisbee, Arizona, developed into a complex mosaic of neighborhoods. The topography helped define these neighborhoods, which soon bore colorful names like Brewery Gulch, Chihuahua Hill, and School Hill. By around the turn of the century, at least thirteen distinctive, topographically defined neighborhoods existed. They persist today, for a person is said to live on "Quality Hill" or "Art Hill" despite the fact that no official map of the city shows these locations.

In order to identify each of these persistent historic neighborhoods geographically (fig. 40), I began to interview Bisbee residents in each of the named areas, asking them to circle their neighborhood on a map. They could do so without much difficulty. In order to verify the boundaries they had drawn, I brought an unmarked street map of the city down to the fire station and asked veteran fire fighters to outline the neighborhoods. "Where," I asked, "would you head if a person reported a fire as being 'on Tank Hill'?" (and so on), until they had quickly marked the dozen topographically defined neighborhoods on the map, with no disagreement as to where each was located.

Bisbee is not alone in this type of diversity, for many mining communities develop tightly clustered neighborhoods or residential areas. Eureka, Utah, is similar: on my January 1988 visit to the community, geographer Gary Peterson pointed out about a dozen neighborhoods in the small, tightly developed townsite, which occupies only a few hundred acres. Some of these neighborhoods may be only a cluster or row of a dozen houses, but to local residents they are what Kevin Lynch calls districts. Like the dozens of small neighborhoods in Butte, Montana, they can usually be distinguished by architectural style.

This geographical (and architectural) diversity extends beyond the limits of the main town and soon shapes the complex character of the entire mining district. Shortly after a mining camp develops, it begins to become a service center for the mining population. It stays closely clustered around the early mining activity; but, if other mines develop elsewhere in the district, they also foster commercial development nearby. Satellite communities may soon develop as the mining district itself becomes more diversified.

Mining populations attract providers of services, and soon a smaller and smaller percentage of the population is actually mining underground: an increasing number of people provide goods and services. Furthermore, as a mining district develops, milling and processing become more complicated and sophisticated because the quality of ore extracted may vary through time and across a district. The original town may often retain its dominant position, but these other satellite communities become indispensable in the production of minerals.

In some mining districts, the topography either may help to foster the growth of satellite communities or may help to define their individual identities further. In writing of her beloved Tintic Mining District in Utah, for example, Beth Kay Harris interprets the creation of numerous towns as follows: "Because of the mountainous terrain, the district was divided into six settlements: Dividend, Mammoth, Silver City, Diamond, Eureka, and Robinson. Ironton (or Junction), six miles to the northwest, was the railroad and shipping center. Eureka was the largest camp of the district, employing, at the height of her production, more than five thousand men in her underground workings."[30]

The typical mining district, then, is a complicated grouping of rather specialized mining/processing communities. Although the natural environment, type of material mined, or regional architectural style may provide some overarching visual unity to a particular mining district, each town or area within that district has its own unique personality and distinctive landscape. This may be surprising if we think of mining as monolithic. If, however, we remember that it is a complicated system of production requiring varied skills, then the diversity is more or less predictable.

By looking carefully at these communities, we can better interpret the character of the entire district. We can also see how complicated the typical mining district really is—it is a whole, dependent on the form and function of its individual parts, all of which are systematically interrelated in the process of mineral extraction, reduction, and shipment. The labor force may be highly differentiated into groups of people who fit into various places along this mechanized processing chain, and housing and settlement may reflect this specialization.

For example, in almost every metals mining district one finds several underground mines (in the case of copper or iron mines, these may have been eclipsed by the development of an open pit), mills where ore is pulverized, concentrators where the percentage of metals is increased through the precipitation of metal-rich sediments, and, in some cases, smelters to increase the percentage of metal into richer matte. Smelting may result in fairly pure anodes that can bear shipping quite some distance to the refinery, where it is rendered virtually pure.

All these processes—and the buildings and structures housing them—are integrated or interconnected, at first by wagon roads and then by railroads, which may later be superseded by improved roads, conveyors, and/or slurry pipelines. The typical mining district provides a complicated transportation system for the movement of mineral products in various states of upgrading, from waste rock to ore and concentrates. Roads and rail lines thread their way through the district, linking the various parts into a system; nearby communities house workers and provide services and goods.

This diversification process has continued into the twentieth century. In his pioneering two-volume work on the railroads of Nevada and eastern California, David Myrick describes the intimate relationship between mining district diversification and the railway lines that permitted them to develop.[31] Several mining districts, including Tonopah, Bullfrog, and Goldfield, boomed into development around 1900 to 1906. They quickly diversified as satellite communities sprang up around each initial boom town. Goldfield, for example, soon developed a number of satellites, including Columbia, Milltown, and Jumbotown. Each community was connected by a road system and a complicated web of competing mining railroads.

Diversification may be fueled by hopes and speculation. Consider "The Bullfrog Map" (fig. 41). It provides an excellent example of the anatomy and physiology of a developing mining district, with the parts identified and compared to those of a self-contained familiar organism. The cartographer, T. G. Nicklin of the *Bullfrog Miner*, used artistic license to show the mines, mills, and towns connected by a circulatory system that consists of railroads, some of which were never built. He placed several townsites in anatomically strategic positions, the railroad junction town of Beatty being the heart, and the gold mining town of Bullfrog—as a wag noted—the armpit. The bullfrog analogy appears a bit fanciful until one remembers the origin of the district's name (a rich, warty green and gold speckled ore), and the inevitable need for people to ascribe a kind of order to places.

To help visitors find their way around Arizona's Warren Mining District, a merchant painted a map on the side of his restaurant in the 1960s. This map (fig. 42) helped orient the hapless traveler to the "traffic circle" (a major circulation node constructed in 1958) at the heart of the mining district. It also depicted the headframes of important mines and used topographic features as points of reference. We can join Kevin Lynch in calling these features landmarks. Like most large mining districts, this area is a complicated system of small communities located near the major producing mines. An equally complicated network of roads must be traversed to get anywhere. The merchant, tiring of giving directions to bewildered travelers, finally painted the map on the stucco wall, where it remained until the early 1980s, when a more sophisticated sign erected nearby by the Chamber of Commerce replaced it.

A visitor to the Flat River area of eastern Missouri could tell from a

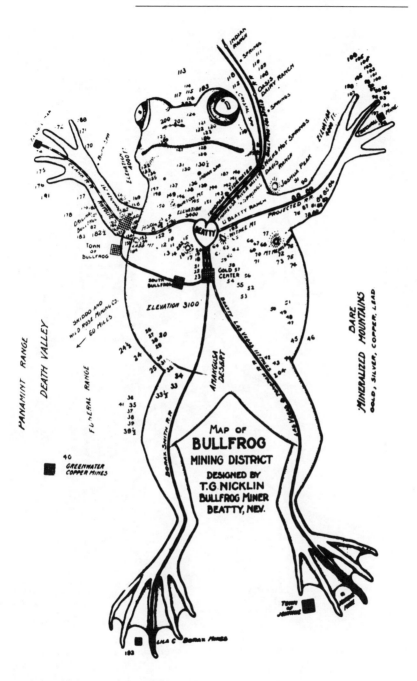

41. *A fanciful map of the Bullfrog Mining District, Nevada, shows that the character of a mining district is determined by the spatial relationship among its parts. From Myrick 1963.*

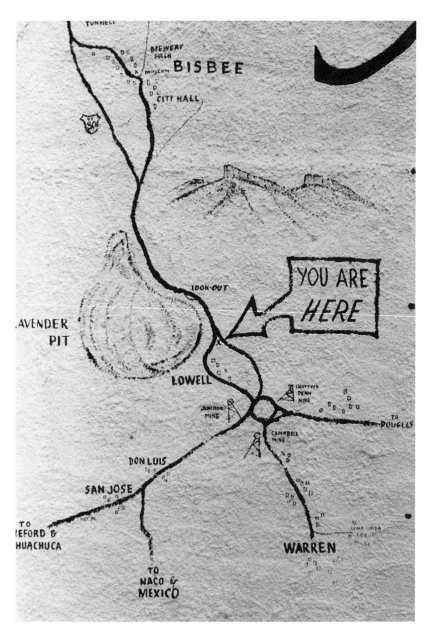

42. *Map of the Warren Mining District painted on the side of a building in Lowell, Arizona, helps acquaint travelers with the complicated positioning of towns in the area. Note that the Lavender Pit is prominent, as are the tilted limestone ridges that form a backdrop to the district: both are landmarks. This map was painted over about 1982. 1980 photo by the author.*

street map alone that this is a former mining district, for the community is really almost a dozen small towns located very close to each other and linked by a sinuous road network that skirts large areas of tailings (fig. 43). To confirm this impression, the traveler need only look at the landscape and see the headframes of lead mines standing in the distance and huge dunelike chat piles rising above the otherwise gently rolling countryside. In the early years of this century, one would have experienced this landscape on foot, in a horse-drawn vehicle, or from an electric streetcar that threaded its way through the district.

In their design and construction, the mining district electric streetcar (or interurban) lines reaffirmed the complexity of mature districts, for they served to interconnect the diverse settlements or neighborhoods. This meant that trolley lines would weave around already-existing features, following roads or using private rights of way where convenient. In his book on the electric railroads of Minnesota, Russell Olson describes the manner in which the Mesaba Railway line was constructed to avoid huge piles of overburden and ore as it ran between Hibbing and Gilbert on the Iron Range. As the open pit operations were enlarged, portions of this electric interurban railway had to be relocated to accommodate the topographic change.[32]

Typically, mining district interurban lines connected the largest (and often the oldest) community in the district with the satellite communities. Each of these satellites might house a different ethnic group or serve a particular function, such as milling or smelting. Under ideal conditions, the major mines were connected to residential and shopping areas. In describing the development of satellite mining communities in the Tri-State lead mining area around Joplin, Missouri, Harry Hood, Jr., notes that "as the mines moved west into Kansas and Oklahoma, the [trolley] line was extended to meet those needs."[33]

The Hocking–Sunday Creek Traction Company, based in the mining and railroad center of Nelsonville, Ohio, appears to be a rather typical mining district traction line. On its route to Athens, it traversed numerous coal mining towns in the Sunday Creek Valley. Its survey report of 1910 tells the reader and potential investor that,

as is well known, miners and their families are great travellers. They make good wages and their hours of work are generally short. They are liberal spenders and a great deal of their pleasure

FLAT RIVER AREA STREET MAP

43. *A street map of the Flat River area of Missouri shows the complicated pattern of interconnected communities characteristic of large, mature mining districts. Certain of the names (Rivermines and Leadington) might indicate mining activity, as would the large tailings or chat piles also shown on the map. 1980 map drawn by L. D. Busenbark to a scale of 1 inch equals 1,600 feet; reduced here to approximately one-fourth original size.*

is in travelling about the immediate vicinity of their homes. We have found it to be a fact that the amount of receipts per capita of tributary population on an interurban line is considerably greater in mining territory than in any other.[34]

The major mining districts usually had fairly sophisticated internal transportation networks. Most of their interurban and streetcar lines were built by mining interests or syndicates beginning just after the turn of the century. Many such lines lasted about twenty years, being abandoned by about 1925 to 1930 when their mining districts fell on hard times; a few were replaced by bus lines, some of which lasted into the 1950s and 1960s. The rise and fall of the Warren-Bisbee Railway, which lasted from 1908 to 1928 and was replaced by a bus system operated by the copper company, illustrates the intimate relationship between diversification and transportation in a mining district.[35]

Despite the passage of time, the diversified settlements or satellites often retain their identity in the present. As we travel through the bituminous coal mining country of southwestern Pennsylvania, for example, we find that the character of each mining community is distinct, despite the fact that they are clustered along the same road or are located in the same valley. Each has a name or number, and residents will tell you that the identity of each place is determined by which mine it served or which ethnic group lived (or still lives) there. Residents are often eager to relate stories about each small mining community or patch, as they are called in the Pennsylvania coal country. Although the origin of the term "patch" appears to have been lost, it has been used for about a century to refer to neighborhoods that, as one local resident at Windber, Pennsylvania, told me in 1989, "sprang up like patches as the mines developed." The term is used with a mixture of affection and disdain today.

Diversity is a trademark of our America mining districts. In fact, acre for acre, they are probably the most varied communities in the country. This internal diversity is found from coast to coast and in mining districts that produce very different minerals. No two mining districts develop exactly the same pattern, of course. A comparison of two copper mining districts in Arizona (Clifton-Morenci and Warren) that were subject to roughly the same economic fluctuations and similar technological changes reveals that their diversification was somewhat affected by local topography and differences in management styles of the major mining companies. But both mining districts diversified, and that diversification helps to identify their character even today.

Diversification is related to the sophistication of the technology and the scale of production in a particular district. We find greater and greater complexity developing when the system of mining, milling, and processing ores is integrated. And the greater the complexity of activities (that is, the more thorough the treatment of ores), the larger the population. This simply means that our largest mining districts are likely to be the most complex. In metals mining districts, the presence of a smelter that can treat a wide variety of regional ores usually assures a dominant role for the district. Typically, large planned communities spring up around such later smelters to minimize the distance workers must be transported.

"Smelterville" or "Smeltertown" is a location where mining meets metallurgy—the place where fire is brought to bear on recalcitrant ores. Because these are often sulfide ores of copper, lead, or zinc, smelter locations are likely to be the smokiest and dirtiest places in the mining district. Sometimes the smelter produces such noxious fumes and smoke that vegetation is killed and agrarian pursuits such as farming or ranching are impossible. In areas where meteorological conditions and topography conspire to trap smoke, smelters may reduce the air quality in the entire district and add to the quality of desolation. We are told that Eureka, Nevada,

> not only produced silver in bonanza quantities; it was the lead capital of the world as well, and the clouds of dense black smelter smoke that constantly swirled over the city yielded a gentle rain of soot. They yielded also other gifts—fumes of sulphur and of arsenic that completely vanquished the native fragrance of the sagebrush. It was not a very pretty place to live, this Base Range city, more like a Pennsylvania coal town than a settlement in the wide open spaces of Nevada.[36]

Smelter workers were usually a separate class of workers, and most lived in their own communities that huddled around the smelter complex. In most metals mining districts, the smelters, which require a lot of water, are located on relatively low-lying land near watercourses

44. The smelter at Herculaneum, Missouri, was constructed to process regional lead ores, and a town developed around it. The smelter stack is a regional landmark. In this photograph, the smelter stack and the community's church help define the economic and social order. 1989 photo by the author.

adjacent to the mines and the mining towns that produced the ore—a seemingly good compromise based on their need for level land, water, and proximity to the ore body. As a district matures, however, smelters tend to be relocated to points more central to the other developing mines in the region. In these cases, the smelter may be located in a rather unmineralized area distant from the mines but close to sources of fuel or water. The copper smelters at Anaconda (Montana), McGill (Nevada), and Douglas (Arizona) provide a case in point, as does the lead smelter at Herculaneum in Missouri (fig. 44).

The smelter may be thought of as the heart of the district or mineral-producing region: ore arrives there for processing from the surrounding mines. The sight of a smelter, or smelters, in full production day and night is absolutely unforgettable. Their metallic, sulfurous smoke fills the canyons or stretches across the open countryside so that the very atmosphere of the entire region is affected. With the demand for clean air, most smelters have been shut down. Actually, the recognition that smelters are a serious problem is not new. The pollution had become so severe in Bisbee by the turn of the century that the smelters were finally relocated to the new town of Douglas, 25 miles away.

The diversification of the Butte, Montana, district was not complete until the huge smelter at Anaconda's Washoe Reduction Works was opened in 1905. This huge smelting complex superseded one across the valley. Its stack is reported to be the tallest freestanding masonry structure in the world: 585 feet. The closing of this smelter a few years ago, like that of the Douglas smelter in 1987, signaled the eclipse of the district as an integrated copper producer. In most mining districts, the tall smelter stack stands as a barometer by which the economic health of the district is measured by the local population.

Differentiation, then, is a geographic expression of technological and economic factors. It is best seen in the land use patterns, which are extremely complicated mosaics. The landscape's complexity mirrors this pattern, for the district is really a mineral production system that is originally placed in a confined setting and later, with improvements in transportation, may spread across the entire region. What may seem chaotic at first glance—a maze of flumes and railroad tracks connecting a mill or concentrator here and a smelter there—is really well ordered. It seems confusing because being in a mining district is like being inside a factory, except that the internal workings of the production system are outdoors. Thus, the mining landscape is inside out, revealing workings of production that are normally hidden behind high fences or factory walls. In an active mining district, conveyors clank overhead, concentrators pound away at recalcitrant ores, and smelters glare and spew smoke and slag across the landscape. The byproducts of this activity are quite unmistakable and readily visible in the landscape.

When we read the landscapes of mining districts, we learn that industry is the dominant factor; everything else—commercial districts and residential areas in particular—serves it. These normally genteel land uses may be shoehorned in among mining properties and subject to their noise and pollution. But as we look closer, we see that they also fit into a pattern: not all parts of town are as good as others, and that determines where people live. In mining districts, as in other industrialized environments, the distance between people can be measured both geographically and vertically—spatially in particular locations and on a social hierarchy or social scale. As we shall see, where people live in any mining district is dependent on their place in the chain of production.

STRATIFICATION

The landscape of any particular mining district is really a mosaic of smaller scenes created by, or for, different groups of people who have diverse tasks to perform. Although the overall unifying theme of a mining district is industrial, there is an underlying social geography. As we travel through a mining district, we see neighborhoods or rows of small houses lived in by miners, other areas for mill hands, and still other areas where the larger, more pretentious homes of managers are found. These residential areas form intricate patterns, fitted between the topographical wastes of industry and their exclamation points—mine machinery and structures. Power and impotence are everywhere juxtaposed, for mining district landscapes are, above all, landscapes of environmental and social control.

Stratification, the process by which things are divided into classes, castes, or social strata, is common in the development of mining districts. Everyone knows his or her place, for social position is defined by occupation. Although this social stratification has always been important in mining districts, there is some evidence that it actually intensified during the nineteenth century as mining required greater and greater investment, that is, became more corporate.

In describing early Nevada mining camps and those in eastern California, for example, geographer Earl Kersten, Jr., notes that "virile, enthusiastic free-livers" who were "unconventional yet honest" pioneered the Bodie Mining District: "But . . . before 1890, mining began to change. The new mines that arose on the heels of new discoveries after 1900 were different. The companies were better organized and financed, and operations were more efficient. Now one group of men labored underground, another group supervised them, and a third group, usually in distant financial centers, provided the operating capital and gained the profits."[37]

This stratification of the mining population into three classes (laborers, supervisors, and financiers) appears to characterize all mining districts and most industry in free-market economies. We see it in most mining districts as early as the 1860s. Shortly after the first mines were developed, outside interests invested heavily in the mines. Those who speculated on mining ventures were among the most rugged of the nineteenth-century capitalists. Many either had a religious, almost Calvinistic bent or, conversely, were part of a new breed of secular materialists; both believed that the worth of an individual was measured by material wealth. They were industrialists, but had an added challenge: to tame a wilderness as they drew wealth out of the earth.

They soon came to understand that mining was more than simply finding a good mineral deposit and hauling it away. What separated the winners from the losers in this business was the knowledge of how to process a particular ore body. That took equipment and laborers. In order to make rational investment decisions, mine owners needed advice, and they sought it from professionals who were to form the middle class of the industry: mining engineers. Indeed, the professional mining engineer helped dictate the character of mining districts from coast to coast. Historian Clark Spence tells us that mining engineers were virtually all males, jacks-of-all-trades, and often came from families of some means.[38] They needed to be knowledgeable about all aspects of mining company operations, including housing and transportation. Many studied mining engineering at colleges or universities, and they formed a kind of pragmatic fraternity.

Their "lace boot brigade" came to symbolize the refinement and growing professionalism of mining—and the control of the industry by outside capital. Spence cites 1917 census figures that show about an equal number having experience in coal mining (1,795), copper mining (1,758), gold and silver mining (1,840), and lead and zinc mining (1,384), with fewer (842) in iron mining and another 500 or so in other metals.[39] Although we tend to romanticize the role of miners and are awed by the power of the mine owners, it was this middle class—the mining engineers—that shaped the developing geography of the mining district: they, more than any other group, made the locational and design decisions that resulted in a distinctive landscape.

Coal and metals mining districts flourished in some of the more remote areas of the country, but they were simply a part of the industrial revolution that helped create strong class divisions throughout American society. The landscape of a typical mining district shows this stratification at every turn; in fact, the densely settled mining district landscape accentuates the differences between wealth and poverty, because it packs so much society into such a small space. This tripartite industrial social class structure (owner, manager, worker) is a dominant feature of mining district landscapes.

It is especially pronounced in housing. Travelers often commented on the large home(s) of the wealthy mine owner(s). In most mining districts, the house of the mine owner or mining company president stands conspicuously, often on a hillside or hilltop some distance from the major ore dumps and tailings or upwind of the smelter. The house is almost invariably done in a high style, its architect either well known or progressive. This symbol of stratification can be found as far back as the early nineteenth century, when, for example, the large house of the mine owner stood on a hillside overlooking the worker's cottages at Hopewell Furnace, an iron mining enclave in eastern Pennsylvania. This pattern extended to the Far West, where the homes of Colorado's mining nabobs stood on hillsides above mining towns crowded with the shanties of mine workers.

These ostentatious residences are all the more remarkable when one remembers that most mine owners owned even more impressive/pretentious houses in the distant cities they called home. In Salt Lake City, for example, we find a row of millionaire's homes on the "Avenues," most of which were erected from the earnings in the silver and gold mines of the state's mountain ranges. Denver had a similar enclave. These serve to remind us that the mining landscape extends, in a manner of speaking, into the heart of the finest residential areas of American cities, hundreds, or perhaps a thousand or more, miles from the source of wealth, reaffirming the colonial quality of mining and its powerful result on the landscape and economy of our country.

In the mining towns that spawned this opulence, the managerial classes were rewarded with protected social status and access to a number of amenities (such as country clubs) often denied to the laboring classes. Their housing reaffirmed their status. The homes of mining company managers are usually identifiable by size or architectural style, almost always fashionable but with fairly restrained detailing.

45. *Social stratification is evident in the landscape of mining country. Here, in the coal mining company town of Roda, Virginia, we see the supervisors' housing (large houses on landscaped lots) juxtaposed with the housing of miners at left (standardized company housing) as photographed in about 1925. Westmoreland Collection, Hagley Museum and Library.*

They are often clustered in an identifiable enclave, sometimes on a hillside or hilltop location, giving validity to the vernacular term "quality hill."

The houses of the managers are usually large, perhaps two stories, and are often painted in the same rather restrained or conservative color scheme. These houses tend to be pattern-book in inspiration, usually looking a great deal like the houses of the middle-class merchants in other cities and towns. They always imply a restrained prosperity—architectural amenity without lavish ostentation. They often have fairly spacious landscaped lots around them, creating a sense of domestic tranquillity in the midst of the hard work of the mining district (fig. 45). We see them in mining districts across the country, from the towns of Pennsylvania's anthracite region to Eureka, Utah, where they cluster in the community of Fitchville, the serene neighborhood where geologists and mining company bosses and superintendents lived. Fitchville was the residential area for the managers of the Chief Consolidated Mining Company: many of its homes were designed by architect Walter J. Cooper, while the chief's residences and offices were designed and erected by N. A. Jones, the mine's surface foreman.[40]

Although the class divisions in a mining district usually are determined by who owns the mines, who manages them, and who works in them, they are in turn complicated by the diversity of mining populations in the laboring classes. If we think of a social pyramid that represents the population that earns a living from mining, we usually find a small number of Anglo-American mine owners at the top, a managerial class that is largely northern European but witnesses some assimilation of other (usually European) minorities, and a progressively larger number of ethnic minorities at the bottom. It is the working classes at the bottom of this pyramid that have the richest ethnic variety. In fact, size for size, mining districts are probably the most ethnically diverse of all communities in America.

Indeed, ethnic diversity is one of the most remarked-upon traits of mining towns. For about 150 years, travelers comparing mining towns to both nonmining towns and other mining towns invariably have detailed the colorful ethnic neighborhoods. The following description of the mercury mining town of New Almaden, California, is typical: "Looking down from Mine Hill into the valley below we see by the character of the houses that there are two divisions in the little burg, one allotted to the Mexican miners, the other to the English speaking, which are mostly Cornish."[41]

Miners and other mine workers lived in neighborhoods or sections that had a rather different character and quality. Their housing varied from region to region, but it was usually modest in size and simple in appearance. Single miners might occupy the very simple one-room miners' cabins, but more often miners and their families lived in three- and four-room houses that were joined by common walls to form row housing (as was common in the coal fields of Pennsylvania) or, more often, were separate houses located very close to others of similar style. Most miners and their families had small yards, in which might be found a garden, clothesline, and—because indoor plumbing was not available—wash buckets and outhouses.

Even after the turn of the century, mining communities were developed as segregated enclaves. McGill, Nevada, a town built by Nevada Consolidated Copper Company after 1906, provides a good example. Expanding upon Georgia Shaver's "memories of McGill," archaeologist/historian Barry Price tells us:

Workers were segregated according to ethnicity, income, and other social factors, with the Greek community assigned to the lower or west side of Main Street below J row, the Japanese to the north end of town above the flume and trestle. Still farther north was "Austrian Town," where Serbs, Croatians, and Slavs from the Austro-Hungarian Empire resided. Hispanics and Blacks also had their own small enclaves behind the commercial district.[42]

In most mining districts, the houses of the miners and mill hands derive from at least one of three different housing traditions: vernacular, speculative, and corporate. Much has been written about the vernacular or folk housing tradition in American rural communities, but virtually nothing is known about such housing in smaller urban places such as mining towns. The few studies that have been done suggest that dominant folk building types were adapted to the relatively urban settings of our American mining districts. Consider, for example, the stone Cornish houses built by the "Cousin Jacks" in Mineral Point, Wisconsin. In addition to their celebrated skills as hard rock miners, we are told that

> the Cornish were also skilled stone cutters and masons. The hillsides on either side of Shake Rag Street were opened here and there as quarries for building stone. The limestone, as it was quarried, was damp, easily cut, shaped, squared dressed and drilled. The early Cornish used the limestone at hand and built about 30 houses along Shake Rag Street. Some of these were only a dozen feet in front of the quarry from which the stone had been taken.[43]

With very few exceptions, our historic mining districts are tapestries of social and ethnic diversity. As we saw in the section on diversification, a visit to a mining district almost always reveals neighborhoods where workers of different classes and ethnic backgrounds lived: such sections may be formally named, like "Spanishtown" and "Englishtown" in the mercury mining community of New Almaden (California) or they may have informal names like "Tintown" or "Jiggerville" (Arizona) that become institutionalized over the years. Some informal pejorative names, like "Nigger Hill" (in the coal mining town of Congo, Ohio) or the numerous "Hunkytowns" or "Dagotowns," are no longer fashionable, but persist in the memories of old-timers.

The indigenous architecture of Chihuahua Hill in Bisbee stood in stark contrast to the frame housing nearby. Historic photographs even

46. The origin of the name "Tintown," an enclave of Hispanic population in Arizona's Warren Mining District, is apparent from this early twentieth century snapshot. Ninety years later, the town still retains its ethnicity, but many of the earlier metal-sheathed houses have been replaced or remodeled. Ethnic neighborhoods were common in most of America's mining districts. Beasecker Collection, Bisbee Mining and Historical Museum.

reveal *jacales*, or stick and straw housing, some of it mud covered. An archaeological study of Candelaria, a Nevada mining camp that boomed in the late nineteenth century, has uncovered traces of Paiute Indian housing.[44] Phil Notarianni's studies of the architectural heritage of coal mining towns in eastern Utah reveal Italian, Slovenian, and Greek roots in the landscape and history.[45] Other research on the gold camps of the West from California to Montana has documented the legacy of Chinese miners. Arnold Alanen's studies of the mining communities of the upper Great Lakes have brought to light the building traditions of Finnish and other ethnic groups. Most revealing of all, perhaps, is the visual image behind the name Tintown, a clustering of Hispanic population in Arizona's Warren Mining District that was located across the railroad tracks from South Bisbee. An early twentieth century snapshot shows the homes, which are little more than shacks, sheathed in corrugated sheet metal (fig. 46).

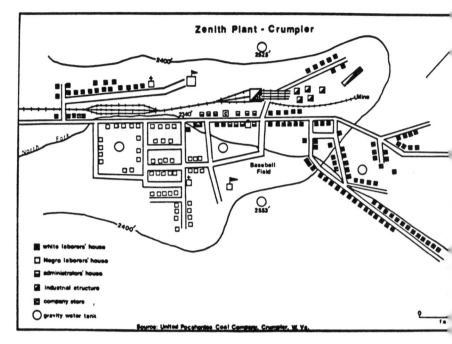

47. A map of Crumpler, West Virginia, clearly shows the social geography:
like many coal towns, Crumpler had a large black population. From
Gillenwater 1972.

Mining communities may have been cosmopolitan, but they were not
necessarily liberal. In fact, it was common to find some ethnic groups
effectively outlawed in some communities, either by law or by mob
rule. This happened to Chinese in many western camps and to blacks
in others. However, mining companies themselves often imported specific groups who could be counted on to keep to themselves and work
hard. Some were brought in specifically to break strikes. Black miners
in particular could be found working coal mines from coast to coast.
Rendville (Ohio), Buxton (Iowa), and Roslyn (Washington) are just
three of hundreds of coal mining towns where imported work forces of
black miners kept production up and costs down.

A look at a map of the coal mining community of Crumpler, West
Virginia, reveals a more or less classic pattern of racial and occupational segregation (fig. 47). The town is essentially divided by a creek,
along which a railroad spur runs to serve the mines and tipples. The
"Negro" section is separated from the housing of white workers and

managers by the creek and the railroad. Note, too, that various small neighborhoods are defined by rows of houses that line roads, a common pattern in mining communities everywhere in America. Crumpler possesses another social feature common in many mining towns—a baseball field or diamond. Wherever enough flat land could be set aside, this most popular of American sports often found a place. In describing the coal mining towns of Wyoming, A. Dudley Gardner and Vera Flores conclude that "since diverse ethnic groups made up coal towns, the baseball teams and bands provided a means of drawing the community together."[46]

Ethnic diversity appears to be common to all of America's mining areas, and their landscapes may still reveal the signs of it despite years of assimilation and social mobility. One still sees the signs that identify Chinese restaurants and laundries in Butte, Montana. According to historical archaeologists/historians Donald Hardesty and Valerie Firby, "ethnicity and ethnic relations are among the most important questions to be asked about mining settlements on the western frontier."[47] Their map of the social geography of Virginia City, Nevada, during its nineteenth-century boomtown period of development reveals several distinct neighborhoods (fig. 48). A black or African-American section was part of the downtown commercial area, a Chinese section lay immediately east of downtown toward the mining areas, the houses of Irish and English families were on the hill above the downtown area, and the Paiute Indian population lived on the periphery of the town. Other ethnic groups also could be found in this cosmopolitan community on the mining frontier.

Hardesty describes the topographic stratification:

On the upper streets of the town were the large and luxurious houses of mine and mill owners and wealthy merchants. The commercial and governmental districts were on B and C streets just below, along with "working class" residences. Below C street in descending social and geographical order were the "red light" district and Chinatown. And at the very bottom scattered around the mill tailings were the Native American residences.[48]

As we study the social geography of mining communities, it becomes apparent that many ethnic groups on the lowest rungs of the social ladder were not actually miners, but provided services to the mining

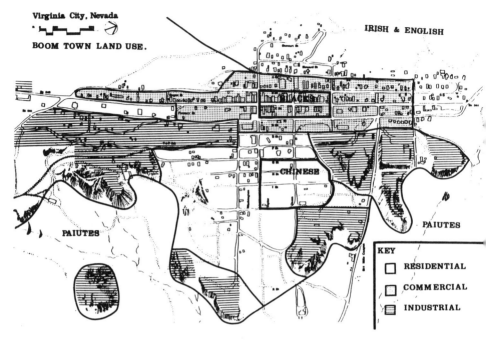

48. *The population stratification in Virginia City, Nevada, was closely related to the topography of the site. From Hardesty and Firby 1980.*

populations. Despite (perhaps because of) their reputation as hard-working miners, Chinese were often banned from working the mines (as they were in Bisbee) and so might be found working in other occupations that served the mining populations. In the West, Chinese populations often farmed or managed laundries and restaurants. In Nevada during the 1870s, Italians and Swiss-Italians were often found in the roles of *carbonari* (producers of charcoal for the smelters), colluded against by teamsters, smelter operators, and merchants.[49]

Discrimination against ethnic groups varied from mining district to mining district. It barred Hispanics from working underground in Bisbee, where they provided water and cordwood that kept the community and its mines functioning. Yet Hispanic miners worked underground in many places, including Arizona's Clifton-Morenci copper mining district and the quicksilver mines around New Almaden, California, where it was said they had a keen "nose" for finding high-quality ore.

New Almaden provides a classic quotation that puts ethnic segre-

gation in visual perspective. The actors in the visual drama are Hispanic and Cornish, and the stage is the tightly controlled, almost feu-
dal mercury mining town in the rugged hills south of San Jose. As
characterized by Mary Halleck Foote, wife of prominent mining engineer Arthur DeWint Foote, during the town's boom period:

> There is no undue propriety about the mining camps on the "Hill."
> Their domestic life has the most unrestrained frankness of expres-
> sion and their charms are certainly not obtrusive. The Mexicans
> have the gift of harmoniousness; they seem always to fit their sur-
> roundings, and their dingy little camp has made itself at home in
> the barren hills, over which it is scattered; but the charm of the
> Cornish camp lies partly in vivid incongruity between its small,
> clamorous activities, and the repose of the vast, silent nature
> about it . . .[50]

Dell Upton's recent book entitled *America's Architectural Roots:
Ethnic Groups That Built America* is recommended for those who
seek a comprehensive overview of ethnic architecture. Although his
examples are predominantly rural, Upton has provided a set of clues
that can help us to read the landscape of our American mining districts. Those who look for ethnic architecture in the landscape of mining districts need to question an assumption stated or implied in many
works by architectural historians—that architectural traditions are
readily lost through urbanization. What would a very careful look at
the more unpretentious houses in mining towns reveal, especially if we
could look under vinyl and aluminum siding? What would a study of
architectural interiors bring to light? What would a closer look at gardens, and even lawn ornaments, reveal? These studies should be done
before the historic material culture changes (or is completely lost)
through modernization.

The mining landscapes of America are rich, but underexplored,
places to look for the traces of ethnic cultures. In many areas, these
traces would be subtle, for sections of town were likely to be developed
by private speculators rather than "folk architects." Even in boom
towns, standardized house types were put up in hopes that they would
be sold or rented to mining populations. Streets were laid out and
clusters of half a dozen or more houses often built on site by itiner-
ant tradesmen and/or contractors. Typically, these houses were of

shoddy construction. As a town developed its railway connections with the outside world, prefabricated housing could be brought in and assembled.

Although the vernacular housing of ethnic workers and the quickly built housing of speculators are an integral part of the fabric of mining districts, our fascination with them should not overshadow a very important design tradition in America's mining towns—company housing, erected (and sometimes designed) by mining companies themselves. These houses usually possess a functional, almost minimalist, simplicity. Their style may vary from simple, unornamented gabled roof boxes sheathed in standard clapboard or capped (board and batten) siding, to hipped roof, bungalow-style dwellings sheathed in novelty siding. They are often a good clue that we are in mining country, though similar houses might also be built in railroad towns or other single-industry communities.

One almost always finds company housing clustered in groups oriented toward geometrically laid out street grids or strung out in linear rows of, say, half a dozen or more. In whatever configuration, company housing possesses a kind of uniformity of both original construction and maintenance often described as monotonous. These dwellings may house the lower-middle-income populations—for example, certain mill hands and miners involved in servicing the mines. This does not mean that their populations are as monotonous as the exterior forms of the buildings. Again, it is inside these houses, and inside their yards, that we may find clues to the ethnicity of their occupants.

If it is true that expressions of grief are among the most genuine, or at least the most conservative, of cultural traditions, then we should explore the cemeteries of mining districts to see what they can tell us. Consider Roslyn, Washington: here, in the handsome but still mine-scarred Cascade Mountains, lies a coal mining town that served as the location for Stanley Kramer's 1979 film *The Runner Stumbles*, a drama that required a rather forlorn mining town whose mineral riches had run out—and whose landscape showed the signs of former mining activity. Roslyn's main street of false-front buildings is deceptively quiet, its miner's cottages dotting the hills hint at its former density, and the mining museum downtown is a dead giveaway that mining put the town on the map in the first place. But it is the town's cemetery or, rather, twenty-six cemeteries that are the longest-lasting testimony to the incredible ethnic diversity that characterized the place at the turn of the century.

Here, on a hillside at the southwest edge of town, is a veritable city—a microcosm of the social stratification that existed in the town itself. Situated on more than fifteen acres, the cemetery is seen to be numerous neighborhoods, many of which are fenced. According to local historian/sociologist Anne Chenoweth, most of the cemeteries were developed by the separate fraternal orders and nationalities. Many of these cemeteries can be distinguished by surnames and by the style and design of tombstones. Many of the graves have encasements or low, curblike walls around them; others have elaborate fences. Chenoweth adds that "these encasements reflect the economic levels of the deceased": "the more elaborate graves can boast cement walls with iron gates and/or fencing on top of them." In Mount Olivet, the black cemetery, one commonly finds simple rocks outlining the graves, a feature not seen in the other cemeteries, perhaps because "the blacks of the area were indeed on the lower end of the pay scale. They had come to Roslyn as strikebreakers, and were forced to take lower paying jobs when the earlier whites came back to work."[51]

The most definitive study of a mining community cemetery to date appears to have been undertaken in Silver City, Nevada, where two researchers, Ramona Reno and Ronald Reno, studied all of the existing grave markers and compared their field evidence with historic records.[52] They determined that the gravestones fit a pattern of stylistic evolution outlined in an earlier historical-geographical study;[53] they also found that the settling or filling of the cemetery occurred in changing spatial land use patterns that could be grouped into distinct periods related to the mining history of the area. By reading the inscriptions on the gravestones (many were no longer legible, having deteriorated), they also learned that the longevity of the mining population generally increased through time. All things considered, the cemetery is one of the most revealing social landscapes associated with mining communities.

A look at cemeteries in most mining districts shows intense social stratification. Despite their inherent beauty and intrinsic architectural interest, cemeteries in mining districts are not harmonious places. From the silver and gold mining districts of the West, to the copper mines of Michigan and Arizona, to the coal mines across the country, we find people separated by fences and encasements and by the architecture of their monuments: they were buried as they lived. Their graves list the rich ethnic surnames of mining country—Kuzara, Petrovich, Caviglia, Kaapinen, Ruiz, McCormick, Schisler, O'Reily—and we can often find verification of their places of birth on their gravestones—Poland, Serbia, Italy, Finland, Mexico, Scotland, Cornwall, Ireland—as well as most of the mining states of America (fig. 49).

There is a deeper theme visible in the socially stratified landscape of mining districts: gender. Whereas some anthropologists have interpreted mining as symbolically female—mother earth yielding her mineral treasures—American history has placed the exploitation of minerals firmly in the hands of males, possibly a result of our Judeo-Christian heritage that puts men in these occupations as far back in Old Testament times. As we look at the three major levels of miners—owners, managers, and laborers—there are virtually no women among them. Although women have worked underground and in smelters in some locations, and a few even became mining engineers, their presence in these jobs is highly unusual, often occurring during times of acute labor shortages.

This is not to say, however, that women have not been important in the life and economy of mining communities, only that they generally have been excluded from the major occupations of mineral production and processing. In fact, few places have been so dominated, either implicitly or explicitly, by male culture. Those who make decisions are male and, moreover, almost exclusively white and of northern European ancestry. Those who physically shape the landscape under the orders of their supervisors are also male, but are more likely to be of varied ethnic backgrounds.

In order to understand the role of women in mining districts, we have to look at a fourth level of the occupational population pyramid mentioned earlier: the nonmining population, which, in most mining districts, may actually be as large as or larger than the mining population. Numerically, we may find that mine owners represent less than 1 percent of the population, managers about 10 percent, and laborers about 40 percent, meaning that about half the population is not directly employed by the mining industry. This sector of the population consists of other males, women, and children. It includes workers in one of the most important and underappreciated categories of all: home-

49. *Grave markers often illustrate ethnic traditions and contain important information about the place of birth, life span, and ethnic character of mining town populations. The grave of a native of Serbia in Tonopah, Nevada, is marked in the Cyrillic alphabet. 1989 photo by the author.*

makers. It also includes workers in the service industries, in which women played important roles.

In a typical mining district, the sex/gender ratio varied through time. Whereas women might have represented a small minority of the population in the earliest boom days of a mining community, this soon changed. Although we are likely to be impressed by the housing for single males, such as the miners' cabins and rooming houses quite visible in historic photographs of mining districts, we should remember that the longer a district operated, the more family-oriented it was likely to become. As a mining district became successful, families arrived, and the population might stabilize at about 35 to 40 percent female.

Women have helped cement the social order in these family roles, and this is most visible in the residential neighborhoods. It is precisely this role we may overlook because the rest of the landscape contains more visually commanding imagery that can be interpreted as unabashedly male: erect headframes, tall smokestacks, towering mine buildings, huge piles of waste rock, for example. In Freudian terms, "hard places" has a subconscious connotation—a male landscape that most fully manifests the power of men in Judeo-Christian (Western) thought: paternalistic, unyielding, confrontational. For those who look for deeper meanings, much of what we see in the mining landscape is patently male, for it involves externalization (of an otherwise internal place, mother earth), a disassembling rather than a putting back together.

The resulting landscape seems unfinished, in a state of flux, restructured through the use of brute force. In short, the landscape represents two basic themes of power; one is social, whereby a few men hold power over many other men and women; the other is environmental in that man has controlled or dominated mother nature. This perception may account for the frequent use of the word "rape" to describe the physical impact of mining on the environment. Carolyn Merchant has traced the development of mining as a reflection of the rise of science/commerce that defied traditional ancient sanctions against defiling female nature. In *The Death of Nature*, she notes that "sanctioning mining sanctioned the rape or commercial exploration of the earth . . ."[54]

Mining landscapes are among the most difficult for us to interpret rationally, for we know that there are strong subliminal messages about power and gender hidden in them. Those who seek answers about gender in these landscapes need to look more closely at the role of women in the social and economic fabric of mining districts. The recently formed interest group Women in Mining has broken some new ground in this area.

Stereotypically, as described in novels about mining districts, women occupy two seemingly polarized roles: as prostitutes who cater to the libidinous desires of the male population and as agents in bringing order and social control—actually propriety and "morality"—to mining districts. Thus, they occupy both the lowest and the highest positions in society. As we have seen, mining districts offer evidence of this dichotomy in the cribs of their red light districts and the picture-perfect homes of the mine managers' families. This distinction has been immortalized in Conrad Richter's novel *Tacey Cromwell*,[55] but does not tell us very much about a much larger group of invisible women between these two extremes.

As with all landscapes, the look of mining districts always reveals the underlying social and economic order. But this is not static: manifestations of control and power may shift or change through time. The process by which power may become more and more centralized in the hands of one large company is especially important, for it assumes a very strong role in shaping the visual geography of most mining districts, a subject discussed in the following section.

HOMOGENIZATION

The early years of a typical mining district find a flourishing of individual mines, each of which may be under separate ownership. As time progresses, however, the mines usually become consolidated, being purchased by large mining interests, and we find fewer and fewer mining companies operating in the district. When large companies take over numerous mines, improve them, and introduce more sophisticated technology, the smaller miners often find themselves unable to compete. The larger corporations adopt sophisticated technologies, such as froth flotation, that increase efficiency and usually reduce labor requirements but call for space-consuming equipment.

Mining companies also have a penchant for standardization. A look at mining supply catalogs is especially informative, for it helps to explain why certain features, from prefabricated buildings to ore cars, can be found in widely separated mining locations across the United States, and even around the world. Much of the hardware in a typical "western" mine, for example, may have been made in cities as far distant as Columbus, Ohio, where the Jeffrey Company manufactured everything from scoops to mine locomotives. The Marion (Ohio) Steam Shovel Company supplied many of the steam shovels for the open pit iron mines of Minnesota's Mesabi Range, and even huge gold dredges for placer mining operations as far distant as Dawson in the Klondike. One immense elevator dredge shipped to the gold workings near Ruby, Montana, required "eighty-five well loaded freight cars" for shipment from Marion.[56] A few of the largest mining companies, among them the Anaconda Mining Company in Montana, had their own shops and foundries that provided most equipment needed in the mines.

Mining is a conservative industry, but technological changes spread fairly rapidly once they are proven in the field. The professional mining engineer—one of the great shapers of the environment—faces an interesting challenge: successfully introducing new textbook technology into unique environments. The mining engineer's counterpart, the metallurgical engineer who designs the smelter, is also an important actor in the design drama. Actually, the jobs of mining engineer and metallurgical engineer became so integrated that they were indistinguishable after about 1910. By the early years of this century, it had become apparent that mining and processing were inseparable. In order to determine the value of an ore, an engineer had to know enough about the reduction and smelting process to be able to determine whether or not it should be mined in the first place. As mining historian Clark Spence puts it, "in practice, no well-defined boundary was drawn between the fields of work of the mining engineer and the metallurgist."[57] Extensive integrated surveying or sampling techniques were introduced into mining, making it a highly scientific process as opposed to the art it had been a century before.

There was also a blurring between engineer and architect. The construction of all functional buildings, whether they were houses or ore bins, might be entrusted to the mining engineer, who, in the role of architect, tackled the design and building of housing, commercial architecture, and industrial facilities. Consider the diversity of these assignments: designing efficient facilities to extract and process ore as well as housing and providing for the needs of workers, which might even include designing and building churches. The engineer working for a mining company sometimes borrowed plans from journals or building supply catalogs in the process. Small wonder that the environment was functional—usually livable, though rarely beautiful. Everything had to be developed in the midst of heavy industry by technicians.

The results are usually not aesthetically pleasing in the traditional sense because they are functional and economical. Visitors to mining districts frequently comment on the bleakness of the settlements and the monotony of the architecture. This condition results when a limited number of designers whose mission is minimizing cost through standardization, and whose aesthetic training may be in engineering rather than fine arts, shape the cultural landscape. In any event, as fewer and fewer large corporations come to dominate a mining district, it loses more and more of its vernacular individuality and becomes more uniform in its design, construction, and maintenance (fig. 50).

Although most mining districts are dominated by a single industry—mining—one of the strongest determinants in how they look is just how many corporations control the location at any particular time. When we look at mining districts, we need to ask a fundamental question: is this area solely owned/operated by a single company or are a number of companies active here? That question is often answered by the landscape itself: the greater the number of companies, the more visual variety in the landscape. Put another way, a mining district usually has less visual variation from location to location, and within any particular location, if one company is in control. Normally, companies try to achieve the greatest degree of design control possible, including regularity of street pattern layout and architectural design of all structures and buildings. From the eastern coal fields to the coal and copper mining towns of the West, one can see the imprint of corporate design on the landscape. The result is a predictable visual order and regulari-

50. *Even from a distance, company housing is easy to spot. In addition to providing a classic view of a mining landscape with a huge culm pile (center) and mine complex (lower left), this panorama photo of Cokeburg, Pennsylvania, shows rows of identical company houses lining streets (right). Note the outhouses at the back of the lots. Photo by the Ellsworth Division, Bethlehem Steel; Hagley Museum and Library.*

zation of design. Houses often line up along roads and are of the same style, carefully planned with regard to commercial and institutional structures (fig. 51).

Regularization does not mean ugliness, however, for some truly interesting and unique town designs were built by mining companies that attempted to introduce design amenities such as parks, plazas, interesting vistas, and themed architecture. These were usually constructed during the period 1900 to 1925, the golden age of the large, nearly autocratic, mining companies. Among the most beautiful of these was Tyrone, New Mexico, designed by New York architect Bertrum G. Goodhue at the request of the wife of a principal in the Phelps Dodge Company. The town was built in 1916 during the World War I boom in mineral production. It featured Mediterranean-style buildings

51. *A historic photograph of the company coal mining town of Cambria, Wyoming, provides a good example of the regularization of landscape and architectural design: the prominent church reaffirms the prevailing sobriety and social order in the typical company town. USGS.*

arranged around a landscaped plaza. The Spanish-style community of Ajo, Arizona, is another example of careful, if not regionally romanticized, town planning designs executed by a mining company. It certainly does not conform to our stereotype of uninspired company architecture. Another example, the St. Joe mining company headquarters building in Bonne Terre, Missouri, is done in the picturesque early twentieth century chateau/Tudor style not usually associated with mining company architecture.

Where mining companies built in elaborate, rather inspired, high styles, it was to make a statement. Consider, for example, the rather atypical company town of Windber, Pennsylvania. Architectural historian Meg Mulrooney has begun detailed studies of the town design and architecture in the soft coal area adjoining Somerset County and is able to compare and contrast Windber with other coal mining towns in the region.[58] In contrast to the other company towns, which were utilitarian if not uninspired, Mulrooney concludes that Windber was a showcase.

Carefully laid out on a spacious rectangular grid in 1897, Windber was designed to serve as the Berwind-White Company's headquarters (fig. 52). All lots along 15th Street between Graham Avenue (the

52. The Wilmore Building in the impressive company headquarters town of Windber, Pennsylvania, served as a post office (lower floor) and company offices. 1989 photo by the author.

town's main street) and Cambria Avenue were reserved for the company's own use, and a central park was developed here. Many residential and commercial buildings were erected in the early twentieth century, including the Palace Hotel, Interurban Station, Arcadia Theater, Eureka Department Store, and Wilmore Building (which housed the firm that developed all company property). The Georgian-style Berwind-White Coal Mining Company Office Building, erected in 1903, remains the most architecturally prominent building in town. Windber's fine homes, large trees, and substantial buildings give it a similar feel to Warren, Arizona, another showcase company town that was also developed in the early twentieth century.[59]

Windber is located at the center of a coal mining district that contains about a dozen separate satellites. One in particular, Eureka No. 40, contained about 110 semidetached houses, called double houses because they are duplexes. A report on Eureka No. 40 settlement by the U.S. Immigration Commission concluded that it was typical of all mine locations in the community in that the engineering precision in its rectangular layout and all houses conformed to a standard plan (fig. 53). The houses are two-family, two-story buildings; the facade of each is symmetrical, and the ornamentation is quite simple. All windows and all doors are standardized, used throughout each building and the entire community. Mulrooney notes that the coal company painted all the houses white with black trim, further creating a sense of uniformity.[60]

Company housing has been criticized as exploitative by later generations, but it served an important purpose—housing miners and their families in areas where no housing existed. A publication by the National Coal Association's Bituminous Coal Institute summarized the situation by contending that "company housing of coal miners was born of necessity, not choice," further adding that "when coal mines are established in sparsely settled sections, living quarters must be furnished in order to attract workers." In a classic characterization of company housing, the report noted that these are "HOMES, NOT CASTLES—NOT SHACKS."[61] The visual repetition of standardization helped cut costs, of course, but it also served to reaffirm social status and defined who was in control.

Company housing varied in quality. Some company housing was well constructed and fairly commodious. Many such houses, however, were hardly more than shacks or shanties (small, crudely built dwellings, usually constructed of wood) huddled close to the mines and tipples. They were poorly situated, poorly ventilated, poorly insulated, and, to critics, unattractive. The shabbiness of this type of miner's housing led to calls for reform at the turn of the century. Implicit in such reforms was the concept that a better-housed work force would be more productive.

In a 1914 assessment of "Houses for Mining Towns," done for the U.S. Bureau of Mines and the U.S. Bureau of Public Health, Joseph H. White offered suggestions that could improve housing conditions in mining towns. He began by noting that "the isolation of a mining town introduces a unique responsibility" to mining companies because "the miners are practically obliged to rent the company house." He advised that while mining companies should "restrain fanciful and unnecessarily expensive building; the other extreme should likewise be avoided" and that "true economy should be distinguished from cheap-

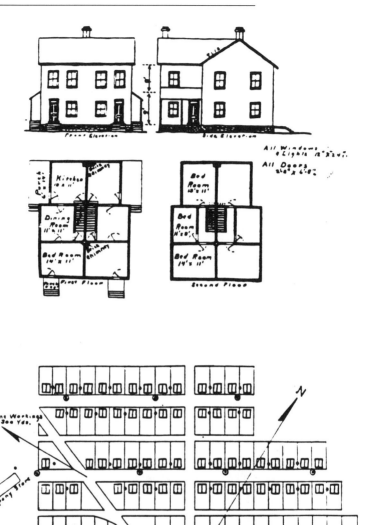

53. Company housing was usually functional and standardized. These attached (duplex) company houses at Eureka No. 40 mine in Pennsylvania were used to illustrate a 1911 U.S. Immigration Commission report.

ness." To create better housing, White urged companies to build towns at a distance from the mines, to avoid crowding, to develop sanitation systems, and to build snug, well-lighted and well-ventilated homes; wood-frame buildings with porches or verandas were recommended. In keeping with the times, White discouraged the use of what was later called gingerbread trim: for porches, "frail, fancy-turned vertical pieces should not be used; plain rectangular pieces, closely spaced, are better."[62]

There is evidence that company housing is part of a rich but poorly studied functional school of American architecture that later influenced subdivision design. Improved industrial housing resulted from the varied interests of mining companies, the federal government, and building supply companies. It established minimum standards for decent, affordable housing and a tolerance for uniformity in streetscape design so long as the resulting monotony represented an improved standard of living. From the coal mining towns of Wyoming to the copper mining towns of the interior West, one sees familiar housing that has a company look about it. This is related in part to specific architectural styles (or rather their simplicity and economy), but is related more to the realization that the building envelopes are both highly functional (usually permitting as much interior living space as possible for the mass of the building) and highly repetitive. One almost never sees one company house standing by itself, but rather assemblages of them. As if to underscore the repetition, companies often built standardized board sidewalks or boardwalks and fences in the residential locations. Even outhouses were usually of a standard design.

After a company ceases operations and pulls out of an area, and sells off its property, one invariably finds a return of individuality. The former company houses slowly take on individual identities; this return to vernacular or popular decoration/treatment underscores the observation that even seemingly monolithic company town architecture is ephemeral. With the demise of the paternalism often associated with large mining companies during the period 1895–1950, the classic, visually uniform company town has become rather rare. This condition has been exacerbated by the general decline in metals mining during the 1970s and early 1980s (which resulted in the abandonment or divestiture of much company housing) and by the recent boom in small-scale mining in the 1990s (which has seen the spread of prefab housing into many historic mining districts in the West). Company town architecture and design is historically important and, in many mining districts, threatened with extinction by modernization.

Mining companies may completely level towns after they seem to outlive their usefulness. Even the toughest of realists wince when they ponder the destruction of Tyrone, New Mexico, which only existed for a few years. The economic downturn in copper prices during the 1920s found the mines closing and the town virtually depopulated. The town was demolished and later became the site of an open pit copper mine. A mining company's response to a downturn in the economy or its interest in new (or renewed) mineral development may find it destroying—with a kind of unbelievable objectivity—the beautiful as well as the ugly. Mining engineers often make little or no distinction between the two—or rather do not use aesthetics as an operative factor in decision-making. Those familiar with historic mining landscapes know, above all, that (to paraphrase a biblical quote) what the mining company giveth, the mining company taketh away.

Until rather recently, James Allen's important book *The Company Town in the American West* was the standard interpretation of company town design. It, however, did not deal with company towns in the eastern United States—a location in which all manner of companies constructed towns, good examples being the coal mining towns of the Appalachian Plateau and iron and copper mining towns from Alabama and Tennessee to the upper Great Lakes states. A recent surge of interest in the topic, as evidenced by numerous reports and presentations at academic conferences, implies that the company town has begun to be recognized as important in shaping the life and landscape of mining districts. Eastern as well as western mining towns should be studied.

The imprint of mining companies extends beyond housing and the design or layout of settlements and ultimately affects all visible aspects of the environment. Whereas most of the maintenance is done by the company, materials and equipment may also be used to improve private homes in the district, especially after the company divests itself of the housing. Miners may have access to the supplies of the company, such as paint, so that features in the landscape may continue to bear a company look: in the Phelps Dodge copper mining towns of the Southwest, for example, one often finds private homes and the fences surrounding them painted PD Green, a pale celery green enamel that is nearly indestructible. PD Green can also be seen on company buildings, giving whatever is painted with it a locker room anonymity.

Mining engineers employed by the mining companies applied their standardized solutions to design problems, including simple maintenance. Given their limited training in aesthetics, the landscape came to have a utilitarian quality: for example, unadorned timbers or cribbing may have served to prop up building sites, and sheet metal sheathed all manner of buildings. In some cases, the work done by mining companies may seem overdesigned or heavy-handed. This is especially true in the twentieth century—for example, a simple roadside ditch may be constructed of concrete; simple sign posts may be made from heavy pipe used in the mines; and supposedly simple fencing may seem like an armor-plated barricade. This results in part from the mining engineering background of surface engineers and illustrates a fascination with the use of standardized materials, such as corrugated metal, for a wide range of purposes, including roofing, siding, and fencing in residential and industrial areas.

Corrugated metal is one of the more ubiquitous building materials in mining districts. It represents the ultimate in functional building material, for it is about as strong and durable as sheet metal can be. Available in standardized sheets, it is unpretentious and inexpensive. The corrugations add strength while keeping down weight. When galvanized (zinc-coated), sheet metal withstands the weather well and, importantly, does not require painting. Sheet metal has another quality; it can be reused. Being simply nailed in place, it can be removed when the company decides to disassemble and relocate a metal-sheathed building, ore chute, or conveyor system. In fact, if one were to choose a building material that personifies mining, it would be corrugated metal, for, like many features in the landscape, it is an industrial product that is portable, easily removed for shipment elsewhere, and standardized. It is understandable that such considerations shape the landscape, for, as we shall see, mining districts experience constant change and reshaping.

TRANSFORMATION

Man puts his hand to the flinty rock,
and overturns mountains by the roots.
He cuts out channels in the rocks,
and his eye sees every precious thing.
He binds up the streams so that they do not trickle,
and the thing that is hid he
brings forth to light.
—Job 28:9–11

This quotation is probably the oldest known reference to mining as a force shaping the landscape. When written several thousand years ago, these verses symbolized man's uncanny ability to obtain nature's treasures through knowledge as well as physical effort. They also described the consequences of this activity: the overturned mountains, channels, and dams described are familiar surface consequences of mining even today.

In the last two hundred years, the mining landscapes of the United States have been created with the westward move of Anglo-American culture. In some ways, this was a sequential process by which the bonanzas were reaped first; then new technology went back and reworked the riches that remained:

An amazing, rapid succession of mineral districts of first rank in the world was found as the westward exploration of the continent progressed. Then, a half century or so later, as the richer ores were running out, deposits of far lower grade but with even greater gross value were profitably exploited as the base of immense enterprises by application of new methods of mining and by concentration on scales that dwarfed any such activities in the past.[63]

This statement, written by the president of the Homestake Mining Company in 1956, summarizes the major changes in technology that have in turn shaped the landscape of America's mining districts. Although there is a timeless quality to digging holes into the earth and dumping mining wastes upon the surface, a person who has a good eye for mining landscapes can tell how, and when, they were created. Whereas miners were undifferentiated and unprofessional in the early years of mineral development on the American frontier, they have become increasingly professional in the way they go about their business. In fact, most of the mining topography in the typical historic mining district shows the handiwork of both the nonprofessional miner and the technician, who later introduced new technology to mine and process ore bodies that the earlier miners had worked.

Since about 1890, the landscape changes brought about by mining have increased in scale and impact. The topographic changes resulting from the adoption of new technologies have been nothing short of phenomenal: as we scrutinize historic mining districts, we may find huge open pit mines where some mining towns once stood or huge tailings piles covering the sites of others.

Transformation—a change in structure or physical appearance—is one of the constants of the historical geography of mining districts. Since the manmade topography is one of the most diagnostic traits of mining country, our discussion of transformation focuses on the physical aspect of landscape change that affects the site or setting: geomorphology. This would appear to be a scientific topic, yet the resulting topography is really shaped by economics, for the physical transformation of the landscape is driven by technology. In the case of mining districts, these changes may completely reorder the geography as earlier mines, and even entire communities, are obliterated in response to the increasing scale of mining activities.

Placer mining may remain very localized if color is found only along the streambed. More often, however, the alluvial deposits themselves contain gold. The ease with which alluvium could be worked, or mined, using relatively primitive tools such as shovels and simple technology (for example, Long Toms or sluice boxes) led to aggressive exploitation of river valley deposits in many areas from North Carolina to California. Even the glacial gravels in some parts of the Midwest, notably Ohio, were the scenes of gold rushes in the nineteenth century. Auriferous deposits were worked (and in some cases reworked) in rich areas, the mother lode country of California being best known. Placer workings that were mined using large dredges and hydraulic hoses left the river valley bottoms a wasteland of deranged and rearranged alluvium. One can still see the effects of this aggressive century-old

54. Hydraulic mining of gold-rich alluvium in many areas has left an impressive legacy. This 1909 view of the McCutchin hydraulic mine near Nevada City, California, reveals a deeply scarred and eroded landscape typical of unregulated placer mining. Photo by G. K. Gilbert, USGS.

placer mining in valleys in California, Montana, and Idaho, where the topography is configured into a maze of hummocks and rounded ridges (fig. 54).

Downstream, the impact of siltation could be enormous; the rather rapid filling of San Francisco Bay with silt resulted from the aggressive nineteenth-century placer mining in the Sierra foothills. Some supporters of the mining industry claimed that these operations actually improved an area's potential for agriculture, but the argument was not very convincing, especially when the visual evidence of desolation was compared to bucolic descriptions of the valleys before mining. The fact that hydraulic mining was outlawed in an era that imposed virtually no constraints on users of the environment says a great deal about its downstream impact.

Hard rock mining leaves a different kind of topography in its wake. Two types of residual landscapes are common, one associated with underground mining (as at Tonopah, Nevada) and the other where open pit mining has been practiced (as in Arizona's Warren Mining District). Most hard rock mining districts begin with underground mining that focuses on extracting the richest ores; typically, the scale of these changes is relatively rather small—their effects are localized. It is here that we see the conical ore dumps and tailings piles dotting the landscape. Donald McLaughlin, a mining engineer by training, has characterized the impact as minimal compared to placer and especially open pit mining; he confidently writes that "the mining of deeper deposits causes little or no marks on the surface except dumps of waste rock or tailings from the mills" and summarizes an aesthetic opinion common among miners that dumps could even "bring an interesting element of relief . . . to an otherwise rather monotonous and unproductive landscape."[64]

As time progresses, the transformation occurs on a larger scale and may culminate in surface or open pit mining activities that leave features occupying square miles instead of acres. Comparatively, the surface area modified by surface mining may vary from fifty to five hundred times greater than areas mined by underground methods. This means that surface mining may obliterate (or bury) earlier evidence of mining as its impact spreads across the landscape. We may think of surface mining and underground mining as being found in different areas, but it is usually time, rather than space, that separates them. The typical mining district may experience at least two types of mining through its history; some, notably the metals mining districts of the West, have experienced all three—placer, underground, and surface mining, usually in that order. This leads to another axiom of landscape development in hard places: in mining districts, large-scale manmade topography is episodic, resulting from technological change that usually occurs in an orderly progression, each successive stage normally being larger in scale than the one immediately preceding it.

These transformations have a visual impact, of course, and are symbolic of the traditional relationship between time (history) and culture (technology) in the exploitation of nonrenewable resources. All mines, and the mining districts in which they occur, have a life cycle. The economic-cultural geographer Homer Aschmann has outlined the four inevitable stages in mine development: prospecting and exploration; investment and development; stable operation; and decline.[65] During the life history of a mine, the geographic impacts of stages of development veneer the landscapes with the kinds of topographic artifacts described in chapter 1. Just as these are not random features in space (bearing a close relationship to the geological features), they are also not random through time: each is a result of technological processes introduced at some point in history.

In the case of the Warren Mining District and the Clifton-Morenci District in Arizona, for example, historical geographers have determined that each economic phase of mining activity produced distinctive landforms that are an integral part of the image of each district.[66] By employing historic maps, historic photography, corporate/oral histories, archaeological techniques, and an analysis of the current landscape features, it is possible to illustrate the topographic changes that have occurred in a mining district sequentially. This spatial approach is important because "each episode of mining activity that takes place potentially destroys part or all of existing archaeological sites."[67] Mining historian Otis Young, in describing the decline of Nevada's Comstock Mining District, notes that new cyanidation processes created new mining activity that transformed the landscape: "The tailing heaps of the original mills were fastened upon, run through the vats, and pumped away. Therefore, although the original waste dumps are still visible in place, the tailing heaps which were once found below them are gone."[68]

These topographic changes that Young describes in the Virginia City–Gold Hill area are common elsewhere, for mining interests are constantly evaluating all materials, not just natural ores, for their mineral content. Thus, older tailings and dumps may be mined (actually reprocessed) in order to reclaim minerals left by earlier, less efficient, processes. These activities create new landscape features, but in so doing may obliterate older features. Few mining district landscapes offer simple, unbroken linear chronologies. The fact that many have been reworked or scavenged at different times helps to make their interpretation more challenging and more interesting. It also complicates the task of determining which features are historic and which are modern.

The features associated with specific mining processes, such as tailings and leach dumps, can best be interpreted and evaluated if they are differentiated both spatially and chronologically. Despite their spatial and chronological complexity, the large-scale topographic changes affecting mining districts occur in an evolutionary manner and can, for convenience, be treated in dated sequences. Several "time exposures" for the Warren Mining District are offered by maps that illustrate the major land use patterns in several critical watershed years (fig. 55).[69] These time exposures or freeze frames exemplify how technology had shaped the landscape at particular points in time: 1885, 1912, 1931, and 1974. They include all major developments from the early mining activities in the early 1880s to the closure of the mines in the mid-1970s.

The topographic change that occurs in a mining district is really a reflection of the changes in both the quality of the ores mined and the techniques used in their processing. It is the job of the mining engineer/metallurgist to separate the metal from the impurities in the most efficient manner. The ore in any particular vein might vary in composition, and improper processing or dressing might lead to more metal going into the mine dumps than to the smelter. In the case of many copper mining areas, for example, the earliest (richest) ores were oxides—colorful copper minerals such as cuprite (copper oxide or ruby copper) or malachite and azurite (green and blue copper carbonates, respectively). These were often found with native (or nearly pure) copper, so that any particular run of ore might be as high as 30 to 60 percent copper. These copper oxides are relatively easy to smelt.

Copper, however, is also found as copper sulfide, in which case it may take several forms, such as chalcopyrite (copper pyrites), chalcocite (copper glance), and bornite (peacock ore). As the percentage of sulfur increases, ores become more difficult to treat and earn the name "refractory ores." Many metals, such as silver, lead, and zinc, combine with various elements, including sulfur. In many districts, the sulfuret ores presented severe challenges. They often required higher temperatures and new techniques, and the smelting process liberated clouds of noxious sulfur dioxide.

As time progresses, lower and lower grades of ore are mined. In the case of copper, for example, the percentage of what constitutes a paying ore has dropped; by about 1915, low-grade deposits of less than 5 percent copper had been developed; and by the 1940s, the percentage had dropped to about 2 percent. This means that upward of 98 percent of the ore was waste material. Mining such low-grade deposits required large machinery and sophisticated ore treatment technology. Flotation (the counterintuitive process by which ores are pulverized

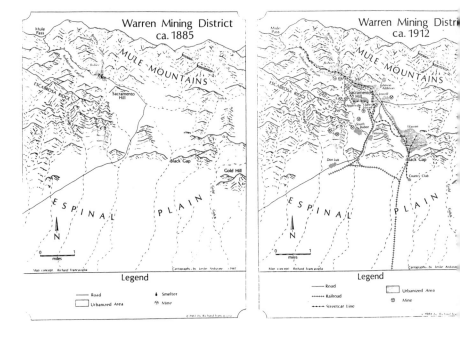

55. *The sequential development of mining over ninety years is illustrated by these four maps. Note the development of large-scale topographic features, including the open pit mine, overburden piles, tailings, and leach dumps. After Francaviglia 1982.*

and their heavier metallic constituents separated by floating on top of the liquid as they are collected on minute bubbles of oil) revolutionized the mining industry after about 1900. It also revolutionized the landscape.

Likewise, the percentage of other metals in ores has dropped with improvements in processing technology. At one time only high-grade ores (about 60 percent iron or virtually pure hematite) could be shipped from the Lake Superior region to the steel mills of Ohio and Pennsylvania. Beneficiation (the process by which impurities are removed from a low-grade iron ore to permit its economical shipment and smelting) has encouraged the mining of lower-grade ores in the Lake Superior region, giving a new lease on life to the open pit mining technology that has transformed the region's landscapes since about 1900. The resulting processed ore, called taconite, can be shipped great distances.

Just as any individual mine may have a life cycle, so, too, does a district. Its life cycle is expressed in the landscape. If we were to study sequential maps for many districts, an overall pattern of landscape evolution might emerge. Many would seem to fit into a predictable, or at any rate orderly, sequence.

1. Exploration: the prospecting phase, in which areas showing color or promise are opened, initial probings reveal information about the extent of the ore body, and a rapidly changing localized mining topography begins to take shape.

2. Initiation: after the quality of the ore and the general parameters of the ore body are understood, capital and energy are invested in the site, resulting in successful exploitation. The richest ores are mined because they must justify the high expenses of shipping to distant smelters. Waste dumps are typically rich and located adjacent to the mines. Most of the features associated with exploration are obliterated during this period, which may last about fifteen years in the typical mining district. This is the bonanza or boom period of development, and mining wastes are often dumped with little regard to future activities.

3. Diversification: improvements in mining technology lead to the exploitation of different, or somewhat lower-grade, ores. Efficient smelting and processing of ore and the development of concentration technologies suited to specific ores characterize operations in this

phase. The landscape becomes increasingly dominated by waste piles and tailings. This phase may last twenty-five years.

4. Intensification: development of large low-grade ore bodies adjacent to the richer deposits exploited in earlier stages occurs during this phase. The method most often selected to develop the ore body is open pit or surface mining, which depends upon the availability of large-scale earth-moving equipment and technologies that reduce the costs of concentrating. Massive reworking of the landscape occurs, and detritus (overburden) or waste materials such as tailings may cover thousands of acres. Tailings and dumps from earlier periods may be reworked. Solution mining (leaching) operations are conducted on leach dumps or leach heaps. This type of activity may last forty or fifty years, depending on the economy, ore body, and other conditions.

5. Cessation: exhaustion of the ore body and/or rising costs of production bring an end to mining operations; major corporate investments are liquidated; mine shaft pumps cease operation, thus flooding the mines. The economic process in the development of topography is superseded by the natural factors of erosion/attrition or the stabilization of the topography through reclamation.

The impacts of these changes are local or perhaps regional, but they result from outside forces being exerted on a particular mining district. That helps to explain why the topography of mining districts has such a familiar look from place to place. Similarities result in places as distant as Arizona, Montana, and Chile because mining companies operate worldwide and respond to worldwide economic conditions. The mining engineers who transformed the landscape were part of a fraternity that traveled widely and maintained close contact with technological developments by visiting other properties, reading mining and metallurgical journals, and attending conferences. Just as the price of metals/minerals helps determine the speed with which change occurs, the technological subculture of mining engineers helps to determine its actual form. As time progresses, mining engineers tend to work for larger companies that may have worldwide interests. The diffusion of corporate technologies has been understated. Mining is not a folk industry. By the early twentieth century, all but the most marginal operations were either influenced by or came under the ownership of large multinational corporations or mineral cartels.

The landscape features in a mining district are a topographic badge

56. *Open pit mining has transformed many mining areas and resulted
in some of the largest manmade topographic features on earth. Terraces
at the Rouchleau Mine at Virginia, Minnesota, are reminiscent of the
canyonlands of the American Southwest. 1990 photo by the author.*

of identity. They affect places as different as Eureka, Utah, where
conical mine dumps and localized tailings brand the landscape as the
handiwork of underground miners; Mormon Bar, California, where the
activity of placer miners left a distinctive landscape; and that "most
conspicuous disturbance of the surface"—to quote a mining engineer—
the cookie cutter topography associated with open pit mining. Industrial archaeologist Jeffrey Brown tells us that large-scale "earthworks" (of all kinds) require vast expenditures of human effort, are a
measure of a civilization's ability to organize human activity, "and produce both intended and unintended consequences for social and natural
systems."[70]

Of all the topographic features associated with mining, none has captured the imagination more than the "desolation" left by open pit mining (fig. 56). In some places, its impact is truly historic, dating from
the early twentieth century. These are overpowering landscapes, for
the transformation from nature to artifact, some might say wilderness
to wasteland, is complete where it has been practiced. Novelists have

provided us some of the more insightful looks at the topography in aggressively surface mined areas. Consider, for example, Phil Stong's description of the development of an open pit iron mine in Minnesota in *The Iron Mountain*: Mr. Sturges, who oversees the explosives used to blast the iron ore,

> always liked to reflect on the fact that thousands of years of nature had done less to this deposit of ferric oxide than a few thousand tons of explosives that he had planted in strategic places at one time or another. When he had left the Range, almost in childhood, this pit had been a tentative and unremarkable little hole hardly big enough to bury all the pyramids. Now the ellipse was two miles long and half as wide; the cancer had bitten about a thousand feet deep, and the waste dump was bigger than the mountain had been. The difference was accounted for by the enormous pit—the mountain inverted and enlarged, and shipped away.[71]

The topography of a district mined using open pit methods is a good example of both landscape by subtraction and landscape by addition. It has been pointed out that, in some metals mining areas where very low-grade ores are mined, the volume of material excavated is actually greater than the hole it was removed from because shattering the ore body increases its volume through restructuring. This means that one could not simply dump the overburden and waste material back into a pit to reclaim the landscape—even if this were economically feasible or environmentally acceptable—because there is actually more of it than when operations began! It also means that mountains are not only excavated, but also created, by this type of mining, as can be seen in the spectular ore dumps that delineate the skyline of Minnesota's Iron Ranges. Visitors to places affected by open pit mining are awed both by the excavations and by the huge piles of debris that are placed on the landscape.

An official United States Steel company report on Minnesota's awesome Hull-Rust-Mahoning Open Pit at Hibbing states that this is "the largest open pit mine in the world, being approximately three miles long and over a mile wide at its greatest width" and that 35,106,296 cubic yards of material have been stripped from the pit.[72] Geographer John Webb's dissertation on the Iron Ranges reveals the phenomenal extent of the pits and dumps, which physically—and perhaps psycho-

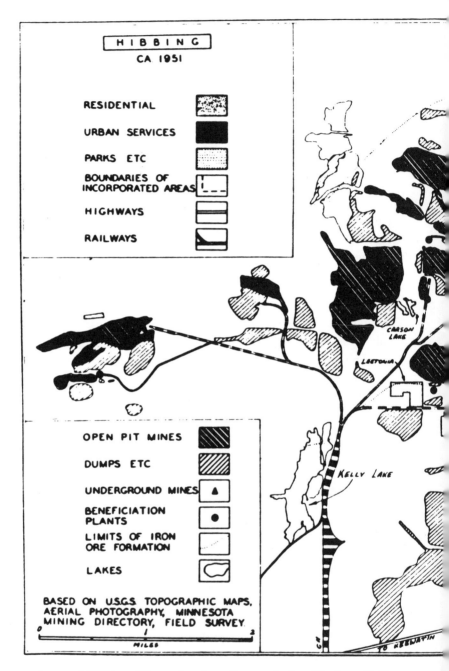

57. A map of Hibbing, Minnesota, shows the proximity of the huge Hull-Rust open pit mine to the downtown commercial district, which is poised at the brink. From Webb 1958.

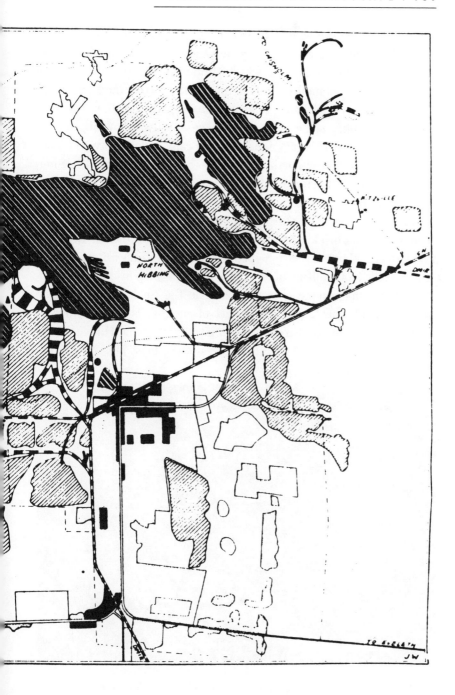

logically—define the edges of settlement and even control the directions of community growth and development.[73] Land use maps of the Iron Range communities, of which Hibbing, Virginia, and Eveleth might serve as examples, reveal the spatial extent and proximity to settlement of such huge topographic features (fig. 57). The Iron Ranges exemplify some of the most awesome earth moving undertaken by man; their legacy is a series of canyonlike excavated landscapes that run across northern Minnesota for dozens of miles. Similarly, the open pit copper mines of the West are among the most awesome of man's creations.

Can such topography affect the psyche of those who grow up in its shadow or at its brink? Could the creation of the spectacular Berkeley Pit at Butte, Montana, have helped local boy Evel Knievel, who would later be billed as the King of the Daredevils, develop his vision of leaping gaping topographic obstacles such as the Snake River Canyon (fig. 58)? And what about the impact of such landscapes on artistic sensibilities: could the incredible open pit mines around Hibbing, Minnesota, inspire genius? Two biographers of the most illustrious prod-

58. An aerial photograph of Butte, Montana, shows the downtown commercial district (center) and its proximity to the Berkeley pit (far right), which removed entire neighborhoods as it grew. 1989 photo by the author.

uct of Minnesota's Iron Range—the enigmatic Bob Dylan—imply that it can. Dylan, born Robert Zimmerman, was himself a product of the isolated but ethnically diverse Iron Range. His music, which has shaped popular culture in the late twentieth century, mixes images of desolation with messages that portend catastrophic change. Like the Iron Range landscape itself, Dylan's musical career has been eclectic and episodic. In comparing what Dylan would have seen in the late 1940s with what his family had seen earlier, we are told that Hibbing was still

> backward and depressing. The only change was that there was seemingly less of it, a wide crater having formed where once-fertile earth had been dredged out by the mines. Only two years before, Truman had ordered the bomb dropped on Hiroshima; an aerial view of Hibbing provided an almost identical picture of reckless abandon: mounds of reddish-brown soil piled high atop the lips of abandoned pits, branchless trees and charred brush growing out of the overburden, a glaring absence of wildlife in the vicinity.[74]

Another biographer reaffirms the impression of the desolation around Hibbing: "There were red iron-ore mining dumps at nearly every fringe of town. 'The richest village in the world' wasn't so rich anymore. They'd cut down the trees and dug the good ore out of the earth." He continues: "The big hole in the ground that haunts Dylan's memory was a 'stripper,' or open-pit mine. By 1964, the Hull-Rust pit covered 1,600 acres, measured 3 3/4 by 1 mile, and reached a depth of 535 feet. From this running sore was extracted a billion gross tons of earth—more than was dug for the Panama Canal—which yielded 500 million tons of iron ore."[75]

This landscape had been in the stages of transformation long before Dylan's birth. As early as 1915, the *Hibbing Tribune* selected the landscape in making a point about taxation of mining companies: "Don't forget: That Hibbing is an island, surrounded by yawning open pits and underlaid by iron ore—you can stand in the center of the business district and almost throw a baseball into four of the biggest open iron ore pits in the world—and mining operations account for by far the greatest portion of Hibbing's expenditures."[76]

With the passage of time, these open pit mines coalesced into huge canyons. Residents of the Iron Ranges have developed a strange affection for the open pit mines, most of which had been abandoned by the 1970s. Enthusiastic travel/tourism efforts led to comparisons of the resulting mining landscape with that of natural features: the Hibbing Chamber of Commerce termed the huge Hull-Rust-Mahoning Open Pit the "Man-made Grand Canyon,"[77] and much of the tourism-related literature describes the awesome impact of technology in creating new landscapes that become more acceptable through time.

We see from these descriptions that it is not only the resulting topography that excites interest, but the actual process by which it is created. Within their lifetimes, people can experience change that might take eons of geological time. Although all mining-related topography reminds us that a resource is disappearing for good, no place reminds us of this more than an open pit mine, for it takes the original landscape with it. Of course, it creates an arguably more interesting landscape at the same time, one that is measured in megastatistics.

Most open pit mines have turnouts or viewpoints where travelers can gaze into the pit and read almost incomprehensible statistics while huge machines are dwarfed in the bowl-shaped terraced canyon landscape below. Even abandoned pits, such as the Berkeley Pit just east of Butte, attract visitors. Here one sees the terraces slowly collapse and the pit filled with an imperceptibly rising emerald green lake whose beauty is exceeded only by its toxicity. In northern Minnesota, the abandoned open pit mines have filled with water and commercial salmon have begun to be raised in these lakes; slowly, these abandoned mines are becoming scenic resources.

This combination—the effects of time and physical processes on the landscape—is exactly what we are supposed to appreciate when we look into the Grand Canyon. The scenery is remarkably similar: an exciting but reassuring landscape of nearly vertical cliffs stratified into a series of benches much like the canyonlands of the Southwest. The topography of mining landscapes does mock natural features, for we can see visual parallels between tailings dams and the large truncated alluvial fans in the Southwest and also in the many barren, conical mine dumps that resemble badlands topography (fig. 59). Conversations with residents and travelers in the West reveal that many cannot tell the difference between natural and manmade topography. In the

59. Mining results in surreal landscapes of erosion: copper mine dumps at Ruth, Nevada, show the characteristic badlands topography of steep-sided, tightly spaced erosion rills in an orange-colored landscape. There is evidence that the general public comes to consider such features natural with the passage of time. 1989 photo by the author.

public mind, mining-related topography may fit so well into a stereotypic visual image of rugged, denuded western landscapes that it seems natural. In the case of the Minnesota Iron Ranges, the desolation of the landscapes left by open pit mining may reinforce a popular perception that the region is a stark, primordial wilderness.

However grand their scale, nature begins to reclaim even the most ambitious topographic works of miners shortly after they are completed, that is, abandoned. Attrition is a factor in the way a mining landscape looks, for it is axiomatic that mining landscapes, like all topography, are further transformed by sedimentation, erosion, and revegetation. From their inception, mining-related topographic features are exposed to, and become part of, the natural environment. Historian Phil Notarianni characterizes this interrelationship for the Tintic Mining District in Utah by noting that "years of mining have parched the land, leaving twisted cedars and hardened conical mine dumps, weathered with age, yet monumental remnants of days past."[78]

Whereas the original design of the manmade topography of a mining district is attributable to technology and economy, its persistence after the cessation of mining is a result of weathering under various climatic regimes. In forested areas, the legacy of mining may be harder to detect as brush and trees return after mining activity ceases. However, the longevity of mining-related topography in deserts is noteworthy: in these regions where rainfall is rare, topographic features may last for centuries. The scars of mining activity dating back nearly three millennia are reportedly still visible in the desert regions peripheral to the Mediterranean Sea. Many of our mining landscapes in the arid West will be visible for at least that long. Even in the coal fields of northeastern Pennsylvania, the landscape is marked by culm banks that remain distinctive years after abandonment, prompting Ben Marsh, a student of the area's cultural landscape, to conclude that "what we see in the hard coal valleys is that it is far harder to end a landscape than to start or despoil one."[79]

Very few detailed studies of the relationship between depositional features associated with mining and their consequences or effect on other aspects of the environment have been conducted to date. How, for example, does an accretionary mining-related topographic feature change through time? How stable, or erosion prone, is it? And, when erosion occurs, how does this weathering change the visual character of such a feature? Historical archaeologist Donald Hardesty describes an impressive tailings flow which today "extends from the [Cortez, Nevada] mill at least a mile down the valley and is greatly dissected from weathering."[80] The finer sediments are often the most easily eroded and thus may be weathered into the eerie badlands topography we see in some mining districts (fig. 60).

The studies of environmentalists may shed some light on the way in which such features erode. Most of their studies focus on either metals (especially copper) mining and the tailings residual to it or coal mining and the effects of spoil banks on water quality. These studies are highly pragmatic and are intended to identify and mitigate environmental impacts. A geomorphological study of the impacts of mining on stream channels in the vicinity of Central City and Nevadaville, Colorado, revealed widespread, documentable topographic changes in a 100-year period.[81] Mining is notorious for accelerating erosion, which is expressed in the downcutting of streams or gullying. Removal of

60. *Appropriately named Slime Wash just north of Tonopah, Nevada, runs through an area of tailings deposited during the early twentieth century. The tailings, which were dumped into the streambed as a thick, slimy liquid, have dried out and are now heavily eroded. 1989 photo by the author.*

vegetation by mining activities in Arizona's Mule Mountains and other nearby ranges is believed to be a major cause of regional arroyo formation,[82] although other factors must also be considered.[83]

The visual impact of mining changes through time, with the greatest visual disturbance occurring during and immediately following mining activities, while erosion is at its most active but before revegetation begins. In the Warren Mining District, Arizona, comparisons of historic photographs, as well as observations of recent features, reveal an initial period of rapid attrition during which the slopes of manmade features either steepen or become more shallow, depending on three factors: frequency and intensity of precipitation events, degree of consolidation of sediments, and particle size. The tailings dams composed of fine, indurated sediments have been documented by photography over a sixty-year period: their topography appears to change in several stages with attendant changes in drainage network (density/pattern) and slope steepness. To the observer looking at the landscape today, it is the deeply rutted, steep, leading edge of the tailings dam that is most obvious: this impressive topographic landmark is also considered an environmental problem—it is very difficult to stabilize, that is, keep in one place. The fine material of which it is composed is exposed to strong winds and blows back over the district from which it was extracted. Sand dunes have actually formed at the north (or leeward) edge of these tailings.

Although reclamation efforts have focused on either blacktopping or revegetating the surfaces, the cost of the former and the futility of the latter due to the relative sterility of the substrate have left a barren surface exposed to the climatic elements. Wind erosion, despite its visibility, is actually a minor force in eroding the tailings piles. As in most areas, running water does the job more effectively. Given current rates of erosion, it is possible that these tailings will be a prominent feature for 16,500 years, possibly longer—unless, of course, they are reworked for their mineral content at some future date.

In other areas of the Southwest where reclamation efforts have been more successful, rates of erosion are significantly reduced on those surfaces that can be stabilized by vegetation, especially grasses. There has been much talk of building housing tracts on top of the tailings south of Green Valley, Arizona, the object being simultaneously to stabilize the surface and to turn wasteland into productive real estate. That tailings can be used as housing sites was demonstrated by Phelps Dodge Corporation's Morenci operation, where company housing tracts and the high school were built on tailings that underlie part of the new (post-1960) townsite.

Determining the age of historic topographic features brings the historical geographer and the environmental scientist together in a unique partnership. Take, for example, the issue of water quality, which is one of the better indices of environmental change. The parameters monitored during flows of highly acidic, heavy metals–laden mine runoff waters so often used to assess the impact of mine spills on the biota also lend themselves to calculating the chronology of events. In the Patagonia Mountains of southeastern Arizona, for example, acidic mine waters served as an index by which relative disturbances of historic mining activity could be determined, their signatures being easily detected fifty or more years after the cessation of mining activity.[84]

Both the surface and the ground waters can be used to locate and determine the processes used in the development of mine dumps. Although interdisciplinary teams should have little difficulty in speculating on the approximate age of a mining-related feature (provided its chemical composition, physical structure, and hydrologic factors such as the rates of runoff are known), it should be understood that these methods are not accurate enough to date specific features. Experimental methods, such as Ezra Zubrow's calcium/metals uptake models, may have applicability in this area of industrial sites chronology research.[85] Nevertheless, at the current time, "our general ignorance of the relevant thresholds separating relatively low rates of process operation from high rates associated with disequilibrium makes the extrapolation game very dangerous."[86]

The process of revegetation is important to those reading the landscapes of historic mining districts. It has been noted that specific types of plants reestablish themselves on or colonize certain types of mine wastes. In southern Arizona and New Mexico, for example, yucca seems to have an affinity for the smelter-derived slag wastes or at least is about the only plant able to grow in such material. Likewise, the ability of certain types of pinyon pines to colonize certain highly eroded and otherwise sterile tailings in Utah and Nevada is widely known among conservationists and reclamationists. Conversely, the common mullein plant of the genus *Verbascum*—which was more or less accidentally introduced from Europe—seems to have little tolerance for pollution and colonizes only in areas with little chemical change; therefore, it is a good indicator of overburden sites in many places, including Butte, Montana, and the Coeur d'Alene mining area of Idaho. After more than a century, birch trees and pine trees have begun to obscure the mine dumps in Michigan's copper country.

More studies should be conducted, for it is clear that plants may help to date various mining-related topographic features in the absence of better indices or written records. The plant communities that reestablish themselves in these types of environments appear to be highly selective and are often imbalanced—that is, overrepresented by volunteering species that may serve as indicators of environmental change. Otis Young describes the tailings of the Rhode Island mine near Virginia City, Nevada, as a "dead white flat of detritus" and notes that "vegetation is only now beginning to creep over this flat, a generation after the last bucket was dumped."[87]

Similarly, it may take vegetation years to reestablish a foothold on areas denuded by smelter smoke, which is highly acidic and laden with heavy metals. The popular press sometimes uses mining-related landscapes as examples of what can be done to reclaim wastelands. An article in *Reader's Digest* describes a landscape that "looked like a no man's land" of what locals called "desert asphalt" in a denuded area in Utah's Oquirrh Mountains downwind of the American Smelting and Refining Company's smelter at Garfield. It documents the efforts of a determined individual, Paul Rockich, who vowed in 1947 "that someday, whatever the cost, he would bring life back to this sterile moonscape" and achieved this dream so that "today, throughout the Oquirrhs, tall trees rise from a sea of grass studded with flowers and shrubs."[88]

Despite an environment's purported ability to heal itself or to be healed in the wake of serious industrial contamination (such as that often associated with mining), it is apparent that the impacts of both historic and contemporary mining activity are likely to be measurable—and visible—for hundreds of years. This is especially true in arid environments, where fluvial and solution processes operate at slower rates than in humid areas. Even in humid areas, where vegetation reestablishes itself more quickly, the legacy of mining may be profound and very long-lasting. The back roads of eastern and southeastern Ohio traverse labyrinthine areas of gob piles deposited from about 1885 to 1935 upon which small trees have only begun to reestablish themselves slowly. The above-ground traces of architectural and engineering features associated with mining have long vanished in many areas. Yet the geomorphology and the consequent irregularity of its drainage patterns and networks clearly mark this as historic mining country.

It is not surprising that mining-related topography—if not reworked by mining interests or reclaimed through conservation efforts—may be the most permanent, and therefore ultimately the most important, of the indices of human activity in a mining district. It is likely to long outlast other above-ground features such as settlements, structures, and transportation systems. In those mining areas neglected by preservationists and historical archaeologists (for example, the coal fields of the western Appalachian plateau, where we were too late to record many vanishing ephemeral features such as tipples and mineheads), those mining-related topographic features become all the more important as our only remaining substantive record of the mining activity that flourished there. Because it is so long-lasting and has such an impact on other features, manmade topography may serve as the ultimate artifact in describing the transformation of mining districts.

SERIATION

We often think of mining districts as having a certain historic character, but may tend to overlook the fact that the personality of a district relates to its stage in a progression of events. Just as Homer Aschmann has been able to document the "natural history of a mine,"[89] it should be understood that there is a natural history, in fact rather predictable evolution, of mining districts. Seriation—the process by which things are arranged in succession—helps to explain what we see in a mining district landscape at any particular time. This not only includes their peculiar topographic features, discussed under transformation, but also other cultural features such as architecture and settlement design.

Historic mining districts have ridden the roller coaster of fluctuating metals and minerals prices, and their landscapes show it. It is common to oversimplify mining as a boom (bonanza) to bust (borrasca) economy, and to assume that a downturn brings about complete ruin that creates ghost towns almost overnight. Actually, many mining districts weather substantial fluctuations in prices. Old-timers know that spurts of production are interspersed with tougher times during the course of a mining district's history. These highs and lows define the character of the place at any one time and, collectively, have helped create the landscape that we see today.

The architectural complexion of any particular mining district changes through time: as the design of buildings that serve certain purposes (such as retail trade) changes, so does a building's relationship to other buildings and to features such as roads and highways. We note, for example, that commercial buildings used to be built closer to the street and that they have come to be set farther back from roads in the more recent past. This repositioning is partially a result of the automobile, whose increased speed reduces what we can see close up and spreads our field of vision horizontally. This change may also explain why newer commercial architecture has a more horizontal, lower profile than the old buildings along main street. Likewise, modern concerns about safety and aesthetics may dictate that miners' housing be located further from the mines than it was in, say, 1900.

Although it is just one of the important visual aspects of landscape (layout and site being the others), architecture provides very good visual clues to the sequences of development in mining communities. As we study historic photographs, we can see a more or less orderly evolution of architecture in mining towns. This is true of all types of architecture, though industrial architecture seems relatively slow to change, housing changes somewhat more rapidly, and commercial building changes the most rapidly of all.

In this section, several major phases of mining district landscape development are described. A search of the literature and a study of long-lived mining districts enables us to generalize and to classify districts into five major stages: formative, developing, maturing, restructuring, and divesting. These are closely tied to the major stages of mineral production described in the preceding section. It should be remembered, of course, that these five stages are arbitrary. They simply are meant to help the reader appreciate the trends that seem to affect mining districts generally. The evolution of any particular mining district may or may not conform to these patterns.

We begin with the formative stage, or what some observers have called the camp phase. During the early years of a mining district's development, the towns often have an embryonic quality, a rude, frontier demeanor that results from their isolation and their youth. During the formative stage, mining activities rather than amenities are capitalized. Things are often thrown together quickly. Local building materials and primitive mining technology dominate, and the high costs of transportation dictate a concentration of all activities. Most studies of mining communities dwell on this most colorful camp period, for we associate it with rugged individualism and hardship that is best observed from a safe distance. The formative stage is important for laying the groundwork, but it soon eclipsed by other, more permanent, developments.

In their visits to mining districts that are in the formative or camp stage of development, writers and travelers often describe main street first because it is the most social place in town and changes very rapidly. Main street does provide one of the best vantage points to observe change, for it is among the most pretentious and style-conscious of the streetscapes. In a mining community, its character may change quickly as makeshift shelters and tents yield to more permanent buildings. Within a matter of months, an entirely new streetscape may blossom as a mining town develops from a rude camp to a substantial town. The formative period may last about a year or two.

Silver City, Idaho, is a good example. Its main street (called Washington Street) came to possess an urban quality almost overnight. In analyzing historic photographs of Silver City, historical geographer and urban planner Steven Dotterrer describes Washington Street as "lined with closely packed wooden buildings," adding:

Most of the buildings had porches which formed a nearly unbroken covered passage along the street. Most were built with the gable end facing the street. Some left the gables exposed and treated them with simple Greek moldings. Most of the later buildings had the false fronts popular throughout Victorian America. The backsides were simply left untreated.[90]

This description implies that the architectural changes we observe through time are rational or orderly. That, in fact, is an underlying premise of architectural history. After we gain experience in reading architecture, it becomes rather easy to predict when a building was constructed by its style alone—provided, of course, that the architect is not deliberately building in a historic or antiquated style. The same is true for landscapes: as we look at photographs of historic communities or observe places that have not changed because they were abandoned or otherwise bypassed, we can often tell by looking at the style of the buildings when the community prospered, for it is usually only during periods of prosperity that new buildings are constructed.

Dotterer's description also implies that buildings have fronts that are meant to be seen and backsides that are not. Of course, those things that are not meant to be seen are at least as interesting as those are showcased, but let us first look at what we are supposed to see, for it shows how styles or fads affect mining towns through time. The later buildings that Dotterer notes—those with wooden false fronts—have become visually synonymous with western boom town architecture. These buildings are usually a good indicator that the mining community is making the transition to the second or urbanizing phase of development.

These false-front buildings make a powerful visual statement to us (fig. 61). They may seem to say West, perhaps Wild West, because we have seen them in western movies. However, we should realize that they are common in all parts of the United States where rapid, inexpensive construction occurred between 1870 and 1900 or so. Because mining towns were among the most rapidly developing places during that period, it is no surprise that false-front buildings are common there and that they have come to symbolize boom towns. Some architectural historians even call them boom town commercial storefronts.

A recent study by Kingston Heath discusses the evolution of commercial buildings in the mining towns of Montana. Like Silver City, Idaho, and hundreds of other towns that boomed in the period 1860 to 1870, the early main street of Bannack, Montana, was at first lined with "gable-ended commercial structures [that] had little to characterize them as business establishments . . . for their facades lacked the distinctive framed false fronts that would later provide a rhythm of rectilinear facades strung along the main street."[91]

*61. A false-front building is designed to look larger and more impressive
than the gable-ended building it disguises. Here, in Black Hawk, Colorado,
a false-front building stands next to a masonry brick building that normally
indicates more lasting prosperity. 1978 photo by the author.*

The false front became popular during this urbanizing phase because
it helped a rapidly developing frontier streetscape look more substan-
tially constructed and finished than it actually was. The false front was
something of a prop erected at the front of an otherwise unimpressive,
gable-fronted building. It provided an air of Victorian architectural
formality that helped the town make the transition from wilderness
outpost to urban center. Heath continues: "The goal was to appear
legitimate by approximating in sawn lumber and plate glass the kinds
of buildings being built of cast iron or brick in more established cities"
In "reproducing the rhythms of urban row buildings, the false fronts
represented an attempt to establish an urban scale that would help to
retaliate against the vastness of the country and extreme isolation."
However, although these pretentious buildings attempted to make the
streetscape look more impressive and urbane, they were often "an expendable but necessary step in a town's rite of passage. If the town
flourished, the humble wooden structures would soon be superseded
by buildings of grander scale and more precious materials; if the min-

ing venture failed, the abandoned buildings remained like a banner of defeat."[92] Historians of Tonopah, Nevada, describe the town's rapid development in the early twentieth century, noting that "the year 1902 witnessed the physical metamorphosis of Tonopah from a camp to a permanent town. Indications of this permanency were seen on Main Street, in Frank Golden's fine stone building, the Merchant's Hotel, the Miner's Union Hall, the Tonopah Theatre, and the big Casino, a huge two-story dance hall."[93]

Early photos often show mining town main streets of the urbanizing stage as having a bustling, densely settled appearance. Part of this quality is generated by the proliferation of signs, which may either be applied flat to the false fronts or designed to project out over the street. Some of this advertising is standardized, while much of it qualifies as vernacular in that it is created in response to local conditions by individuals within the region. The profusion of signs in the typical mining boom town is probably related to the diversity of activities in any one establishment. Because each merchant might offer duplicative services, visual competition was intense. This theory would seem to be substantiated by the relative scarcity of garish advertising in company towns, where one company controlled all the commercial trade.

In terms of their architectural styles during this urbanizing phase, mining town commercial districts appear to have experienced an evolution similar to that of other developing commercial areas—but the development is often rather compressed in time. Despite their physical isolation, mining communities were not cut off from current trends in architectural styles. As we look at the way their main streets evolved, for example, we see patterns in time: early (pre-1875) commercial structures were frequently rather simple gable-roofed buildings oriented with their gables toward the street: Greek Revival styling was common, as seen in numerous commercial buildings in the early Idaho, Utah, and Nevada mining camps. Thompson's Opera House in Pioche, Nevada, is a gem of Greek Revival architecture on the urban mining frontier, but this style was soon to become outmoded.

Between 1870 and 1900, Victorian false fronts became common, helping to give an urban feel to the community and to disguise the modest size of many establishments. Where prosperity was sustained, or fires were particularly effective, brick and stone Victorian Italianate architecture became a common idiom. This helps to explain why many mining towns from this period (for example, Virginia City and Austin in Nevada and Central City and Black Hawk in Colorado) present a substantial, detailed masonry image associated with the Victorian period throughout the United States. That urban commercial landscape could not have developed were it not for the mining enterprises in the background. An urbanizing mining district has a wealth of mining-related structures such as headframes and ore bins. It is also veneered with ore dumps and other mine wastes that stand out like conical hills in an often denuded landscape.

One need not travel to Colorado or Nevada to see such Dickensian mining landscapes, for the hard coal country around Jim Thorpe (formerly Mauck Chunk) Pennsylvania has that feel, having prospered during the 1870s and 1880s. The main street is lined with impressive Victorian Italianate commercial buildings. In the towns of the anthracite region, huge hard coal breakers stood astride railway tracks, and workers' housing huddled nearby. These landscapes epitomized the concentration of wealth during the period when mining companies were consolidating. Massive investment in the mines led to a flourishing commercial development on main street and the proliferation of housing throughout the mining district. During this period of consolidation, the landscape itself becomes more polarized. While some parts of the mining district become more genteel, others are neglected.

Tonopah, Nevada, was among the last of the single-industry, multiple-company mining districts to develop, and its townscape had that familiar, uncoordinated laissez-faire appearance so typical of urbanizing nineteenth-century mining districts. Historians of Tonopah's early twentieth century mining boom tell us that "there had been no idea among the directors living in Eastern cities of making life more pleasant for the employees in the way of homes, parks, and entertainment for the employees. Much of the discontent and poor efficiency of the employees was due to the unchecked liquor, gambling, and prostitution interests."[94]

As we look at Tonopah, however, we see that it is somewhat different in appearance from other mining towns, such as Virginia City, Nevada, that had flourished a couple of decades before it. Much of the difference can be explained by architectural fashions. In Tonopah, for example, the new construction was less heavily ornamented than it was in those towns that flowered in the mid-Victorian period. The rea-

62. *The impressive ruins of the John S. Cook bank building in Rhyolite, Nevada, vividly tell the story of a mining boom and bust. The recent (1908) date of the building is apparent from its architectural style, making this scene of desolation all the more poignant. 1940 photo by David Myrick.*

son, of course, is that by the time Tonopah boomed in the early 1900s, steel beam construction and the use of concrete had become more common. This change permitted larger window openings because it freed the building from the restrictions of load-bearing walls. It also coincided with major stylistic changes in American architecture, with trim (such as cornices and brackets) becoming less ornate and rising use of terra cotta for building facades. The ghost towns of Goldfield and Rhyolite provide some of the most interesting mining town imagery because their abandoned commercial buildings are surprisingly modern ruins that are given bizarre connotations of antiquity through disintegration. The landscapes of these places show that they were cut down in their prime (fig. 62). The richest ores ran out just as they were urbanizing in about 1910.

Residential architecture is also a good indicator of change. When we look at the house types in a particular mining district, we find that they, too, have fairly clear chronologies. In determining both the spatial and chronological distribution of certain housing types and building materials in the silver mining town of Park City, for example, Deborah Lyn Randall has been able to speculate on the cultural or social trends involved in their acceptance. During the camp stage of development, for example, we learn that "wood, the cheapest, most readily available, and most easily manipulated material was used. Prior to 1890 houses were almost exclusively built of single wall construction. . . . This preference for single wall construction may be explained by the fact that single wall houses could be constructed with greater speed than balloon frame houses because they had no frame."[95]

Most of the houses constructed using this technique were rectangular cabins, the most common house type in the early years of the community. Randall notes that "the rectangular cabin was a logical choice for the first major wave of house building in Park City for a number of reasons," among them its small size, simplicity, ease of construction, and familiarity to miners from Ireland, England, Scotland, and Wales.[96]

In the 1880s, the T-cottage became popular; houses of this style were built until about 1895. The T-cottage introduced visual complexity into the housing stock: it lacked symmetry and often featured quite a bit of Victorian detailing. The T-cottage would appear to be a good indicator of the urbanizing phase, for it was more expensive to construct, more detailed, and often of more substantial construction. The third major house type in historic Park City, the pyramidal roofed cottage, became popular after 1890 and remained so until about 1910. It possessed an element of symmetry and an almost classical formality that, according to Randall, may have been reassuring. In concluding that "what distinguished each house type was its formal appearance,"[97] Randall's study reaffirms that external appearances are important, for they can tell us much about the values of people who create cultural landscapes.

People may make statements with the buildings they construct, and time has a way of dictating how long those messages will last. Consider, for example, the expeditious single wall construction that is so common during the formative stage of mining district development. Because single wall construction provides only marginal rigidity and structural strength to buildings, it helps to explain the tumbled-down condition of many buildings in historic mining camps. They may lean at precarious (or picturesque) angles because they lack the internal bracing that a frame would provide. The buildings constructed during the earliest phase of a mining district's development were temporary, and it is remarkable that many have survived as long as they have. It should not be surprising, however, that they have come to epitomize the hardship and initiative that went into settling the mining frontier during the formative stage.

Seriation expresses itself in unique ways in mining landscapes. Consider, again, the western Nevada mining towns—like Tonopah, Rhyolite, Bullfrog, and Goldfield—that boomed during the first decade of the twentieth century. Architecturally speaking, they are surprisingly complex for several reasons; technological changes may have brought new techniques and building forms into the region, but this progressiveness was counteracted by the high cost of building materials. This, in turn, led to three common solutions (often also seen in other mining districts) that may at first confound architectural historians and other landscape interpreters: the ingenious use of available building materials (such as barrels, cans, and bottles); the construction of purely functional, even primitive, buildings such as dugouts and lean-to shelters that have no formal style; and the pragmatic tradition of moving buildings from earlier camps, such as Candelaria, a mining town that had seen better days.

Thus, interpreting the look of a mining landscape at any particular time must account for pragmatism that sometimes overrides formal stylistic trends. Usually, however, there is a fairly close relationship between architectural style and stage of development.

As soon as a district develops its satellite communities and its mineral processing facilities, it can be said to have urbanized. It enters a mature stage during which the district achieves its basic form and all systems operate to exploit, process, and distribute the ore and its by-products. The entire mining district operates like a machine: functional, efficient, and integrated. A relatively long period of maturation typically finds a district operating in both prosperous (usually war) and lean (usually peace) times.

In most of our historic mining districts, the period of maturity began about 1890 to 1900 and lasted into the 1920s. World War I was probably the most prosperous period: mining companies achieved almost unlimited political power in supplying the war effort. Iron, copper, lead, and zinc mining in particular operated around the clock and left a landscape legacy that is still visible today from the iron mines around Birmingham, Alabama, to Marquette, Michigan, from the lead and zinc mines of the Tri-State District (of Missouri, Oklahoma, and Kansas) to Mineral Point, Wisconsin; and the copper mines from Duck-town, Tennessee, to Magna, Utah. The coal mines from coast to coast prospered along with the metals mines, for they were part of the same industrial system.

In studying the "cultural landscape of the Athens County coal region" in Ohio during the period of prosperity (1885–1927), Eugene Palka focuses on four features in particular: company housing, company stores, tipples, and mine buildings. Most of these remaining company buildings date from 1900.[98] These features can be contrasted with the early (pre-1885) structures, most of which have vanished, and the later tipples and structures constructed to handle strip-mined coal. Palka's study describes only five major house types and notes their clustering in separate communities, each of which had its own character; this clustering, of course, is common in mature mining areas that have diversified.

In many mining districts, the period of maturity or urbanization is also a period when corporations shaped the landscape with seeming impunity, and they often did so with help from the public sector. In fact, it may be difficult to tell who built something, for there may be a blurring between what we normally think of as public versus private improvements. In a mining district, it is not safe to assume that the city built the roads, the municipal swimming pool, or even the city hall. As discussed under homogenization, the further we move into the twentieth century, the more likely we are to see the work of mining companies in the landscape. Where numerous large companies are operating, they may agree to support urban improvements such as roads, streetcar lines, and public facilities that improve the moral well-being (and hence the character) of workers.

A kind of pragmatism may bring these competing mining companies together; surprisingly, their inherent suspiciousness is more often directed toward outside sources of control, such as unions and regulatory authority, than toward their competitors. In any event, this mature phase of mining district development often involves the most aggressive planning of any large-scale environments in the United States. During the mature stage, the quality of public life begins to become an issue in mining districts. Sanitation systems may be installed, roads improved, and amenities (such as street lighting) added.

The mature stage marks the heyday of underground mining, but it sets the scene for future developments that will radically transform the landscape. Depletion of the richest parts of the ore body and/or high labor costs bring about the next, or fourth, phase of mining district development—restructuring. This phase coincides with the aggressive pursuit of lower-grade ores. Previously existing settlements may be relocated or demolished as the overburden is stripped and entire mountains removed. The mining industry also has a tendency to cause further impact on the settlement of a particular mining district by depositing waste material in the interstices or vacant areas, through what geographer John Webb calls "progressive enclosure" in his study of urban communities in the Minnesota Iron Ranges.[99]

We have seen how this type of enclosure can transform the physical topography of a mining district and lead to distinctive manmade features such as topographic landmarks and precipitous edges that define the visual geography. It can also reshape the economic geography of any particular district, for differences in ores mined require different milling, concentrating, and smelting techniques. Restructuring involves massive investment and affects the life and landscape of a mining district.

Although open pit mining began as early as the 1890s in Minnesota's Mesabi Range, most of the major open pit mining projects in the United States developed after 1910. This type of mining required massive amounts of explosives and large earth-moving machinery. This was the undisputed age of electricity, which was, symbolically, the heir of copper, iron, and coal mining. The materials taken from the earth were shaped into machines that, in turn, made even more aggressive, place-consuming mining possible. It was a time of scientific calculations of efficiency, a time of systematization of all mining operations. It coincided with the rise of the automobile and the simplification of architecture during the early years of the twentieth century. In the second decade of this century, gasoline and diesel power began to be used for some tasks (such as hoisting, pumping, and haulage), but it was still the undisputed age of steam. Steam produced electricity, which began to power most of the mine hoists at this time.

Residential architecture continued to become more efficient and standardized into the 1910s and 1920s. New housing was as likely to meet minimal expectations about dwelling size and healthful living as it was to be beautiful. Pressed brick and concrete cinder block became common building materials. Sears and Roebuck began marketing catalog houses, and many of these found their way into mining districts.

Automobiles had become a common sight in the mining districts by the late 1910s, and automobile ownership brought with it a greater demand for public roads. Garages became a common feature in the 1920s, at least in housing areas occupied by miners who held better jobs. Indoor plumbing became more common as sanitation was addressed in various neighborhoods of the mining districts, and the outhouse began to disappear about this time. The early twentieth century marked a time of greater and greater government involvement in a wide range of activities, from road building and sanitation to housing. In some places, mining companies provided these services; in others, they worked hand in hand with the public sector.

A look at a mining district developed during this later period, such as the copper-rich area around Ruth and Ely, Nevada, is revealing. Upon entering Ely, county seat of White Pine County, we find an orderly community laid out in a checkerboard pattern. The community was platted in the late nineteenth century, and its wide main street is lined with substantial commercial buildings that date from the period 1910 to 1920—a time of nearly unprecedented prosperity for the copper industry. Thus, Ely's architectural character is quite different from other Nevada mining communities, such as Austin and Eureka, that prospered during the silver boom about forty years earlier. Ely is a mining community, but we can see that a great deal of planning, if not imagination, went into its design. A large public square with shade trees and even a bandstand marks the center of town. One must glimpse the mine workings and mine dumps on the hillsides or see the rows of pattern-book miners' housing lining the side streets to know that this is mining country.

This period of restructuring lasted through good and bad times. The tempos of mining activity and construction were directly correlated. The 1920s were not especially good times for many mining districts, but economies of scale permitted many mines to operate at a profit. Open pit mining was less labor intensive, but the jobs that were available often paid fairly well. As labor costs dropped, and the price of purchasing and operating machinery increased, underground mines continued to be worked in some districts along with open pit mines.

The 1930s were generally hard times, and activity wound down considerably in many districts. Layoffs occurred in many areas, and the depression reduced many operations to skeleton crews as the nationwide demand for metals declined. Architects and designers continued to shape architectural styles in the 1930s, but the demand for new construction was low. That explains why we see very little of the sensuous art deco styling of the 1930s in mining towns, some notable exceptions being larger mining districts (for example, Anaconda, Montana). Where art deco was found, it introduced curves and arcane, almost mystical imagery; the interior of the Anaconda theater was one of the best examples of the genre in that part of the country. We now interpret the smooth streamlining of art deco as an attempt to foster new construction, and sales, through design hype. Art deco styling may have caught the fancy of the public, but the economy was too moribund for much to happen until the boom brought about by World War II.

World War II found prosperity returning to the mining areas, which supplied strategic metals for the war effort. Given constraints on building, however, only the most necessary new construction could occur until the postwar boom that followed. In the late 1940s, art moderne styling was a popular architectural idiom, seen on service stations and cafes. The postwar period also witnessed the wholesale acceptance of prefabricated housing, which was no stranger to the mining districts. Postwar housing was eclectic, embracing a wide variety of styles, including Colonial Revival. In the late 1950s, ranch-style houses began to appear in mining districts.

One of the most interesting fusions of mining and housing occurred during these later years—construction of metal houses. Although the idea predated the war, Lustron's steel houses were manufactured in the late 1940s. They were enameled in standard colors and were available in a few styles. However, they could not compete with houses of more traditional materials, and production ceased in the mid-1950s. An even more interesting use of metal for housing was promoted by Kennecott Copper Company, which built an entire neighborhood of copper

63. Colonial Revival and other modern suburban-style housing began to be built in mining districts on the eve of World War II and continued into the 1950s, to be replaced by ranch houses in the 1960s. This home in Copperton, Utah, is sheathed in copper—a unique marketing experiment by the Kennecott Copper Company. 1988 photo by the author.

homes near its mining operation in Copperton, Utah. These were simple Colonial Revival cottages, with all siding and trim made of copper. Even the roofing material was copper sheeting. These homes never became a commercial success, but are now listed on the National Register of Historic Places (fig. 63).

The trailer or mobile home became a common sight in mining districts following World War II. Since miners often move in response to better mining opportunities elsewhere, mobile housing was a perfect solution to a lifestyle that called for short-notice mobility and an environment that featured small, narrow lots (fig. 64). To miners, who are likely to be very pragmatic about what they call home, the mobile home would appear to be a perfect alternative to the historic miners' cabins, which, for all their charm, were often poorly constructed, poorly maintained, and drafty. Mobile homes were easily placed on vacant lots (some of which were the sites of earlier homes). They be-

64. *Mobile housing is particularly well suited to the needs of miners and the small, narrow lots of mining towns. Mobile homes contrast visually with historic structures, but they tell us much about the population and economy of mining communities. This example in Tonopah, Nevada, features a wooden deck (left) and an additional room with a wood-burning stove (right). 1989 photo by the author.*

came a common feature in mining landscapes in the latter half of the twentieth century, which—depending on economic conditions—are likely to feature a mixture of historic and modern housing. Mobile homes are standardized and introduce a horizontal element in the landscape. They are usually metal-sheathed, and their unpretentious aluminum skins are about as functional as the unpainted corrugated metal seen elsewhere in the mining district. In a number of cases, mining companies have used mobile homes to house miners in areas that were experiencing rapid development or relocation following the destruction of old housing that stood in the way of new mining operations.

Restructuring may not always require new construction; sometimes the relocation of previously existing housing accomplishes the purpose. As one reads the landscape of a mining district, one must be prepared for some surprises. Saginaw, Arizona, in the Warren Mining District, seems to be an anomaly. Looking at the community, which clusters at the base of a metal headframe and large leach dump, we see several dozen miners' homes that were obviously built in the early twentieth century; we can tell their age by their architectural style, for they are mostly pyramidal roofed and T-cottage miners' houses. We might be stunned to find that this community dates from 1958— until we learn that the houses were moved here from the historic Upper Lowell area in order to make way for the expansion of the Lavender Pit in the late 1950s.

The transformation of the physical landscape by mining interests, then, makes our understanding of seriation all the more important. If we had simply been told that Saginaw was developed by Phelps Dodge in 1958 and had not sensed that something was wrong with the chronology of its architecture, we might not have asked why such old housing is in such a new area. Like other detective work, reading the landscape depends on interpreting all clues. The landscape of a typical mining district is often so complex and so reworked by mining activity that the factor we normally assume is constant—location or place— may become as transitory as time.

The march of time in a mining district is relentless, for the fate of the district is determined by decisions made miles away. High energy and labor costs and a depleted ore body may lead to the last stage of a mining district's evolution, divestiture—the decision of the mining company or companies to close the mines. Sometimes the decision is made and announced with stunning rapidity, as in the case of "Black Sunday" (May 2, 1982), when Exxon pulled out of the booming oil shale town of Parachute, Colorado. Andrew Gulliford has masterfully told the story of how Exxon's sudden departure affected both the landscape, which is marked by abandoned projects and empty buildings, and the residents, who reacted much as they would have to an unexpected death.[100]

More typically, however, the end of mining in a district occurs in several agonizing stages, including the leasing of mines to smaller operators who can function more efficiently by circumventing labor costs or using less expensive machinery. The pumps may be shut off in some mines, and the mines may flood. Companies stop improving the existing mines, and the handwriting is on the wall. This phase usually finds large numbers of the most employable workers and their families leaving the district. The district's economy enters a major slump, with houses going on the market for a fraction of their boom-time value. Businesses close, and the landscape of the district takes on a forlorn, shabby look: maintenance either ceases or the inhabitants make do with low-cost repairs.

Whether or not the district is really finished as a mining community at this point depends on many unknowns, including geopolitics, the price of minerals, labor costs, and so on. Quite a few mining districts that were considered dead have popped back to life, and those experienced in mining learn to pronounce a district dead only with great reluctance. The area around Austin, Nevada, in the early 1990s provides a case in point. Long considered nearly a ghost town, at least as far as mining activities were concerned, the town began to experience a miniboom in the late 1980s and early 1990s as gold and silver mines developed in the area. New construction was evident, and travelers had difficulty finding motel rooms during the week as miners moved into the area.

The changes that geographer Gary Peterson has witnessed in the Tintic Mining District of Utah could describe conditions elsewhere in the region: "generally, higher metals prices have joined heap leaching and ion exchange extraction processes to cause old mines and waste dumps to suddenly assume 'ore' status in the current economics."[101] Relaxation of environmental restrictions and an increase in the price of silver helped renew mining activity in many areas, including Tombstone, Arizona, in the 1980s. In many cases, however, the remaining ore may be of too low a concentration to be mined in the foreseeable future, at which time most people acknowledge that the mining district is dead, at least as far as mining is concerned.

It is at this juncture that the last phase of a mining district begins: its primary economic reason for being now gone, the district either may decline and ultimately vanish or may regroup to find a new economy, such as tourism or other service-related industries, to sustain it. Across the country, many mining districts have been experiencing a surprising revitalization that is based not on mineral production, but rather on the marketing of amenities. What is happening to mining landscapes in the late twentieth century is both a result of the historic forces that shaped them and a result of a relatively new phenomenon: a growing appreciation of history that characterizes postindustrial societies. Mining country provides powerful visual settings in which "technostalgia"—the romanticizing of the industrial past—can thrive. This sentiment has been a major factor in the preservation of mining communities. It is so significant, and so contemporary, that it is treated separately in the following chapter.

3

PERCEIVING

THE

LANDSCAPE

THE PERSISTENCE OF MINING LANDSCAPES

Mining towns seem to be unusual, perhaps unique, among
American settlements in being problems when they are booming
but desirable when they have failed. Just as Americans have
created romantic heroes out of their movie cowboys . . . , so too
have they remade into romantic sagas the histories of their early
mining towns.
—Thomas R. Vale and Geraldine R. Vale, *Western Images,*
Western Landscapes: Travels along U.S. 89

Although America is littered with thousands of ghost town
sites, many of which are associated with mining activity, a surprising number of our former mining towns have survived despite the
closing of their mines. Their survival, and their popularity, surprises
the cynics. Like the "Unsinkable Molly Brown," that feisty Colorado
mining matron who caught the popular imagination with her resolve
and heroism, many mining towns have simply refused to give up.
From the Iron Ranges of the upper Midwest to the historic mining
towns of the West, travelers will find hundreds of historic mining communities that seemingly should have vanished after their mines closed
down—but did not. This chapter looks at why mining landscapes persist, and how these landscapes fit into the American mind and the
American scene.

What enables a place to survive after its main reason for existing
disappears with the closing of the mines and mills? How can a single-
industry town survive after that industry closes? The answer usually
lies in its ability to market other amenities, which is to say adapt to
change. Ironically, a number of the factors that lead to the development of mining communities in the first place, including isolation, diversification, and nucleation, may help them survive postmining dives-

titure. A look at mining districts that have experienced significant revitalization shows that they have done so for several reasons, including economic diversification, recreation and amenity marketing, and the promotion of tourism. Many of these are tied, in some way or another, to image.

HISTORY AS CATALYST

To a greater or lesser degree, the historic heritage of former mining towns has been a factor in their survival. The growing popular appreciation of history as a cultural amenity has affected the entire country and is especially pronounced in mining districts, for few places capture the passage of time and the excitement of history in the public imagination better than our mining landscapes. This appreciation is one of the most characteristic features of life in the late twentieth century, for never before has the country been so obsessed with history.

Although a few visionaries began documenting and saving the physical heritage of mining towns (especially in California) as early as the turn of the century, and their efforts finally began to take root in the 1920s and 1930s, it was during the period following World War II that our mining heritage gained widespread appreciation. Before mining landscapes could be valued, however, a romanticized vision of their place in history and nature had to be developed. It took a merging of prose, poetry, and art to depict the landscapes that had been left in the wake of mining; among the most effective were the popular drawings by Muriel Wolle, whose works on Colorado ghost towns defined the image for a generation of Americans. Spectacular natural scenery had something to do with it, but so did the rich bonanza history of the mining West. Colorado, once viewed by the public as forlorn and desolate, was among the earliest centers of mining landscape nostalgia. The state had a wealth of abandoned mining communities and a surprising amount of surviving heritage of the narrow gauge railroad that had gone hand in hand with the development of the mining camps. Both were promoted simultaneously. This may explain, in part, why mining towns and western railroads are so closely linked in the public mind.

Few people could capture the sentiment of time and place better than the dean of popular historians—Lucius Beebe—and his associate Charles Clegg. Among the lines of classic prose penned by these devotees of Gilded Age railroad and mining history, we find this ode to the western mining landscape:

> The false fronts of once populous mining camps are good for a decade or so of Colorado winters at the most. The tailings and mine dumps are only a little more lasting and a few centuries will have eroded them past discerning to the most perceptive archeologists. The elemental earth is quick to reclaim the cuts and fills of vanished railroads. Thus, while for a brief period the tangible souvenirs are at every hand, their impermanence is there also, implicit in the very nature of the society and its economics that mined the hillsides for precious metals. A rags-to-riches social emergence was not notably aware of its mortality. It didn't build for the ages.[1]

Descriptions like this helped create a sense of urgency while they also generated an appreciation for the venerability of our mining landscapes. Beebe and Clegg were among the first to recognize the greatness of our mining heritage even though it was both ephemeral and pretentious: here, in formerly remote settings now reached by good highways, was a landscape of theatrical proportions, a montage of quickly built, ornate sets that emulated the high cultures of the East and Europe. The relentless march of time and the elements underscored the vulnerability of this historic fabric while providing an almost perversely beautiful sense of desolation and decline. If every culture needs ruins to emphasize its past accomplishments and its relationship to nature, then our once-prosperous mining towns are among the most powerful of our cultural symbols.

This means that two very different motives lie at the roots of our fascination with mining history, affecting how we perceive, and how we preserve, mining landscapes. On the one hand, we need to recognize the former greatness of mining communities and to show how they dominated nature to win mineral riches; and on the other, we need to venerate their abuse by nature in order to emphasize their antiquity.

Small wonder, then, that two types of mining town landscapes are preserved today for tourists: boom towns and ghost towns.

THE GHOST TOWN IMAGE

Few places capture the imagination more readily than ghost towns. Just how one defines a ghost town is open to debate: some authorities claim that the place should be completely depopulated but should contain standing buildings or ruins; others say that a few living hangers-on (say ten or fewer) may be permissible as long as the place once had a much larger population; still others say a true ghost town is a place where all above ground signs of people, including buildings, have vanished. These distinctions, of course, are academic, for the public understands a ghost town to be a tangible but depopulated place inhabited only by the memories of former occupants. The term "ghost town" implies former activity, perhaps even former greatness, as manifested in decrepit buildings and other ruins. A ghost town is a place that is being reclaimed by nature, and we seem to take a perverse interest in the aesthetics and symbolism of time marching into, and over, such forlorn places.

They are also instructional, for they depict the results of risk-taking, a revered trait in our culture. In creating the popular Knott's Berry Farm in Orange County, California, in 1953, Walter Knott recognized the iconography. He was among the pioneers of a politically conservative school of educators who created mythical places to reaffirm values of American greatness. Ghost Town was built anew in the fertile farmlands of the Los Angeles basin, but depicted a wild and wooly, roughhewn mining town main street wherein visitors could even pan for flecks of real gold. We are told that "Ghost Town depicts an era in our nation's history when men were forging ahead and crossing new frontiers. Ghost Town also represents an era of free people who carved out their individual empires from a new land, asking only to work out their own salvation without let or hindrance. The people, the things, the buildings of Ghost Town are long dead, but the same pioneer spirit still lives on."[2]

Although Ghost Town was a fictional, recreated mining town, it stood as a model for real places, such as the long-abandoned silver mining town of Calico, in California's Mojave Desert. It was Walter Knott, "a direct descendant of early day pioneers," who recognized the deeply held American fascination with the past and capitalized on it. Calico, "site of one of the most spectacular silver strikes ever made in California," was one of the earliest ghosts to be resurrected: in 1953, the public was told that "today the townsite, with its handful of ruins, is gradually being restored by the Knott family."[3] Calico emerged as one of the more popular booming ghost towns, an attraction not too far from the otherwise uneventful highway from Los Angeles to Las Vegas. Sequestered in the colorful, rock-strewn Mojave Desert hills that gave it its name, Calico became the liveliest of our mining ghost towns and one of the region's most successful tourism ventures.

Most ghost towns are far more somber than the lively Calico. Many, like Ballarat in the Panamint Valley of eastern California, are little more than historic markers standing near melting adobe and splintered wooden walls of former mining town buildings. Some, like Terlingua and Shafter, in the spectacular Big Bend country of west Texas, are promoted as important historic sites that help tell a story of regional development and decline. The grandest of our mining ghosts is the silver mining town of Bodie, California (fig. 65). It symbolizes our culture's desire to stop time. Set in a sagebrush-covered, bowl-shaped valley in the high desert, it was one of the roughest and most isolated of the boom towns. It had, and still has, a rigorous climate: huge snowfalls in winter, high winds, and searing summer days that may alternate with frosty nights. Bodie has virtually no growing season, but sits on top of a highly mineralized area rich in silver and lore.

Like most of its sister mining towns, Bodie has experienced devastating fires, one of which (in 1932) burned down half of the business district and further contributed to the forlorn quality of the place. The only reason that the remainder of the town was not carted off by souvenir hunters and scavengers was the presence of a watchman who looked after it throughout the 1940s and 1950s. Bodie's nearly sure fate of being obliterated was averted through private ownership by the wealthy Cain family. If it had been left unattended, the elements and scavengers would have reduced the place to an archaeological site in a few seasons.

In contrast to the gold rush town of Columbia in California's mother

65. Once-prosperous Bodie, California, is now the classic ghost town. Cattle graze the empty lots near the remains of the commercial district, and forlorn commercial buildings stand along main street. 1978 photo by the author.

lode—another state park that attempts to capture the vibrant spirit of an active mining town—Bodie is dead, and proud of it. Since its opening as a state park in 1962, visitors to Bodie have found themselves face to face with solitude. The town appears to be desolate and unoccupied, but in reality everything is carefully preserved in a state of arrested decay. Some buildings lean at precarious angles, seemingly ready to topple with the next windstorm. They will not, however, for they are carefully propped up. All the buildings in Bodie have a weather-beaten look.

In Bodie, the preservation of the ghost town image finds our culture resisting the elements and forestalling the inevitable. Recognizing the extreme fire danger, state park preservationists painted the buildings with a clear coating of fire retardant, which, to their chagrin, they later learned was actually accelerating the deterioration of the wood that they were trying to protect. But the overall effect of all this behind-the-scenes stabilization of ruin is stunning, for Bodie has an artistic patina—the Standard Mill sits at the edge of town, its corrugated zinc metal sheathing burnished to a dull whitish-blue; basaltic rock foundations stand forlorn and geometrical; a hundred seasons have given the ramshackle wooden buildings a silvery-golden hue; the gray-green sagebrush flourishes along with fat cattle that graze the site. Bodie is preservation as theater, and its landscape is so provocative that the drama needs no actors, only a stage of deserted buildings.

BOOM TOWNS AND TOURIST TRAPS

By the late twentieth century, travel and tourism had become one of the major industries in the United States. As the public became more history-conscious, in part as a result of the nation's Bicentennial in 1976, history became a major factor in the tourism equation. When quizzed about their preferences in tourism, a greater and greater number of people have selected "historic sites" as their destination. This is true of both American tourists and, significantly, tourists visiting the United States from abroad.

The landscapes of mining communities often conveyed enough of a sense of the past to attract visitors, a point not lost on merchants who saw a potential gold mine in the marketing of history. Tombstone, Arizona, was one of the earliest to capitalize on its mining-related boom town heritage. A state park was established at the historic Cochise County courthouse—a further catalyst to visitation. Tourists get something of the spirit of the place when they drive past Boot Hill cemetery on the way into town and soon find themselves on a main street lined by false-front buildings emblazoned with gaudy Wild West signs and elaborate fake porches (fig. 66). The spirit of the place is best revealed by a bumper sticker promoted by the merchants in the late 1970s: *Tombstone: The Town Too Tough to Die*. Actually, toughness had less to do with Tombstone's survival than television, for the town was saved from oblivion by its popularization in television westerns— including *Tombstone Territory*—beginning in the 1950s. However, relatively little of Tombstone's mining history was preserved in the process of emphasizing the rough and tumble "shoot 'em up" downtown along Allen Street. By the 1960s, Tombstone had become a tourist town that capitalized on its bawdy, violent history as a frontier out-

66. The power of television westerns: highly commercialized Allen Street in Tombstone, Arizona, hides a number of historic structures, but preservationists recommending that they be properly restored received a hostile reaction from the business community in the early 1980s. 1990 photo by Damien Francaviglia.

post. Around 1980, a mine tour opened, its main purpose being to expose visitors to the historic silver mining that put the town on the map in the first place.

Hoping to capture some of the tourist trade after the closure of its copper mines in the mid-1970s, nearby Bisbee (25 miles south of Tombstone) launched into an aggressive history/tourism marketing campaign in the early 1980s. It promptly resurrected the slogan *Queen of the Copper Camps*, in honor of its historic Copper Queen Mine. As if not to be outdone by Tombstone, wags in Bisbee designed a sequel bumper sticker that also said something about the town's tenacity and sense of humor: *Bisbee: The Town too Dumb to Die*. Other equally enigmatic bumper stickers appeared, including the ambitious *Bisbee: Greatest Happening Since the Grand Canyon*, perhaps an oblique reference to the huge abandoned Lavender Pit copper mine that lies at the heart of the mining district.

DIVERSIFICATION AND SURVIVAL

Tourism, however, is usually only one aspect of the economy of former mining towns. Some, like Central City (Colorado) and Deadwood (South Dakota), hope that legalized gambling will help bring another boom. Most of the former mining towns that are making a comeback are doing so by promoting several types of economic development. Diversified revitalization is a major factor in the survival in many mining communities, for they often possess a critical mass of services that accommodate a large tributary area.

Bisbee, Arizona, and the towns of its Warren Mining District show us that our mining districts are surprisingly tenacious. In engineering its turnaround since the closing of the mines, Bisbee has developed a more balanced economy based on a mixture of service industries, craft industries, government, retirement, and tourism.[4] Despite a mid-1970s University of Arizona study predicting that Bisbee would become a ghost town within about a decade after the mines closed, the town has survived. A detailed study of the processes by which this mining town defied dire predictions was completed at the same time that another popular bumper sticker appeared: *Bisbee Arizona Ain't No Ghost Town!*[5] Once again, a mining town whose mines had closed refused to die. In describing why Bisbee and places like it survive, geographer Lay Gibson has noted that the effects of major shifts in employment "probably will be exaggerated. In fact, positive impacts probably will not be as great as initially claimed by optimists, and negative impacts likely will be less severe than anticipated by pessimists."[6]

There is a down side to marketing the amenities of former mining towns too aggressively. For some, like Aspen, Colorado, the combination of history and scenery has proven overwhelming. The place has become so popular, and expensive, that it has developed a completely new identity in the space of a few years. Its character as a mining community has been virtually lost in the process. Skiing and solitude—two amenities not especially appreciated by the early miners—attracted a wealthy population that priced everyone else out of the community. Promoters recognized the town's picturesque setting and historic architecture as irresistible, and they were correct. That other historic mining communities (for example, Telluride and Crested Butte) are succumbing to a similar fate proves that Aspen is not a fluke, but rather a regional model. The 1980s and 1990s find the historic community gentrified as condos fill the valley and the remaining historic miners' houses—even small miners' cabins—sell for astronomical figures.

HISTORIC PRESERVATION AND ITS CONSEQUENCES

Many of our historic mining communities would look quite different today were it not for the growing sense of history that has swept the country since the 1960s. In the twenty-five years since the passage of the Historic Preservation Act of 1966, the historic preservation movement has become a powerful economic and social force, and its impact is obvious in today's landscape. A Gallup Poll conducted for the Urban Land Institute in 1986 revealed that a large majority of the population supported the objectives of historic preservation. "Retaining a sense of the past" was rated as the most important objective of historic preservation,[7] reaffirming that historic preservation is inextricably linked with the image of historic places.

Professional preservationists direct a program aimed at identifying and evaluating all historic resources—and preserving those that are historically significant. However, the landscape shows that preservation has been a selective (and subjective) process that favors properties that are attractive, desirable, or marketable—those historic properties that the culture feels are worthy of preservation. This selective preservation has resulted in the saving of certain residential and commercial properties, while many industrial features owned by the mining interests have vanished. Included in the latter are mine buildings, headframes, flumes, and other structures. Therefore, preserved mining landscapes are usually lopsided assemblages of genteel buildings—not the gritty landscape of everyday industrial life that characterized the mining district during its active period(s).

Historic preservation often beautifies the landscape that it seeks to

preserve. In this sense, the landscape that is preserved is less an artifact of history (the past) than of current values (the present). An
early (1962) description of the preservation process in Mineral Point,
Wisconsin, provides a case in point:

> The miners were totally unconcerned about the appearance of
> their town; that tendency has continued, generation after genera-
> tion. The town continues to reveal the effects of the mining days,
> of the vast ruins of the zinc works and its spoil area. Somewhat
> recently the people have awakened to the natural charm of their
> city and have made progress in changing the appearance of the
> place from an old mining and smelting town to a village with ir-
> regular and picturesque streets and alleys and with well-kept
> homes, lawns and gardens.[8]

We find in this statement the roots of a conflict surrounding the preservation of mining landscapes: the miners who shaped these landscapes are often the last to want to preserve them, while the most
active proponents of preservation are often newcomers who appreciate
the uniqueness and charm of the place.

Historic preservation—the act of maintaining the historic environment in order to preserve its character—has become law in certain
former mining communities—like Park City, Utah, and Jacksonville,
Oregon—through the passage of local historic preservation legislation.
When this happens, historic properties and districts are identified, and
restrictions are placed on what can be done with them. In so doing,
preservation exercises control over current or future actions by in effect redefining the public's interest in private property—at least as far
as exterior appearances are concerned. It also implies a collective re-
spect, almost a reverence, for the past that may prohibit what some
pragmatists might consider to be more or less natural change from
occurring.

The issue of change versus preservation in miners' housing provides
a good example. Whereas historic preservationists concerned about
retaining the character of the community have argued against mobile
homes being moved onto narrow lots in mining towns like Bisbee and
Crested Butte, those mobile homes may actually be as much in the
spirit of pragmatic, expendable, movable housing as the ninety-year-

67. Neotraditionalism and image-building. According to the Architectural
Record, *the new (1988) Main Post Office in Julian, California, "reinterprets
the Old West character" of a historic mining town in order to introduce
motorists to the town's distinctive character. Photo © Sandra Williams.*

old miner's cabin next to them. It is worth remembering that miners
never built things to become historic, but rather to be used—if not
used up—and their landscape shows it.

The historic preservation movement and its postmodernist/neotra-
ditional architecture has given a new/old look to much recent construction in the American landscape, and many restored or revitalized
mining towns have been affected by it. Consider, for example, the
new (1988) post office constructed in the historic gold mining town of
Julian, California. An *Architectural Record* article cites Julian's "well-
preserved Old West atmosphere" as one of the factors that the architects (Keniston & Mosher) sought to build upon. The post office, situated on the main highway into town, "is meant to introduce passing
motorists to Julian's distinctive character"; the architects designed a
"stepped false-front facade [that] mimics the most distinctive feature
of turn-of-the-century Western architecture,"[9] as well as a cupola that
helps identify the post office as a public building (fig. 67). This attractive building is a caricature that serves to remind us of the power of
history in image-building.

The relatively recent preservation/revitalization of former mining
towns may be interpreted as having an associated cost—the devel-

opment of a historic image that in turn becomes dependent on what has already been arbitrarily selected to be saved. While this has resulted in the preservation of parts of the mining landscape, it may also result in the loss of the historic industrial landscape context of the community. This condition, of course, mirrors the American pattern of preservation: attractive or popular pieces of history, such as the mansion of a mine owner, are sequestered and severed from their true context and meaning as they become icons separated from the industrial structures and workers' housing that helped to create them. In other words, mining towns are usually preserved at the cost of being sanitized. Ironically, the least welcome residents of all may be new miners who have moved into many older districts as improved mining technologies, relaxed environmental controls, and changes in metals prices reopen closed mines. Their carefree ("rowdy") ways and their penchant for making no long-term commitments are often too much for staid historic mining communities to take. In a strange twist of fate, the metal booms of the late 1980s and early 1990s found a vigorous mining population unwelcome in the very places that catered to just this "type" in the boom days a century or more ago.

These new miners do pose a threat to the historic landscape through renewed mining development—if we consider the historic landscape to be static. By the early 1990s, renewed mineral exploration threatened further to transform the landscape of numerous historic mining communities, among them Silver City (Idaho), Bisbee (Arizona), and even Bodie (California). In all of these locations, mining interests have attempted to reassure local preservationists that there is little threat to the historic towns themselves because any open pit mining would stop short of consuming the actual historic resources. This assurance, of course, does not account for the fact that preservationists consider the overall site or setting of a mining community to be part of the historic ambience. Preservationists argue that considerable visual damage can be done by mineral exploration, which may result in the digging of innumerable test holes, the grading of roads, and the removal of certain historic features—even before any serious mining begins. As we have seen, renewed mining activity is a natural part of the sequential development of a mining district. Looked at objectively, preservation is a recent sentiment that may actually add so much to the costs of mining that it may redirect mining activity. In the scheme of things, preservation—like reclamation—is simply yet another environmental or economic factor that miners must deal with as they transform the face of the land.

THREATS TO HISTORIC MINING LANDSCAPES: A SUMMARY

Mining landscapes are in a constant state of flux as cultural values and natural forces continue to exert themselves. What are the major threats to the historic mining landscapes we see today? As we witness the disappearance of historic mining-related features and landscapes, we can observe at least one of four forces coming into play.

1. Neglect may result in short-term preservation, but ultimately finds the resources obliterated by natural forces.

2. Preservation, especially gentrification, transforms the landscape into something that may seem historic but has little basis in fact.

3. Reclamation removes many features considered to be hazardous or unsightly in an effort to make the area productive or attractive.

4. Renewed mining may completely obliterate the historic landscape or result in the relocation of historic features.

Regarding this last issue, a fundamental battle is taking shape as mining landscape preservation advocates tackle mining development interests. The former cite local and state preservation legislation, as well as the aesthetic sentiments associated with history, as establishing a legal basis for preservation, while the latter cite the Mining Law of 1872 and mining's nearly inalienable right to develop mineralized properties as sufficient reasons to proceed with new mining developments. The General Mining Law of 1872 guarantees that all valuable mineral deposits in lands belonging to the United States are "free and open to exploration and purchase" and helps to explain the seeming omnipotence that mining companies have in transforming landscapes under the jurisdiction of the federal government. Even though this law requires that mineral development must occur within regulations prescribed by applicable state and federal laws, it has found many regulatory agencies adopting a hands-off policy, especially when confronted by mining company attorneys and irate legislators backed by mining interests.

Recent developments in the vicinity of Bodie and/or other historic mining communities are almost sure to result in challenges to the 1872 law by preservationists. The outcome will be hard to predict, but it is safe to say that the mineral development lobby—especially when backed by arguments that strategic minerals/metals must transcend aesthetics and even the wishes of conservation interests in order to keep the country strong—has seldom failed. The same industry that has persuaded Congress to change seemingly sacrosanct National Monument boundaries in the past still maintains considerable clout, especially in the context of future national emergencies. One can expect the 1990s to witness renewed attempts to amend the Mining Law of 1872, and it is likely to be the historic preservationists interested in historic mining landscapes who mount the challenge.

That debate would force us to confront the issue of mining landscape preservation versus development on a national scale. If and when this happens, we should remember that mining interests will be acting according to an episodic pattern of mining development that is even more deeply rooted, and consequently more historical, than the historic preservation movement itself. Mining interests will contend that the very actions that left Hibbing, Minnesota, and Lowell, Arizona, poised at the brinks of huge open pit mines helped the United States win two world wars. These gaping mining landscapes removed earlier historic settlements, but, paradoxically, are now just as historic as the towns that remain. Will preservationists be able to view the continued development of mining landscapes—that is, the relentless seriation/transformation processes discussed earlier—as part of history?

The country's obsession with historic preservation leaves one to ponder the thoughts of David Lowenthal, who warns against a culture becoming so captivated by history that it loses the ability to act in the present.[10] Time will tell whether the historic preservation movement has ossified, but there is some concern among its strongest advocates and leaders that it has begun to do so. William Murtagh notes that "inexplicably, many preservation leaders have lost sight of the motives that once fueled their movement and have become preoccupied with *how* to preserve, either politically, economically, or technically, with little or no discrimination as to *what* they are preserving and *why*."[11] Historic mining landscapes will be among their biggest challenges.

LANDSCAPE AND MEMORY

Whether we attempt to preserve them or not, historic mining landscapes provide a visible connection with the past and reveal much about the attitudes and the lifestyles of those who created them. Even after mining landscapes have been so altered that their content is virtually devoid of the architectural features that branded them as mining country in the first place, they linger in the minds of old-timers. Consider, for example, the comments of Frank C. Dunlavy of the Tooele County Historical Society in Utah, who concludes an elaborate description of the extensive works of the Tooele Smelter with this emotional litany: "I have taken my grandchildren up to the old site and told them, 'There is where the lead plant stood, and the copper plant was over there, and the concentrator was up there.' 'Where, grandfather, where?' they asked. To the untrained eye there was nothing left. Perhaps it had all been a dream? But it was no dream to me. It was real to me, it had been a part of me."[12]

It is natural to want to recapture such lost landscapes, and this is done in many ways. One of the more artistic approaches to recapturing a lost mining landscape is found in Steubenville, Ohio—which now calls itself the "City of Murals." A visitor finds a dozen colorful murals painted on the sides of buildings in the downtown area: one of these, entitled *High Shaft*, commemorates a mine of the same name that operated for more than a century in the downtown area (fig. 68). Created by Canadian artist Dan Sawatsky, the mural depicts the High Shaft mine in the 1860s. This mural is accompanied by a text that educates the viewer and is an excellent example of how urban art can serve history. Louise Snider, executive director of Steubenville City of Murals, notes that the murals provide a success story of "a small, hard core steel and coal town fighting back and winning."[13] The mural symbolizes the community's tenacity, and the fact that the other murals

68. The High Shaft *mural painted on the side of a commercial building in downtown Steubenville, Ohio, depicts a mine that operated for several generations. The mural symbolizes this former coal and steel town's move away from industry to tourism, and its educational potential should not be overlooked. Photo by Steubenville City of Murals.*

also feature local historic scenes says much about the community's need for visual continuity through landscape imagery.

More typically, it is the local historical society in a mining district that becomes the major institutional force in perpetuating the memory of the historic landscape and the community's heritage "before it is lost forever," as a retired copper miner from Calumet, Michigan, put it. To do so, the local historical society is assisted by diverse elements in the community, including those who have both blue-collar as well as managerial experience in the mines. Significantly, little or no funding may be provided by the mining companies themselves—especially if (or when) the company has pulled out of the area for good. As a brief history of the World Museum of Mining in Butte, Montana, puts it: "In the early days we expected the mining industry would flock to our doors with grants to further our cause, however this did not come to be."[14] Given the pragmatic attitudes of many mining companies, and their seeming aversion to history, this should not be surprising.

Bisbee (Arizona), Eureka (both Nevada and Utah), Ely (Nevada),

Platteville (Wisconsin), and Roslyn (Washington) are a few of about fifty mining district communities that have active historical societies and museums. Because a mining museum's archival records usually include primary and secondary source materials such as letters, reports, written descriptions, and historic photographs (as well as recorded oral history interviews), it is a logical spot from which to begin any serious study of a mining district's landscape history.

The more progressive mining museums often use the entire community and landscape as their classroom—they interpret the historic environment through public programs, walking tours, and brochures. The traveler who finds himself or herself in Pioche, Nevada, for example, discovers a remarkable historic silver mining town whose museum on main street is but the central point for a communitywide historic interpretation effort focusing on the historic features in the landscape.

In Pioche, the serious tourist can take a comprehensive self-guided tour using a map marked with numbered historic sites. These include the house of a merchant, an early miner's cabin, commercial and civic buildings, an ore bin, a nearly intact aerial tramway, and the cemetery. Each historic location is marked with a distinctive interpretive sign that gives a brief historic overview (fig. 69). Pioche's historic tour is remarkable for its breadth: it identifies the locations of most major activities, from ore processing to social life. Such mining-based "theming," of course, is likely to be pursued very enthusiastically by merchants and others along main street. In Pioche, one finds historic mine tram buckets serving as street furniture or sculpture of sorts, and the local vest pocket park has become the site of a simulated mine opening, complete with a trestle and mine dump (fig. 70). The historic hardware of the mining industry has become Pioche's connection with the future.

The temptation for the artifacts of the mining industry to become the playground of the tourist is strong. Take, for example, the exhibit of mining equipment that was placed on the front lawn of the Bisbee Mining and Historical Museum in Arizona in the mid-1970s. Here we find several large objects associated with the underground mining history of the district, including a huge sheave wheel, mine hoist cage, and a nearly complete narrow gauge mine train that includes ore cars of various sizes and even a latrine car. This equipment, which was

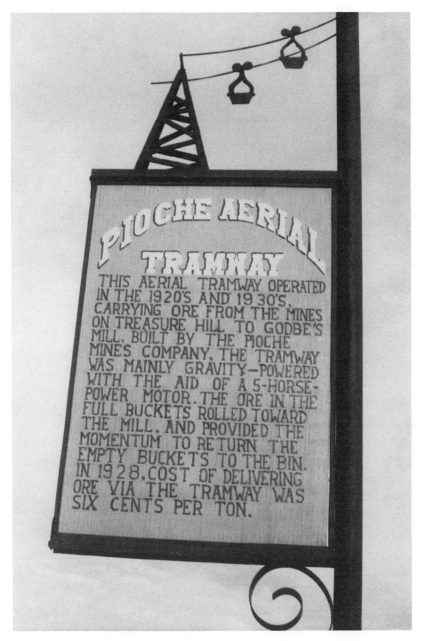

69. Pioche, Nevada, has done an interesting job of preserving and interpreting its mining heritage. Here a distinctive historic marker sign outlines the history of the aerial tramway that connected the mines with the mills (see fig. 35). 1989 photo by the author.

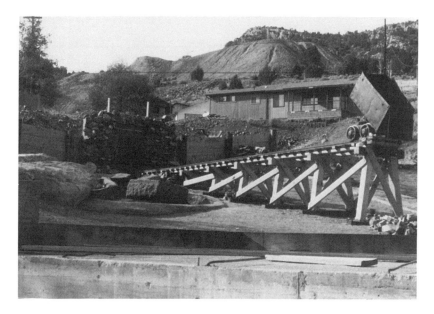

70. Enthusiastic use of the theme of mining history is seen in a park in downtown Pioche, Nevada, where a simulated mine opening and a mine dump trestle, complete with ore car, face main street. 1989 photo by the author.

originally intended as an exhibit and, perhaps, a kind of interpretive sculpture, is an irresistible playground for visitors of all ages. Mining historian Robert Spude calls uninterpreted collections of mining technology "'artifact gardens'—where machinery was drug [*sic*] in and displayed like so many *objets d'art.*"[15] In the best of exhibits, equipment is used to demystify the processes that hauled ore out of the mines and men and equipment into them and to show how the technology fit into the landscape.

A few mining museums attempt to preserve or recreate the historic mining landscape itself. Eckley Miner's Village, which is one of four regional mining museums developed in the anthracite country in the vicinity of Scranton, Pennsylvania, has the feel of a company town in about 1880. According to Mary Ann Landis, the museum's director, Eckley represented a rare find when discovered in the 1960s: it possessed a remarkably complete collection of miners' houses that lined the main street. Moreover, many of the ancillary structures, such as outbuildings and summer kitchens, were still extant in the back yards.[16] Each of these houses represented historic architecture, but, more importantly, each contained a wealth of information about everyday family life in Eckley.

In Eckley we find more historic architecture than we normally would, making the place seem too good to be true. And that is partly the case—several of the historic structures were moved into the community in the late 1960s. Eckley's historic look relates, in part at least, to its having served as the location of the 1970 Paramount film *The Molly Maguires*, a powerful drama starring Sean Connery and Richard Harris as two Irish miners on opposite sides of the labor-management dispute. In order to film this epic, technical advisor of mine operations Joseph Lawrence and others had to recreate a townscape that had the feel of a typical coal mining community in the 1870s. Eckley's townscape was enhanced through the building of several semihistoric structures and buildings, including a convincing breaker (or tipple and hoisting mechanism) and general store/depot (fig. 71). Both assumed major roles in the film, and both remain two decades later, the breaker forming a striking backdrop, the store serving as the museum's gift shop. The railroad tracks, constructed for the movie, also remain, adding a great deal of texture and character to the scene and reminding the public of the inseparable relationship between mining and railroading. As mining landscapes go, Eckley is remarkable for its blend of authentic history and cinematic history. Whereas purists would urge that the movie sets be dismantled, they are extremely important: if properly interpreted, they can tell us much about the mining landscapes of popular culture.

Hell Roarin' Gulch (fig. 72) at the World Museum of Mining in Butte, Montana, is a recreated hypothetical mining town. A museum report states that "in the construction of the village we have taken care to be authentic." The mining town here is a diverse collection of thirty-two buildings located at the site of the historic Orphan Girl silver and zinc mine. Some of the buildings are real or parts of real buildings: "We look around the area for the proper materials and so often will tear down old structures to get the materials that are needed for an exhibit." Some of the reconstructed buildings are contrived: their main purpose is "to preserve a segment of American

71. *The huge breaker at Eckley Miner's Village near Scranton, Pennsylvania, was constructed to serve as an on-location movie set for the 1970 film* The Molly Maguires. *This breaker is rather accurate and lends a great deal of character to the landscape today, despite the fact that it is a movie prop. 1990 photo by Mary Ann Landis.*

History which has heretofore been neglected, to bring to the people of America a realization of the glorious and ingenious heritage which is theirs." [17]

The designers of Hell Roarin' Gulch attempted to capture something of the serendipity of boom town design: the highly nucleated or clustered townscape has a narrow, crooked, main street lined with commercial buildings, fraternal lodges, churches, and even a hospital. The town's designers did not shy away from depicting the ethnic/social history: a row of Chinese businesses (including a drug store) is represented, and even a bordello, complete with a curvaceous mannequin dressed in red, is implied. Purists will criticize such recreations, but if we recall that landscapes are not good or bad, but rather statements, then these mining landscapes of popular culture have much to tell us about what those living today believe, or want us to believe, mining towns looked or felt like in the past. In the case of the World Museum of Mining, the more traditional kind of museum facility is located

72. *Hell Roarin' Gulch recreates a boom-era mining town at the World Museum of Mining at Butte, Montana. Its buildings are a combination of historic structures moved in from the area and stereotypical recreations that use parts of historic structures. 1989 photo by the author.*

nearby in the large museum building—a former mining building at the Orphan Girl mine whose interior now serves as a center of historic interpretation for the mining district, and whose exterior has a rich collection of artifacts and other materials pertaining to the district's mining history, including ore-hauling equipment from the Butte, Anaconda, and Pacific Railroad.

One of the more ambitious and interesting landscape-related mining museums is found at the Missouri Mines Historic Site at Flat River in southeastern Missouri's Old Lead Belt. Here an abandoned lead/zinc mining and milling facility, Federal Mill No. 3, is being converted into a museum and interpretive center by the Missouri Department of Natural Resources (fig. 73). This is an industrial museum: the entire complex, including a powerhouse, Dorr thickeners, shaft houses, and mill buildings, will be developed to tell the story of lead mining in Missouri. The facility was dedicated in 1980 "in recognition of its significance in the history of the state's mining industry, and in industrial architecture and technology."[18]

73. The Missouri Mines Historic Site, showing part of the huge Federal Mill No. 3 complex that is being interpreted. The former powerhouse serves as the museum building, whose exhibits treat the mining history of the state. 1989 photo by the author.

The first building to be readapted from mining to museum facility at the Missouri Mines State Historic Site was the former powerhouse, which features exhibits that interpret the state's mining history and the technology associated with it. According to its director, Warren Wittry, this is a major historic preservation project in adaptive reuse, for the goal is to retain the entire milling complex while having it serve to interpret the history of the industry.[19] The surrounding landscape is classic mining country, with large tailings ponds and chat piles that may also be preserved and interpreted. The entire complex is part of a large 8,244-acre state park, and its development as an interpretive area is reminiscent of what is now called an *ecomusée* —"a museological way to preserve the link between the human being and his environment in space," which is to say "a system comprised of the major components of heritage, territory, and population and their interrelationship through time."[20]

In Nevada, the Berlin-Ichthyosaur State Park is developed around the theme of historical geology. As the name implies, part of the park is a fossil site. The other portion pertains to economic geology, for the community of Berlin was built at a silver and gold mine. Although most of the town is gone, a number of interesting mining-related structures remain; these include a stamp mill/concentrator, ore bins, and wooden settling vats—just the kind of industrial structures that often vanish after mining operations cease. The huge ore dumps stand behind the site, an uncompromising reminder that this is hard rock metals mining country. At Berlin, even a few miners' cabins have been preserved and interpreted, further celebrating the working-class industrial roots of the fledgling mining operation that failed here more than seventy years ago. Why, one might ask, is it the public sector that most often initiates saving the mining landscapes created by the private sector?

On a regional level, a recent study by the Marshall University Center for Regional Progress identifies "mining related resources and facilities such as mines, tipples, company stores and houses . . . that could be developed into tourist sites." In addition to generating tourism revenue for eight former coal-producing counties, the alternatives presented would "provide the visitor with opportunities to appreciate the mining heritage and enjoy the scenic beauty of southern West Virginia." Plan A would disperse tourist activities throughout the region and be based on museum exhibits and selected examples of mining towns; Plan B would "preserve and upgrade one mining town to 1920 decor to tourism standards" and would "focus on miner's houses, community elements and mine related activities."[21]

The study concludes that "if the success of mining related tourism in the Rocky Mountains, northern Minnesota and eastern Pennsylvania are [sic] indicative, then tourism has the potential of serving as the catalyst for a diversified economic base while retaining critical vestiges of mining culture in southern West Virginia."[22] A look at a map of the United States showing locations that are effectively promoting mining-related history reveals concentrations of activity, much of it initiated by museums, in areas of former mineral production that have turned the closing of mines into an important local industry: tourism (fig. 74). This map reveals an interesting phenomenon—most of our mining history sites focus on metals: very few interpret coal mining, which is equally important, but less romantic in that it did not tend to make the individual prospector rich. This reaffirms that our culture is selective

74. *A map of the United States showing selected historic mining-related tourism sites. Although the concentrations of sites generally represent historic mining areas, many former mining localities are not yet represented. Map by the author.*

TOWER
CALUMET
HOUGHTON
IRON MOUNTAIN

EVILLE MINERAL POINT
GALENA

EAST GRANBY
SCRANTON
WILKES-BARRE
ECKLEY
ASHLAND
FRANKLIN

CADIZ
CALDWELL

HUNTINGTON
BECKLEY
BLUEFIELD

TERRE
AT RIVER
URG
LIN

STEARNS

ASHEVILLE
CHARLOTTE

MONTEAGLE

DORA DAHLONEGA

LEGEND

● Metals Mining

○ Coal Mining

Cartography by Wm. Mahon

about how it tells the story of mining history and what landscape features it uses to do so.

MINING LANDSCAPES AND POPULAR CULTURE

In addition to depicting history, mining is associated with thrills and fun. The flourishing of theme amusement parks, such as the pioneer Knott's Berry Farm (1953) and Disneyland (1955) in Orange County, California, had their own romanticized stories to tell about mining. They did so by creating sets that involved the visitor as a participant. It is not coincidental that these theme parks began to flourish with the rise of television—a visually kinetic vehicle of entertainment and learning—and that mining, a most dangerous and romanticized industry, would be among the first of the theme occupations. We saw earlier that even townscapes such as Tombstone, Arizona, came to confuse popular imagery of television westerns with reality. This popularization also had another effect: the public came to expect a tactile or hands-on involvement in mining landscapes through the use of rides.

What better way to experience mining landscapes than to don miner's gear and go underground? By the 1960s, the use of abandoned or even simulated mining facilities as a way of getting the public underground became popular. A statement by the Heritage Museum in Leadville, Colorado, helps us understand the link between education and entertainment: "We have found an overwhelming need for a mine that people can go down into and study rock formations, methods of mining, etc. A well-planned replica might suffice."[23] Several museums, including the Bisbee Mining and Historical Museum (until its recent renovation) and the Arizona Historical Society's museum in Tucson, feature simulated underground mining landscapes. The popular coal mine at Ohio's Center for Science and Industry (COSI) in Columbus is another example. These permit the public vicariously to experience the paths used by miners underground.

The most memorable underground experiences, however, occur in real mines. In Bisbee, the Copper Queen Mine tour is considered a high point by tourists. Visitors are trundled along on a narrow gauge mine train after being outfitted with slickers and lamps and given elaborate safety instructions. Such tours are intended to give the visitor some idea of the uterine surroundings of the underground miner; in order to comply with safety requirements, however, the equipment and underground environment are rendered about as hazard-free as the rides at an amusement park. Many such rides are staffed by retired miners. Bisbee's tour elicits awe when, deep in the bowels of the earth, the lights are momentarily extinguished to reveal the sensation of total darkness—a condition miners constantly avoided. This performance does, however, reaffirm what miners and tourists instinctively know—underground is no place for those who are prone to claustrophobia.

Minnesota's Tower-Soudan mine historic site features the most spectacular of America's underground mine tours. An illustration of this iron mine in its productive days (see fig. 6) gives one an idea of its design: this is a classic deep mine, and its workings are connected to the outside world by a steeply sloping (nearly vertical) shaft. Visitors descend more than 2,300 feet and then transfer to an electrically powered mine train that trundles them along horizontal tunnels for almost three quarters of a mile. The remaining portion of the trip into large excavated cavities or stopes is accomplished on foot. Here one finds simulated mining activities underway, with mannequin miners operating ear-splitting machinery.

Most mine tours are educational, but many, like the lead mine tours at Bonne Terre, Missouri, also have something of an amusement or theme park quality. Heavy industrial machinery, the railroad, and the headframe have come to symbolize connections with the underground in the popular mind. At the Bonne Terre, a headframe serves to accentuate the tie between recreation and mining (fig. 75). Even Dollywood, Dolly Parton's amusement theme park in Tennessee, features a stylized version of a coal mine—a nostalgic reminder of the rugged, working-class Appalachian roots of its popular founder.

Back in the 1960s, the masters of themed entertainment, Walt Disney enterprises, designed a memorable mining town landscape as part of the Thunder Mountain mine train ride. It perpetuates the popular image of a densely built-up crooked main street lined with false-front buildings (fig. 76). Like other caricatures developed by Disney to epitomize historic places (for example, Main Street USA), it has popu-

75. *Since the rise of theme parks, mining history has become fun as well as educational. This reconstructed headframe at the Bonne Terre, Missouri, historic mining site symbolizes the connection. 1989 photo by the author.*

76. Caricature: a simulated recreated mining town landscape in Disneyland shows that certain architectural and design features, such as ornate Victorian boom town architecture and irregular placement of structures, can be stereotyped. 1991 photo © Gary Peterson.

larized the American landscape. It is likely that such sentimental/ nostalgic imagery influenced historic preservation and may even lie at the roots of the neotraditionalism that swept the country in the late 1980s and early 1990s. Whatever the architectural differences between the new Post Office in Julian, California, and Disney's Thunder Mountain townscape, both perpetuate stereotypical regional and historic mining landscape images.

The Disney organization took the image one step further by making it a tactile/kinetic experience: vistors ride the mine train that whisks them out of the memorable mining boom town and through a barren mining country landscape as it careens past teetering rocks, dynamite sheds, and other frontier hazards. This type of kinetic/participatory experience is reassuring because it combines a sense of action and motion (even danger) with the stability and familiarity of history—a combination that may also explain the appeal of popular films like *Bill and Ted's Excellent Adventure* and *Back to the Future* and its sequels.

There is another type of amusement associated with historic mining landscapes: model miniatures. At the interface between popular cul-

77. *Preservation in miniature: long-vanished coal mines and coal mining towns come to life on the HO-scale Guernsey Valley Model Railroad in Cambridge, Ohio. This scene by Jake Davis features the tipple and other structures of the Black Top Mine; note the row of drab company houses facing the mine and railroad. Photo by the Guernsey Valley Model Railroad Club.*

ture and recreational psychology, we find pursuits such as model rail-roading, which, having attained the respectable age of about fifty years, is now considered a valid expenditure of adult leisure time. In their efforts to record the passing railroad scene, individual modelers and clubs have not overlooked the landscape or scenery, as they call it. These are often renderings of actual historic mining landscapes.

Indeed, if one wishes to view a historic landscape depicting coal min-ing in early twentieth century southeastern Ohio, for example, the best place to do so today is at the Guernsey Valley model railroad club in Cambridge, Ohio. Here one can find highly detailed dioramas de-picting nine individual mines as they appeared during their heyday in the early twentieth century. Like their prototypes, the mines vary in size and type, from a small hillside tipple serving a nearby drift mine, to large complexes, like the spectacular Black Top mine that occupies an entire small valley or hollow (fig. 77). They are all done in HO scale, that is, 1/87th of the prototype.

Jake Davis, creator of the mining landscapes on the Guernsey Valley model railroad, combined an interest in miniature railroads with skills in historic research to help build the highly detailed historic scenes. Most of the real mining scenes depicted are today archaeological sites, but Davis has "brought them back to life," as one visitor put it. According to a reviewer of his impressive model building, Davis "searched the archives of local libraries and historical societies to find old photographs and books and magazines that depict coal mines in operation in the area."[24] His resulting scenes convey much of the character of this mining area: large weather-beaten metal-sheathed tipples straddle railroad sidings that are embedded in cinder-strewn roadbeds; powerhouses and sheds flank the mine buildings; rows of pattern-book company houses, all painted in the same drab colors, line the tracks; huge purplish-black gob piles loom behind the mines, with rusty rubble and machinery strewn everywhere.

Davis has captured, through technical and artistic skills, the gritty character and feel of mining country. These scenes are animated: long strings of hopper cars are pushed or pulled up to the mines by grimy, slow-moving locomotives of the era. For the edification of the visitor, each mining scene is flanked by historic photographs showing the real location in its heyday. Thousands of people view such model railroad scenery annually and come away with vivid impressions of historic mining landscapes—perhaps more realistic than the preserved and restored mining towns they visit. It is not surprising that two mining areas, Appalachia and the Colorado Rockies, are among the most popular of those modeled.

MINING LANDSCAPES AND VISUAL SYMBOLISM

Both the real (or authentic) historic mining landscapes and the contrived landscapes of popular culture are cultural artifacts. What do they tell us about our culture? What do these cultural artifacts—such as miners' cabins, headframes, and ore dumps—mean to those who experience them today? Discussions with tourists at mining-related sites have helped me to understand how evocative mining landscapes are to the general public. Mining is considered to be tough business—dirty work that someone had to do, which contributed to the greatness of America. The fact that the dirty business of mining makes a better life possible excuses certain excesses, and this shows in our ambivalent attitudes toward mining landscapes themselves.

To the general public, the business districts of mining towns may signify both prosperity and vice; their colorful topography may signify our power not only to reshape, but to destroy the face of the earth. Whereas mining companies and those who supply mining equipment may use the mining landscape as evidence of their ability to control the environment in order to bring us the good life (fig. 78), the public senses that something—innocence, perhaps—is lost in order for such progress to be achieved. Mining, like warfare, is the kind of activity that someone, preferably someone else, has to do. Both diminish the productivity of the earth in order to win, a term that, importantly, mining engineers use to describe gaining metals from ores. Both also leave heroes and, significantly, are regarded with nostalgia only after they are finished, that is, become history.

To the general public, these mining landscapes contain powerful, even conflicting, symbolism. Although objects in the landscape (and entire landscapes) are actually neutral, those who view them are not. Like all symbols, those in the mining landscape need a cultural context in order to be understood and interpreted. Our context is provided by cultural traditions and beliefs about the individual's place in nature and society that run very deep. Reward (victory) and punishment (loss) are two pervasive themes in our dealings with nature and culture and seem operative in the way we perceive mining landscapes.

Just as most truly powerful cultural symbols (for example, a crucifix) may have dual meanings (life and death), so, too, our mining landscapes are capable of evoking conflicting meanings: a stark gallows headframe standing on an eroded hillside above a mining town may become a symbolic reminder of both life—economic prosperity, energy, activity—and death—depletion of resources and even actual loss of human life (fig. 79). Even a mundane ore dump piled onto the landscape is a powerful symbol: it may mean prosperity (reward), on the

78. Mining landscapes as symbols of power: a giant figure of a miner looms above a Mountaineer power shovel, as a string of loaded hopper cars is pulled away by a steam locomotive. A transformed landscape of extraction on this scale symbolizes the power of modern technology and the supremacy of the culture that can create it. From Haddock 1984.

79. Landscape and symbolism: an abandoned headframe and a mine dump stand above the town church at Randsburg, California. The icons of mining, like other symbols, can have dual meanings: both the headframe and the cross can symbolize life (and the vitality of the community), but they can also symbolize death (through the loss of a resource and lives of miners). 1975 photo by the author.

one hand, or loss and decline (punishment), on the other. Mining landscapes remind us that our actions have consequences.

That we can read messages of hope and desolation into mining landscapes today says much about the way we view industry, culture, and nature. The fact that an appreciation for preservation of historic mining landscapes is growing at a time when concern for the pristine natural environment is also growing need not be considered contradictory: both appear to be inevitable in a postindustrial culture that is losing its immediate dependency on heavy industry. In other words, "it is significant that an appreciation of industrial landscapes is developing at what may be the end of our reign as an industrial nation and the beginnings of our development as a service-oriented society."[25]

When they are being created, mining landscapes embody what landscape architect Robert Thayer, Jr., has called the "consumptive" technologies; we may either ignore these landscapes or attempt to conceal as much about them as we can.[26] We may treat them very pragmatically, as in the case of a recent recommendation by Southern Pacific to use the site of the recently abandoned Kaiser iron mine in the southern Mojave Desert as a disposal site (dump) for nonhazardous waste materials hauled by rail from the Los Angeles area. After all, many reason, what else could be done with a huge hole in the ground that nobody wants? Extending the reasoning just a little further, however, we may ask why some people are so quick to recommend that such holes be filled up—that is, removed from sight.

As we have seen, our culture is fascinated by places that once served industry, but are now abandoned. Operations such as open pit mines and mine tailings may come to represent nostalgic technologies after abandonment. Some, like the impressive Hill-Annex open pit mine in Minnesota, have become historic sites, but most lie abandoned. Sometimes these features are all that mark sites of aggressive mining activity in the past, but nature may soon soften them. In fact, as time progresses, the public often considers such mining landscapes part of, or at least confused with, the natural environment. Therefore, "the one hundred year old gravel tailings from the gold-rush mining along the Sacramento River can be looked upon as pleasant landscape remnants of California's past."[27] Time softens the impact of these landscapes, both physically and psychologically. By transforming them from wastelands to scenery, it resurrects them and exonerates those who created them: us.

Thus, Thayer notes that "technological landscape guilt" (or TLG) finds us trying to conceal the visual consequences of contemporary industry, while at the same time romanticizing historic industrial landscapes. He differentiates the technologies that shape industrial landscapes into several categories.[28]

Iconic technologies are highly conspicuous and local, such as a strip mine or open pit mine and ore dumps. These command our attention.

Explicit technologies are quite visible, but their products are so widespread that they are simply considered to be part of the contemporary landscape and we do not see them as readily: roads, railroad lines, and commercial developments can be included here.

Implicit technologies have come and gone, leaving telltale patterns that become part of the landscape with the passage of time—for example, erosion associated with earlier mining activity.

Invisible technologies leave little or no visible effect, but may profoundly affect the environment—for example, metals or acidic or radioactive pollution from mining activities.

Using this system, we see that the most powerful symbols of mining are iconic, but that even more commonplace (explicit) landscape features are always present. Moreover, mining leaves implicit features, and its most profound environmental impacts may be invisible, that is, microscopic.

Because they are so localized, and so visually significant, most of our attention focuses on iconic mining landscapes. The fact that few of us experience mining landscapes on a daily basis makes them more unusual, exotic, and hence even more iconic, as pictorial or symbolic representations of a process or system. At this level, mining landscapes have much to tell us.

They should be viewed as icons of power. Forged as a result of aggressive investment and speculation in reaction to more or less uncontrollable economic and political situations, they are battlegrounds that show victory and defeat. Mining landscapes may vary widely, but they all reveal a great deal about power in at least three areas.

1. Economic: wherein the system or process of production concentrated mineral wealth in order for it to be exported elsewhere. Mining district landscapes are a manifestation of ambivalence about the permanence of the place, for the more capital that was invested, the more effectively the resources were diminished and the location was exhausted.

2. Social: wherein ethnic minorities were highly stratified and women placed in polarized, invisible/visible roles. This stratification resulted in a series of distinct neighborhoods; like most segregation, class was also found in the elaborate cemeteries of mining districts.

3. Environmental: wherein actions that may have had no seeming consequences at the time have left either a powerful visual legacy of waste and degradation or the honest manifestation of industry, depending on how one views (and defends) the system. The changing attitudes of our culture toward nature now define the landscapes of mining districts and will continue to redefine them in the future.

The more closely one studies individual mining districts, the greater one's understanding (and awe) of the attitudes of their developers and settlers. Few places better reveal the consequences of virtually unreg-

ulated economic activity than our historic mining landscapes. The further one stands back to view mining districts collectively, the more
impressed one becomes at the familiar iconic landscape features, and
sometimes patterns, that repeat themselves in strikingly different
geographic locations and political systems.

THE PLACE OF MINING LANDSCAPES IN THE AMERICAN LANDSCAPE

The landscape of any particular mining district is quite easy
to distinguish from other natural and cultural landscapes in any particular area or region.

1. Mining activities profoundly affect the physical environment and
result in visually distinctive topographic features and distinctive vegetation patterns.

2. Mining settlements are spatially arranged in patterns that are
different from other settlements in an area: they often cluster around
extractive features and form interconnected urban networks of small
communities.

3. Architecturally, mining communities are often easily differentiated from other settlements in an area: their social architecture is
frequently characterized by relatively limited diversity and standardization as well as revealing class differences, and their industrial architecture is diagnostic.

4. Mining landscapes undergo change differently from other places,
for their evolution is often episodic and the changes themselves so profound that they may obliterate earlier mining communities.

To a greater or lesser degree, all mining landscapes are likely to
exhibit many of the visual traits common to mining country—such as
waste rock piles, ore loading and/or processing facilities, and workers'
housing—but what would we find if we carefully compared them to
each other? What, in other words, would a detailed comparison of *all*
American mining district landscapes reveal? Would there be any subtle
regional or geographical differences in the look of these mining landscapes? Would these differences relate to chronology—would we find
that mining districts developed in certain periods look more alike re-

gardless of their geographic locations? Or would other factors, such as the type of mineral mined, be determinants in the way a particular mining district looks? Finally, would the imprint of certain powerful companies or schools of technology vary from place to place? Some tentative answers to these questions are set out below.

The look of any landscape is a result of three factors: innovation, cultural diffusion, and physical conditions. We can tell a mining landscape almost instantly anywhere in the United States, indeed, the world, because of its general visual characteristics that brand it as a system: mining landscapes that developed in the last two hundred or more years are the result of rapid, pragmatic technological diffusion. That explains why mining landscapes in Australia, South Africa, South America, and the United States exhibit such strong similarities. Consider even their names: the Mojave Desert gold mining town of Ballarat, California, was named after the gold mining center of the same name in Australia, and the name Randsburg was applied "as a good omen" after the fabulous Witwatersrand, or the "Rand," in South Africa, one of the richest gold mining areas in the world.[29]

If one of the major factors shaping mining landscapes is ownership and control, then there are two fundamentally different mining landscapes: those that involve a large number of individual speculators and those that represent the interests of a large corporation. The former manifest themselves in nineteenth-century boom towns and account for the frenzied look of the landscape in everything from commercial and industrial design to residential architecture. The latter account for the uniformity we see in many mining landscapes, especially those created shortly after the turn of the century by huge corporations. As we have seen, the larger mining corporations wielded nearly complete monopolistic power over the districts they controlled. Could this help to explain why their resulting landscapes are in some ways similar to those mining landscapes that developed under formerly communist regimes in the USSR and eastern Europe? Both have been described by critics as drab, paternalistic, and highly functional technological landscapes that leave little doubt as to who wields power. No doubt both systems viewed themselves as transforming the landscape to advance civilization: could they exemplify the saying that the end justifies the means?

Mining not only controls the environment, it must also respond to conditions. Despite its power rapidly to transform mineralized places into distinctive mining landscapes, the mining industry never develops without national, regional, and local constraints: the prevailing regulations, labor conditions, and natural environment affect how things are done—and how the landscape looks. These have been considered ecological factors by anthropologists. Take, for example, three copper mining areas, one developed in Connecticut around 1800, one in Michigan in the 1860s, and one in Arizona about 1910. Consider the differences in the physical (and geological) environment first. Connecticut's copper industry developed in a well-watered hilly area of moderate climate where copper deposits were found disseminated throughout metamorphosed rocks. Michigan's Keweenaw Peninsula is an area of rigorous, snowy winters and short summers where native copper was found in huge deposits in moderately tilted, tough basalt-conglomerate rock. The copper deposits of Arizona exploited in the twentieth century are often found in a mountainous, semiarid area where copper sulfides are disseminated throughout a porphyry ore body. These environments require different mining techniques.

Then consider the labor situation: mostly British Americans worked the Connecticut copper deposits, immigrant eastern and northeastern European labor worked the mines in Michigan, and western Europeans and Hispanics were drawn to the mines in Arizona. To these differences must be added the technological differences in copper mining over the period. And, of course, even though mining may have been among the earliest activities in certain of these areas, it developed as regional identities were being evolved: certain architectural styles, foodways, rural activities, speech patterns, and the like developed at the same time. These, too, affect the character of our mining districts.

Looked at this way, mining transcends the regions in which it occurs while also being developed in a regional context. Thus, the copper mining towns of Arizona are home to (among others) Hispanic populations and their traditions, and the copper mining towns of Michigan have Finnish populations and traditions. Add to these cultural factors the basic physical environments of the regions. Both Arizona and Michigan have distinctive industrial mining landscapes that are in part related to the climate: the terraced tailings ponds of arid Arizona are not seen in Michigan, and the elaborately sheathed mine headframes, protected from the heavy winter snows of Michigan, are not seen in Arizona.

MINING LANDSCAPES AND REGIONAL IDENTITY

When geographers describe American regions, they normally focus on the rural countryside and agrarian market towns as the nuclei of regional identities and tend to overlook mining communities. However, a comparative look at mining district landscapes across the country reveals a regional identity that has never, to my knowledge, been described. As depicted in figure 1, America's historic coal and metals mining regions occur in three large areas: the eastern (Appalachian) highlands, the Mississippi Valley, and the western mountain (cordilleran) provinces. Within these large areas, one finds many smaller regions that contain particular mining districts—and distinctive mining landscapes. The geology (types of minerals and configuration of ore bodies), date of exploitation, type of ownership, and regional conditions such as ethnicity and climate affect the look of any particular mining landscape, but certain patterns become apparent. America's mining regions are discontinuous. As geographic systems, they are spatially isolated and internally nucleated, but they are also interconnected and interrelated by management and capital. Therefore, they have their own identities, but are also part of a larger national (and international) system.

Among the most visually recognizable of our regional mining landscapes are the following.

The hard coal (anthracite) mining region of northeastern Pennsylvania actually consists of three separate coal fields with their deep mines, rows of workers' housing, and large breakers that stand amid huge purplish colored culm banks.

The Tri-State lead/zinc mining area around Joplin has clusters of grid-patterned mining towns huddled in the shadow of huge chat piles and large, heavily capitalized mining and milling facilities.

The Mississippi Valley lead/zinc mining districts (from eastern Missouri to Wisconsin) show more than two centuries of sequential metals development and a remarkable continuum of settlement types, from vernacular/folk to corporate, in their landscapes.

The distinctive nineteenth-century western silver/gold mining districts of the Rocky Mountain and intermountain West are developed around nucleated, highly speculative linear towns located in canyon settings and surrounded by ore dumps on the honeycombed mountainsides.

The mining districts of the Black Hills of South Dakota, really an outlying island of Rocky Mountain mining activity, are characterized by a mosaic of interrelated towns and extensive surface alteration resulting from aggressive development of refractory ores.

The Iron Range locations of the upper Great Lakes—whose frames of reference are the hematite red escarpments of open pits, huge overburden dumps and ore stockpiles, and towns and smaller locations with ethnic European populations—include Minnesota's Mesabi, Vermilion, and Cuyuna Ranges and Michigan's Gogebic Range.

The Copper Country of Michigan's Upper Peninsula, an area of interconnected mining communities that sit in the shadow of large deep mines and their waste dumps of dark basaltic rock, stretches in a line for almost one hundred miles, and activities here set the stage for much of the corporate development that characterized the powerful copper industry by the late nineteenth century.

The well-designed early twentieth-century copper mining company towns of the intermountain West, with their ever-growing (or disappearing) backdrop of porphyry terraces and dazzling white tailings ponds, form a regional topography as distinctive as the tabular alluvial *bajada* slopes they occupy.

The historic mining area of California's gold rush country, with its extensive placer mining remnants later veneered with the detritus of quartz mills and remarkable commercial architecture, contains fabled locations where the ethnically diverse forty-niner miners toiled.

The Appalachian Plateau has numerous soft coal mining towns that exhibit strong company control and related mining features, such as company stores, gob piles, large tipples, and coke ovens.

The perceptive observer will find certain connections between widely separated mining landscapes. For example, the technology of coal mining and coal car loading finds similar tipples straddling railroad spurs in places as distant as southeastern Ohio, central New Mexico, Wyoming, and Washington. Their towns, too, may bear certain visual similarities, especially where powerful coal companies have been dominant. These coal towns are more likely to have housed black miners and their families than metals mines. Although mining landscapes have a regional identity while at the same time transcending it, we can also speak of subregional mining landscape identities: the Appalachian coal mining region itself fits into several landscape systems that appear to be based on particular coalfields, which is to say the identity of major companies that controlled these areas as well as a host of other factors, including ethnicity.

Spatially, America's mining landscapes may occupy a rather small percentage of the larger geographic regions in which they occur, but they are always an important element in the overall character of those regions. However, they are often either geographically peripheral to the regional identity (as in the case of the coal mining areas that essentially ring the agrarian Midwest) or psychologically peripheral (as in the case of silver and gold mining centers of the intermountain West, which, despite their near geographic centrality and ubiquity, are still considered remote). Therefore, mining landscapes have been relegated to the periphery of our national psyche, and this may help to explain why the public and scholars alike know so little about them. Nevertheless, they are as distinctive as other regional archetypes, and it is hoped that students of the landscape will further identify them: only by so doing shall we gain an appreciation for the regional diversity of the country and better understand the relationships among America's regional landscapes.

CONCLUSION: MINING LANDSCAPES IN THE AMERICAN MIND

Where, then, do America's mining landscapes fit in the overall mental image of our countryside? If, as geographer D. W. Meinig contends, America's ideal environmental icons are the New England village, the middle western main street, and the California suburb,[30] then America's mining districts must be the antithesis, for their scenery provides an unsettling vision. These hard places are characterized by environmental abuse, pragmatism, and economic exploitation, and their landscapes do not often conceal these facts. These landscapes of extraction do not compare favorably with ideal landscapes because they seem unfinished, crude, and imperfect; perhaps they are too honest a depiction of how we have treated the environment and each other.

This seemingly harsh assessment is contemporary. In the eighteenth and nineteenth centuries, mining landscapes were not held in disdain. To Victorians, they may even have epitomized civilization's inevitable victory in the quest for knowledge and superiority over nature. This attitude may be linked to historic sources that portray mineral exploitation as coexisting with pastoral settings. If the Bible provides our earliest descriptions of mining's impact on the land, then it is worth remembering that Deuteronomy 8:9 describes the promised land (or good land) as well watered, a land of rich crops, "a land whose stones are iron, and out of whose hills you can dig copper." To the nineteenth-century capitalist and entrepreneur, mining was seen as an indispensable part of the mission of Western civilization, and our religious roots very likely helped to place it there.

As we progressed into the twentieth century, it appears inevitable that mining landscapes would come to symbolize the turmoil between what our culture elects to view as two opposing forces: culture and nature. Active mining landscapes are now seen as being in disequilibrium. Therefore, it is not surprising that we have relegated them to our distant vision. It is in these hard places that the dirtiest work occurs to sustain our ever-demanding technology and culture. Small wonder that we would just as soon keep them out of sight and out of mind.

Nevertheless, we cannot put such hard places completely out of our thoughts and are drawn to them—perhaps because they embody a number of deeply held values such as competitiveness, risk-taking, and dominance over nature. That may explain why we are not content to watch them disappear after their main reason for existing is gone, but either preserve them or resurrect their memory through novels, movies, or television miniseries and in theme parks and historic sites. In this regard, mining landscapes are among our most interesting, for it is in such isolated locations that the consequences of our actions as Americans are, paradoxically, most visible and least understood.

NOTES

1. READING THE LANDSCAPE

1. Leo Marx, *The Machine in the Garden: Technology and the Pastoral Ideal in America* (New York: Oxford University Press, 1967).

2. Duane A. Smith, *Mining America: The Industry and the Environment, 1800–1980.*

3. Kevin Lynch, *The Image of the City.*

4. Frances Downing and Thomas Hubka, "Diagramming: A Visual Language," in *Perspectives in Vernacular Architecture, II*, ed. Camille Wells (Columbia: Univerity of Missouri Press, 1986), pp. 44–52.

5. Emil W. Billeb, *Mining Camp Days*, p. 4.

6. Christopher Davies, "Dark Inner Landscapes: The South Wales Coalfield," *Landscape Journal* 3/1 (Spring 1984): 38–39.

7. William Ralston Balch, *The Mines, Miners, and Mining Interests of the United States in 1882*, p. 782.

8. Mrs. Hugh Brown, *Lady in Boomtown: Miners and Manners on the Nevada Frontier*, p. 126.

9. Richard V. Francaviglia, "Copper Mining and Landscape Evolution: A Century of Change in the Warren Mining District, Arizona," *Journal of Arizona History* 23/3 (Autumn 1982): 287.

10. Mack H. Gillenwater, "Cultural and Historical Geography of Mining Settlements in the Pocahontas Coal Field of Southern West Virginia, 1880 to 1930," p. iii.

11. Barbara Bailey, *Main Street Northeastern Oregon: The Founding and Development of Small Towns* (Portland: Oregon Historical Society, 1982), and Randall Rohe, "The Geography and Material Culture of the Western Mining Town," *Material Culture* 16/3 (Fall 1984): 99–120.

12. Duane A. Smith, *Rocky Mountain Mining Camps: The Urban Frontier.*

13. Richard V. Francaviglia, "Mining Town Commercial Vernacular Architecture: The 'Overhanging Porches' of Ohio's Hocking Mining District," *Pioneer America Society Transactions* 13 (1990): 50.

14. Richard Longstreth, *The Buildings of Main Street: A Guide to American Commercial Architecture*.

15. Deborah Lyn Randall, "Park City, Utah: An Architectural History of Mining Town Housing, 1869–1907."

16. Eugene J. Palka, "The Cultural Landscape of the Athens County Coal Region: A Reflection of Its Mining Activities from 1885–1927."

17. Robert H. Richards, Charles Locke, and John Bray, *A Text Book of Ore Dressing*, p. 412.

18. Donald Hardesty, *The Archaeology of Mining and Miners: A View from the Silver State*, pp. 18–66.

19. John Hays Hammond, "The Milling of Gold Ores in California," in *Eighth Annual Report of the State Mineralogist*, pp. 696–735.

20. Richards et al., *A Text Book of Ore Dressing*, p. 415.

21. A. J. Wallis-Tayler, *Aerial or Wire Rope-Ways: Their Construction and Management*.

22. Richard V. Francaviglia, "The Cemetery as an Evolving Cultural Landscape," *Annals of the Association of American Geographers* 61/3 (1971): 501–509.

23. Gillenwater, "Cultural and Historical Geography of Mining Settlements."

24. Hardesty, *The Archaeology of Mining and Miners*, pp. 9, 11–12 (quotation on p. 11).

25. David M. Gradwohl and Nancy M. Osborn, *Exploring Buried Buxton: Archaeology of an Abandoned Iowa Coal Mining Town with a Large Black Population*, p. 5.

2. INTERPRETING THE LANDSCAPE

1. David Lowenthal and Hugh Prince, "English Landscape Tastes," *Geographical Review* 55 (June 1965): 191–220.

2. Donald H. McLaughlin, "Man's Selective Attack on Ores and Minerals," in *Man's Role in Changing the Face of the Earth*, ed. William L. Thomas, Jr., p. 860.

3. Georgius Agricola, *De re metallica*, Herbert Hoover and Lou Hoover, p. 14.

4. Spiro Kostof, *America by Design*, pp. 88–89.

5. Mrs. Hugh Brown, *Lady in Boomtown: Miners and Manners on the Nevada Frontier*, p. 28.

6. Stanley A. Kuzara, *Black Diamonds of Sheridan: A Facet of Wyoming History*.

7. Leonard J. Arrington, *Great Basin Kingdom: An Economic History of the Latter-Day Saints* (Lincoln: University of Nebraska Press, 1958), pp. 241–243.

8. Page Smith, *As a City upon a Hill: The Town in American History* (New York: Knopf, 1966).

9. William Ralston Balch, *The Mines, Miners, and Mining Interests of the United States in 1882*, p. 769.

10. Ibid., p. 783.

11. *Off-Hand Sketches: A Companion for the Tourist and Traveller over the Philadelphia, Pottsville, and Reading Railroad, Describing the Scenery, Improvements, Mineral and Agricultural Resources, Historical Incidents, and Other Subjects of Interest in the Vicinity of the Route* (Philadelphia: J. W. Moore, 1854), p. 53.

12. Ibid., p. 90.

13. A. Dudley Gardner and Vera R. Flores, *Forgotten Frontier: A History of Wyoming Coal Mining*, pp. 1–32.

14. David F. Myrick, *The Railroads of Arizona*, vol. 1, *The Southern Roads*, pp. 177–254.

15. David F. Myrick, *The Railroads of Nevada and Eastern California*, vol. 1, *The Northern Roads*, pp. 236–288; and *The Railroads of Nevada and Eastern California*, vol. 2, *The Southern Roads*, pp. 454–503, 544–593.

16. Patrick C. Dorin, *The Lake Superior Iron Ore Railroads*, p. 6.

17. Mallory Hope Ferrell, *Southern Pacific Narrow Gauge* (Edmonds, Wash.: Pacific Fast Mail, 1982), p. 27.

18. Frank King, *The Missabe Road: The Duluth, Missabe and Iron Range Railway*, pp. 218–219.

19. Phil Stong, *The Iron Mountain* (New York: Farrar, Straus, and Giroux, 1941), p. 17.

20. Ralph D. Williams, *The Honorable Peter White: A Biographical Sketch of the Lake Superior Iron Country*, p. 273.

21. Randolph Delahanty and Andrew McKinney, *Preserving the West*, p. 94.

22. Roberta Martin Starry, *Gold Gamble*, p. 25.

23. James B. Allen, *The Company Town in the American West*, p. 47.

24. Brown, *Lady in Boomtown*, p. 29.

25. J. Eugene Haas, Robert W. Kates, and Martyn J. Bowden, *Reconstruction following Disaster* (Cambridge: MIT Press, 1977).

26. Arnold R. Alanen, "The 'Locations'—Company Communities on Minnesota's Iron Ranges," *Minnesota History* 48/3 (Fall 1982): 94–107 (quotations on pp. 99 and 101).

27. John W. Reps, "Bonanza Towns: Urban Planning on the Western Mining Frontier," in *Pattern and Process: Research in Historical Geography*, ed. Ralph E. Ehrenberg, pp. 271–289.

28. Donald Hardesty, *The Archaeology of Mining and Miners: A View from the Silver State*, p. 14.

29. David A. Wolff, "Pyritic Smelting at Deadwood: A Temporary Solution to Refractory Ores," *South Dakota History* 15/4 (Winter 1985): 313.

30. Beth Kay Harris, *The Towns of Tintic*, p. 13.

31. Myrick, *The Railroads of Nevada*.

32. Russell L. Olson, *The Electric Railways of Minnesota* (Hopkins: Minnesota Transportation Museum, 1975), pp. 445–467.

33. Harry C. Hood, Jr., *The Southwest Missouri Railroad* (n.p.: Harry C. Hood, Sr., 1975), p. 1.

34. The Hocking–Sunday Creek Traction Company, *The Proposed Hocking–Sunday Creek Traction Company's Extensions, Report of Preliminary Survey, Estimates of Costs of Construction, of Cost of Operation and of Earnings* (Nelsonville, Ohio: n.p., 1910).

35. Richard V. Francaviglia, *Mining Town Trolleys: A History of Arizona's Warren-Bisbee Railway*.

36. Gilbert Kneiss, *Bonanza Railroads*, p. 79.

37. Earl W. Kersten, Jr., "The Early Settlement of Aurora, Nevada, and Nearby Mining Camps," *Annals of the Association of American Geographers* (December 1964): 504.

38. Clark Spence, *Mining Engineers & the American West: The Lace Boot Brigade, 1849–1933*.

39. Ibid., p. 233.

40. Philip F. Notarianni, *Faith, Hope & Prosperity: The Tintic Mining District*, p. 104.

41. Arthur Lakes, "The New Almaden Mines," *Mines and Minerals* 19/8 (March 1899), as cited in Milton Lanyon and Laurence Bulmore, *Cinnabar Hills: The Quicksilver Days of New Almaden*, p. 67.

42. Barry A. Price, "McGill, Nevada: An Example of Company Town Architecture As Social History," paper presented at the Building the West Conference on Vernacular Architecture West of the Rockies, Reno, Nevada, September 21, 1989, p. 4.

43. George Fiedler, *Mineral Point—A History*, p. 165.

44. Rolla Lee Queen, "Historical Archaeology and Historic Preservation at Candelaria and Metallic City, Nevada."

45. Philip F. Notarianni, ed., *Carbon County: Eastern Utah's Industrialized Island*.

46. Gardner and Flores, *Forgotten Frontier*, p. 144.

47. Donald Hardesty and Valerie Firby, *Managing Archaeological Resources on the Comstock*, p. 1.

48. Hardesty, *The Archaeology of Mining and Miners*, p. 14.

49. Charles D. Zeier, "Historic Charcoal Production near Eureka, Nevada: An Archaeological Perspective," *Historical Archaeology* 21/1 (1987): 88.

50. Mary Halleck Foote, "A California Mining Camp," *Scribner's Monthly* 19 (October 1865), as quoted in Lanyon and Bulmore, *Cinnabar Hills*, p. 63.

51. Anne Chenoweth, "Roslyn Cemetery" field work paper, Anthropology Department, Central Washington University, Ellensburg, Washington, December 1978 (quotations on pp. 37, 41).

52. Ramona Reno and Ronald Reno, "The Historic Cemetery at Silver City, Nevada: Recording Methods and Initial Findings," *Nevada Archaeologist* 7/1 (1989): 14–27.

53. Richard V. Francaviglia, "The Cemetery as an Evolving Cultural Landscape," *Annals of the Association of American Geographers* 61/3 (September 1971): 501–509.

54. Carolyn Merchant, *The Death of Nature: Women, Ecology, and the Scientific Revolution*, pp. 1–41.

55. Conrad Richter, *Tacey Cromwell* (Albuquerque: University of New Mexico Press, 1942).

56. George W. King, *The Marion Steam Shovel Company Family: History—Biography—Autobiography* (New York: Century History, 1915), pp. 79–80.

57. Spence, *Mining Engineers & the American West*, p. 235.

58. Meg (Margaret) Mulrooney, Coal Patch Workshop Tour Notes, Coal Patch Conference, Johnstown, Pennsylvania, June 23, 1989.

59. Richard V. Francaviglia, "Copper Mining and Landscape Evolution: A Century of Change in the Warren Mining District, Arizona," *Journal of Arizona History* 23/3 (Autumn 1982): 278.

60. Mulrooney, Tour Notes.

61. National Coal Association, *Bituminous Coal Mining Towns, North, South, East, West: Pictorial Study of Their Progress*, pp. 10, 71.

62. Joseph H. White, *Houses for Mining Towns*, pp. 6, 33.

63. Donald H. McLaughlin, "Man's Selective Attack on Ores and Minerals," in *Man's Role in Changing the Face of the Earth*, ed. William Thomas, Jr., p. 855.

64. Ibid., p. 860.

65. Homer Aschmann, "The Natural History of a Mine," *Economic Geography* 46/2 (April 1970): 171–190.

66. Richard V. Francaviglia, "Copper Mining and Landscape Evolution: A Century of Change in the Warren Mining District, Arizona," *Journal of Arizona History* 23/3 (Autumn 1982): 267–298; Udo Zindel, "Landscape Evolution in the Clifton-Morenci Mining District, Arizona, 1872–1986."

67. Donald Hardesty, "Industrial Archaeology on the American Mining Frontier: Suggestions for a Research Agenda," *Journal of New World Archaeology* 6/4 (1986): 51.

68. Otis E. Young, Jr., *Western Mining: An Informal Account of Precious-Metals Prospecting, Placering, Lode Mining, and Milling on the American Frontier from Spanish Times to 1893*, p. 265.

69. Richard V. Francaviglia, "Time Exposures: The Evolving Landscape of an Arizona Copper-Mining District," in *Mineral Resource Development: Geopolitics, Economics, and Policy*, ed. Harley Johansen, Olen P. Matthews, and Gundars Rudzitis, pp. 258–268.

70. Jeffrey L. Brown, "Earthworks and Industrial Archeology," *IA: Journal of the Society for Industrial Archaeology* 6/1 (1980): 1.

71. Stong, *The Iron Mountain*, pp. 52–53.

72. Lake Superior and Canadian Iron Ore Properties Operated by Pickands Mather & Co.," United States Steel Company report dated August 1959, pp. 15–16.

73. John W. Webb, "An Urban Geography of the Minnesota Iron Ranges."

74. Bob Spitz, *Dylan: A Biography* (New York: McGraw-Hill, 1989), p. 19.

75. Robert Shelton, *No Direction Home: The Life and Music of Bob Dylan* (New York: Beech Tree Books, 1986), pp. 22, 26.

76. April 17, 1915, editorial in the *Hibbing Tribune*, as quoted in Paul H. Landis, *Three Iron Mining Towns: A Study in Cultural Change*, p. 89.

77. *The Hull-Rust Mine, The Man-made Grand Canyon of the North* (Hibbing: Hibbing Chamber of Commerce, n.d.).

78. Notarianni, *Faith, Hope & Prosperity*, p. 13.

79. Ben Marsh, "Continuity and Decline in the Anthracite Towns of Northeastern Pennsylvania," *Annals of the Association of American Geographers* 77/3 (September 1987): 351.

80. Hardesty, "Industrial Archaeology on the American Mining Frontier," p. 49.

81. William L. Graf, "Mining and Channel Response," *Annals of the Association of American Geographers* 69/2 (June 1979): 262–275.

82. William H. Rodgers, "Historical Land Occupance of the Upper San Pedro River Valley since 1870," (M.A. thesis, Department of Geography and Regional Development, University of Arizona, 1965).

83. Richard Francaviglia, "The Upper San Pedro River Valley: A Century of Change in Cochise County, Arizona," *Cochise Quarterly* 14/2 (Summer 1984): 8–26.

84. Sheila Ann Dean, "Acid Drainage from Abandoned Metal Mines in the Patagonia Mountains of Southern Arizona," report submitted to the Forest Supervisor, Coronado National Forest, September 1982.

85. Ezra Zubrow, interview, Columbus, Ohio, October 19, 1987.

86. Scott Morris, "Geomorphic Response to Mining Disturbance," in *Mineral Resource Development*, ed. Johansen et al., p. 304.

87. Young, *Western Mining*, p. 266.

88. Jack Fincher, "One Man against a Wasteland," *Reader's Digest* (August 1990): 99–103.

89. Aschmann, "The Natural History of a Mine."

90. Steven Dotterer, "Cities and Towns," in Thomas Vaughan, *Space, Style and Structure: Building in Northwest America* (Portland: Oregon Historical Society, 1974), p. 76.

91. Kingston Heath, "False-Front Architecture on Montana's Urban Frontier," in *Perspectives in Vernacular Architecture III* ed. Thomas Carter and Bernard L. Herman, p. 203.

92. Ibid., pp. 206, 211, 201.

93. Jay A. Carpenter, Russell R. Elliott, and Byrd Fanita Wall Sawyer, *The History of Fifty Years of Mining at Tonopah, 1900–1950*, p. 14.

94. Ibid., p. 123.

95. Deborah Lyn Randall, "Park City, Utah: An Architectural History of Mining Town Housing, 1869–1907," p. 140.

96. Ibid., p. 73.

97. Ibid., p. 145.

98. Eugene Palka, "The Cultural Landscape of the Athens County Coal Region, A Reflection of Its Mining Activities from 1885–1927," p. 80.

99. Webb, "An Urban Geography of the Minnesota Iron Ranges."

100. Andrew Gulliford, *Boomtown Blues: Colorado Oil Shale, 1885–1985.*

101. Gary Peterson, "Down the Shaft or Up?—Silver and Heritage in the Tintic Mining District," in *Making Money out of Dirt*, papers of the Utah Mining Symposium, sponsored by the Utah Centennial Foundation, the Utah State Historical Society, and the Utah Mining Association, Salt Lake City, 1987, p. 1.

3. PERCEIVING THE LANDSCAPE

1. Lucius Beebe and Charles Clegg, *Narrow Gauge in the Rockies* (Berkeley: Howell-North Press, 1958), p. 8.

2. Knott's Berry Farm, *Ghost Town & Calico Railway* (Buena Park, Cal.: Knott's Berry Farm, 1953), p. 59.

3. Ibid.

4. Richard V. Francaviglia, "Bisbee, Arizona: A Mining Town Survives a Decade of Closure," *Small Town* 13/4 (January–February 1983): 4–8.

5. Steven Lee Vierck, "Regional Impacts of Substantial Reduction in Basic Employment: Economic/Demographic Impacts of the 1974–75 Mine Closures on Bisbee, Arizona."

6. Lay James Gibson, "Restructuring the Landscape," *Yearbook of the Association of Pacific Coast Geographers* 50 (1988): 19.

7. *A Gallup Study of Public Attitudes towards Issues Facing Urban America*, 2 vols. (Washington, D.C.: Urban Land Institute, 1986).

8. George Fiedler, *Mineral Point—A History*, p. 205.

9. "Western Front," *Architectural Record* (November 1990): 94, 95.

10. David Lowenthal, *The Past Is a Foreign Country.*

11. William J. Murtagh, *Keeping Time: The History and Theory of Preservation in America*, p. 167.

12. Quoted in Orrin P. Miller, ed., *Mining, Smelting, and Railroading in Tooele County*, p. 81.

13. Louise Snider, personal communication, July 27, 1990.

14. World Museum of Mining, Butte, Montana; one-page report on the

"World Museum of Mining," n.d., included in correspondence from David Johns, president of the World Museum of Mining to David Duffy, planner, Southeastern Arizona Governments Organization, January 16, 1984.

15. Robert L. Spude, "Historic Mining Resources Conference," *CRM Bulletin* 13/4 (1990): 16.

16. Mary Ann Landis, interview at Eckley, Pennsylvania, May 31, 1990.

17. World Museum of Mining, report.

18. "Missouri Mines State Historic Site" brochure, Missouri Department of Natural Resources, Jefferson City, Missouri, n.d.

19. Warren Wittry, interview, Flat River, Missouri, April 23, 1989.

20. William A. Tracy, "The Planning of the Ecomusee," paper presented at the Annual Meeting, Society for Industrial Archaeology, Philadelphia, Pennsylvania, June 2, 1990, in which the work of Sabrer in France is cited.

21. "The Coal Road: A Survey of Southern West Virginia Mining Tourism Potential—A Preliminary Study," p. vii.

22. Ibid.

23. Sherrill Warford, secretary to the president of the Lake County Civic Center Association, Leadville, Colorado; letter to David Duffy, planner, Southeastern Arizona Governments Organization, Bisbee, Arizona, November 29, 1983.

24. Robert Schleicher, "Gurnsey [*sic*] Valley HO Scale Model Railroad Club," *Model Railroading* 19/6 (May 1989): 9.

25. Richard V. Francaviglia, "Aesthetic Lessons from Industry," *Religious Humanism* 17/1 (Winter 1983): 40.

26. Robert L. Thayer, Jr., "Pragmatism in Paradise—Technology and the American Landscape," *Landscape* 30/3 (1990): 1–11.

27. Ibid., p. 9.

28. Ibid.

29. Erwin G. Gudde, *California Place Names: The Origin and Etymology of Current Geographical Names* (Berkeley: University of California Press, 1965), pp. 19, 249.

30. D. W. Meinig, "Symbolic Landscapes: Models of American Community," in *The Interpretation of Ordinary Landscapes*, ed. D. W. Meinig.

BIBLIOGRAPHY

Agricola, Georgius. *De re metallica*. Trans. Herbert Hoover and Lou
 Hoover. London: Mining Magazine, 1912.
Alanen, Arnold R. "The 'Locations': Company Communities on Minnesota's
 Iron Ranges." *Minnesota History* 48/3 (Fall 1982): 94–107.
Allen, James B. *The Company Town in the American West.* Norman:
 University of Oklahoma Press, 1966.
Allen, James P., and Eugene J. Turner. *We the People: An Atlas of America's
 Ethnic Diversity.* New York: Macmillan, 1988.
Ames, Ethel Marie. *The Story of Coal and Iron in Alabama.* Birmingham:
 Book-Keeper's Press, 1972.
Aschmann, Homer. "The Natural History of a Mine." *Economic Geography*
 46/2 (April 1970): 171–190.
Balch, William Ralston. *The Mines, Miners, and Mining Interests of the
 United States in 1882.* Philadelphia: Mining Industrial Publishing Bureau,
 1882.
Billeb, Emil W. *Mining Camp Days.* Berkeley: Howell-North Books, 1968.
Blackwelder, Eliot. *Regional Geology of the United States.* New York: G. E.
 Stechert, 1912.
Bornhorst, Theodore J., William I. Rose, Jr., and James B. Paces. *Field
 Guide to the Geology of the Keweenaw Peninsula, Michigan.* Houghton:
 Michigan Technological University, May 1983.
Brace, Charles L. *The New West.* New York: Press of Wyncoop and
 Hollenback, 1869.
Brothers, Beverly J. *Historical Butte: The Richest Hill on Earth.* Butte,
 Mont.: Artcraft Printers, 1977.
Brown, Mrs. Hugh. *Lady in Boomtown: Miners and Manners on the Nevada
 Frontier.* Palo Alto: American West Publishing, 1968.
Brown, Jeffrey L. "Earthworks and Industrial Archaeology." *IA—Journal of
 the Society for Industrial Archaeology* 6/1 (1980): 1–8.
Burgess, Opie Rundle. *Bisbee Not So Long Ago.* San Antonio: Naylor, 1976.
Cain, E. M. *The Story of Bodie.* San Francisco: Fearon Publishers, 1956.

Campbell, Thomas Jr. "Galena, 1820–1830: The Creation of a Mining Boom Town." *Historic Illinois* (June 1985): 8–13.

Carpenter, Jay A., Russell R. Elliott, and Byrd Fanita Wall Sawyer. *The History of Fifty Years of Mining at Tonopah, 1900–1950.* University of Nevada Bulletin (Geology and Mining Series No. 51) 47/1 (January 1953).

Cheek, Lawrence W. "The Dreamers of Silver City—How a New Mexico Mining Town Is Recapturing Its Heritage—And Its Vitality." *Historic Preservation* (March–April 1989): 58–61.

Clark, James I. *Life on Wisconsin's Lead Mining Frontier.* Madison: State Historical Society of Wisconsin, 1976.

"The Coal Road: A Survey of Southern West Virginia Mining Tourism Potential—A Preliminary Study." Marshall University Center for Regional Progress, Huntington, West Virginia, March 1989.

Conzen, Michael P., ed. *The Making of the American Landscape.* Boston: Unwin Hyman, 1990.

Crowell & Murray, Inc. *The Iron Ores of Lake Superior—Containing Some Facts of Interest Relating to Mining, Beneficiation and Shipping of the Ore and the Location of Principal Mines.* Cleveland: Pentonn Press, 1927.

Davies, Christopher. "Dark Inner Landscapes: The South Wales Coalfield." *Landscape Journal* 3/1 (Spring 1984): 36–44.

Davis, E. W. *Pioneering with Taconite.* St. Paul: Minnesota Historical Society Press, 1964.

Davis, Jake, and Robert Schleicher. "Ohio Coal Mines—Prototype and in HO Scale." *Model Railroading* 19/6 (May 1989): 11–19.

Davis, Sarah Ann, Elizabeth L. Egenhoff, Mary Hill, and Elinor Rhodes. *Guide to Virginia City, Nevada, and the Comstock Area, Wherein Are Described Points of Interest in the History of Mining the Lode.* Sausalito, Cal.: Pages of History, 1959.

Delahanty, Randolph, and Andrew McKinney. *Preserving the West.* New York: Pantheon Books, 1985.

Dorin, Patrick C. *The Lake Superior Iron Ore Railroads.* Seattle: Superior Publishing, 1969.

Fiedler, George. *Mineral Point—A History.* Mineral Point, Wis.: Mineral Point Historical Society and Iowa County *Democrat-Tribune,* 1962.

Francaviglia, Richard V., "Copper Mining and Landscape Evolution: A Century of Change in the Warren Mining District, Arizona." *Journal of Arizona History* 23/3 (Autumn 1982): 267–298.

———. "Bisbee, Arizona: A Mining Town Survives a Decade of Closure." *Small Town* 13/4 (January–February 1983): 4–8.

———. *Mining Town Trolleys: A History of Arizona's Warren-Bisbee Railway.* Bisbee: Copper Queen Publishing, 1983.

———. "Time Exposures: The Evolving Landscape of an Arizona Copper-Mining District." In *Mineral Resource Development: Geopolitics,*

Economics, and Policy, ed. Harley Johansen, Olen P. Matthews, and Gundars Rudzitis. Boulder: Westview Press, 1987.

———. "Reading the Landscape and Other Historical Detective Stories." *Local Historian* (September–October 1988): 7–9.

———. "Mining Town Commercial Vernacular Architecture: The 'Overhanging Porches' of Ohio's Hocking Mining District." *Pioneer America Society Transactions* 13 (1990): 45–51.

Gardner, A. Dudley, and Vera R. Flores. *Forgotten Frontier: A History of Wyoming Coal Mining*. Boulder: Westview Press, 1989.

Gillenwater, Mack H. "Cultural and Historical Geography of Mining Settlements in the Pocahontas Coal Field of Southern West Virginia, 1880 to 1930." Ph.D. dissertation, University of Tennessee, 1972.

Gradwohl, David M., and Nancy M. Osborn. *Exploring Buried Buxton: Archaeology of an Abandoned Iowa Coal Mining Town with a Large Black Population*. Ames: Iowa State University Press, 1984.

Graf, William L. "Mining and Channel Response." *Annals of the Association of American Geographers* 69/2 (June 1979): 262–275.

Greever, William S., *The Bonanza West: The Story of the Western Mining Rushes, 1848–1900*. Norman: University of Oklahoma Press, 1963.

Gulliford, Andrew. *Boomtown Blues: Colorado Oil Shale, 1885–1985*. Niwot: University of Colorado Press, 1989.

Haddock, Keith. *A History of Marion Power Shovel's First 100 Years*. Marion, Ohio: Marion Power Shovel Division, Dresser Industries, 1984.

Hammond, John Hays. "The Milling of Gold Ores in California." In *Eighth Annual Report of the State Mineralogist*. Sacramento: California State Mining Bureau, 1888.

Hardesty, Donald. "Industrial Archaeology on the American Mining Frontier: Suggestions for a Research Agenda." *Journal of New World Archaeology* 6/4 (1986): 47–56.

———. *The Archaeology of Mining and Miners: A View from the Silver State*. Special Publication Series No. 6. Society for Historical Archaeology, 1988.

Hardesty, Donald L., and Valerie Firby. *Managing Archaeological Resources on the Comstock*. Washington, D.C.: Heritage Conservation and Recreation Service, National Park Service, 1980.

Harris, Beth Kay. *The Towns of Tintic*. Denver: Sage Books, 1961.

Heath, Kingston M. "Defining the Nature of Vernacular." *Material Culture* 6/4 (1986): 47–56.

———. "False-Front Architecture on Montana's Urban Frontier." In *Perspectives in Vernacular Architecture III*, ed. Thomas Carter and Bernard L. Herman. Columbia: University of Missouri Press, 1989.

International Correspondence Schools. *A Textbook on Metals Mining*. Scranton: International Textbook Company, 1899.

Johnson, Ronald, and John Paige. "Looking for the Mother Lode: Hard Lessons Learned by the NPS." *CRM Bulletin* 13/4 (1990): 18–20.

Jones, James B., Jr. "Coal Mining in the Cumberland Plateau, 1850–1920." *Courier* (Tennessee Historical Commission) 27/3 (June 1990): 4–7.

Kersten, Earl W., Jr. "The Early Settlement of Aurora, Nevada, and Nearby Mining Camps." *Annals of the Association of American Geographers* (December 1964): 490–507.

King, Frank. *The Missabe Road: The Duluth, Missabe and Iron Range Railway.* San Marino, Cal.: Golden West Books, 1972.

Kneiss, Gilbert. *Bonanza Railroads.* Stanford, Cal.: Stanford University Press, 1941.

Konrad, George. "Modeling Mines." *Narrow Gauge and Short Line Gazette* 2/4 (September 1976): 24–36.

Kostof, Spiro. *America by Design.* New York: Oxford University Press, 1987.

Kuzara, Stanley A. *Black Diamonds of Sheridan: A Facet of Wyoming History.* Cheyenne: Pioneer Printing & Stationery, 1977.

Landis, Paul H. *Three Iron Mining Towns: A Study in Cultural Change.* Ann Arbor: Edwards Brothers, 1938.

Lanyon, Milton, and Laurence Bulmore. *Cinnabar Hills: The Quicksilver Days of New Almaden.* Los Gatos, Cal.: Village Printers, 1967.

Longstreth, Richard. *The Buildings of Main Street: A Guide to American Commercial Architecture.* Washington, D.C.: Preservation Press, 1987.

Lowenthal, David. *The Past Is a Foreign Country.* New York: Cambridge University Press, 1985.

Lynch, Kevin. *The Image of the City.* Cambridge: MIT Press, 1960.

McLaughlin, Donald H. "Man's Selective Attack on Ores and Minerals." In *Man's Role in Changing the Face of the Earth,* ed. William L. Thomas, Jr. Chicago: University of Chicago Press, 1956.

Magnuson, Richard G. *Coeur D'Alene Diary: The First Ten Years of Hardrock Mining in North Idaho.* Portland, Ore.: Binfort & Mort Publishing, 1968.

Marsh, Ben. "Continuity and Decline in the Anthracite Towns of Northeastern Pennsylvania." *Annals of the Association of American Geographers* 77/3 (September 1987): 337–352.

Meinig, D. W. "Symbolic Landscapes: Models of American Community." In *The Interpretation of Ordinary Landscapes,* ed. D. W. Meinig. New York: Oxford University Press, 1979.

Merchant, Carolyn. *The Death of Nature: Women, Ecology, and the Scientific Revolution.* San Francisco: Harper & Row Publishers, 1983.

Miller, Orrin P., ed. *Mining, Smelting, and Railroading in Tooele County.* Tooele, Utah: Tooele County Historical Society, 1986.

Molinelli, Lambert. *Eureka and Its Resources: A Complete History of Eureka County, Nevada, Containing the United States Mining Laws, the*

Mining Laws of the District, Bullion Product and Other Statistics for 1878, and a List of County Officers. Reno: University of Nevada Press, Vintage Nevada Series, 1982.

Morris, John W., ed. *Drill Bits, Picks, and Shovels: A History of Mineral Resources in Oklahoma.* Oklahoma City: Oklahoma Historical Society, 1982.

Morris, Scott. "Geomorphic Response to Mining Disturbance." In *Mineral Resource Development: Geopolitics, Economics, and Policy,* ed. Harley Johansen, Olen P. Matthews, and Gundars Rudzitis. Boulder: Westview Press, 1987.

Murtagh, William J. *Keeping Time: The History and Theory of Preservation in America.* Pittstown, N.J.: Main Street Press, 1988.

Myrick, David F. *The Railroads of Nevada and Eastern California*: vol. 1, *The Northern Roads.* Berkeley: Howell-North Books, 1962.

———. *The Railroads of Nevada and Eastern California*: vol. 2, *The Southern Roads.* Berkeley: Howell-North Books, 1963.

———. *The Railroads of Arizona*: vol. 1, *The Southern Roads.* Berkeley: Howell-North Books, 1975.

———. *The Railroads of Arizona*: vol. 3, *Clifton, Morenci and Metcalf Rails and Copper Mines.* Glendale, Cal.: Trans-Anglo Books, 1984.

National Coal Association. *Bituminous Coal Mining Towns, North, South, East, West: Pictorial Study of Their Progress.* Washington, D.C.: Bituminous Coal Institute, 1946.

Navin, Thomas R. *Copper Mining & Management.* Tucson: University of Arizona Press, 1978.

Noble, Bruce J., Jr. "A National Register Perspective: Evaluating Historic Mining Resources." *CRM Bulletin* 12/2 (1989): 1–4.

Notarianni, Philip F., ed. *Carbon County: Eastern Utah's Industrialized Island.* Salt Lake City: Utah State Historical Society, 1981.

———. *Faith, Hope & Prosperity: The Tintic Mining District.* Eureka, Utah: Tintic Historical Society, 1982.

Palka, Eugene J. "The Cultural Landscape of the Athens County Coal Region: A Reflection of Its Mining Activities from 1885–1927." M.A. thesis, Ohio University, 1986.

———. *Artifacts of the Coal Age–Athens County Region.* Athens, Ohio: Athens County Historical Society & Museum, 1988.

Parkinson, George (with the assistance of Claire Collier and Joseph Preston). *A Guide to Coal Mining Collections in the United States.* Morgantown: West Virginia Library, 1978.

Paul, Rodman Wilson. *Mining Frontiers of the Far West, 1848–1880.* New York: Holt, Rinehart and Winston, 1963.

Peterson, R. H. *The Bonanza Kings: The Social and Business Behavior of Western Mining Entrepreneurs, 1870–1900.* Lincoln: University of Nebraska Press, 1977.

Poliniak, Louis. *When Coal Was King: Mining Pennsylvania's Anthracite.* Lebanon, Penn.: Applied Arts Publishers, 1970.

Queen, Rolla Lee. "Historical Archaeology and Historic Preservation at Candelaria and Metallic City, Nevada." M.A. thesis, University of Nevada, Reno, 1987.

Ragsdale, Kenneth Baxter. *Quicksilver: Terlingua and the Chisos Mining Company.* College Station: Texas A&M University Press, 1976.

Randall, Deborah Lyn. "Park City, Utah: An Architectural History of Mining Town Housing, 1869–1907." M.A. thesis, Department of Art, University of Utah, December 1985.

Raymond, Rossiter W. *Mines, Mills, and Furnaces of the Pacific States and Territories: An Account of the Condition, Resources, and Methods of the Mining and Metallurgical Industry in Those Regions, Chiefly Relating to the Precious Metals.* New York: J. B. Ford, 1871.

———. *Mines and Mining of the Rocky Mountains, the Inland Basin, and the Pacific Slope, Comprising Treatises on Mining Law, Mineral Deposits, Machinery, and Metallurgical Processes.* New York: J. B. Ford, 1871.

Renner, Gail K. *Joplin: From Mining Town to Urban Center.* Northridge, Cal.: Windsor Publications, 1985.

Reno, Ramona, and Ronald Reno. "The Historic Cemetery at Silver City, Nevada: Recording Methods and Initial Findings." *Nevada Archaeologist* 7/1 (1989): 14–27.

Reps, John W. "Bonanza Towns: Urban Planning on the Western Mining Frontier." In *Pattern and Process: Research in Historical Geography,* ed. Ralph E. Ehrenberg. Washington, D.C.: Howard University Press, 1975.

Reynolds, Terry. "Iron in the Wilderness: The Michigan Iron Industry Museum." *Technology and Culture* 30/1 (January 1989): 112–117.

Richards, Robert H., Charles Locke, and John Bray. *A Text Book of Ore Dressing.* New York: McGraw-Hill, 1925.

Richason, Benjamin F. *Atlas of Cultural Features: A Study of Man's Imprint on the Land.* Northbrook, Ill.: Hubbard Press, 1972.

Rickard, T. A. *A History of American Mining.* New York: McGraw-Hill, 1932.

Roark, Michael. "Early American Lead Mining in Southeast Missouri." *P.A.S.T.—Pioneer America Society Transactions* 5 (1985): 55–62.

———. "The Effect of Lead and Iron Mining on the Cultural Development of Eastern Missouri, 1860–1880." *P.A.S.T.—Pioneer America Society Transactions* 11 (1988): 9–17.

Rohe, Randall. "The Geography and Material Culture of the Western Mining Town." *Material Culture* 16/3 (Fall 1984): 99–120.

Sackheim, Donald E. *Historic American Engineering Record Catalog.* Washington, D.C.: National Park Service, 1976.

St. Clair, Hillary W. *Mineral Industry in Early America.* Washington D.C.: U.S. Department of Interior, Bureau of Mines, 1977.

Schilling, J. H. *Metal Mining Districts of Nevada*. Nevada Bureau of Mines and Geology Map 37, 3rd ed., 1976.

Shideler, John C. *Coal Towns in the Cascades: A Centennial History of Roslyn and Cle Elum, Washington*. Spokane: Melior Publications, 1986.

Smith, Duane A. *Rocky Mountain Mining Camps: The Urban Frontier*. Lincoln: University of Nebraska Press, 1967.

———. *When Coal Was King: A History of Crested Butte, Colorado, 1880–1952*. Golden: Colorado School of Mines Press, 1984.

———. *Mining America: The Industry and the Environment, 1800–1980*. Lawrence: University of Kansas Press, 1987.

Spence, Clark. *Mining Engineers & the American West: The Lace Boot Brigade, 1849–1933*. New Haven: Yale University Press, 1970.

Spratt, John S., Sr. *Thurber, Texas: The Life and Death of a Company Coal Town*. Austin: University of Texas Press, 1986.

Spude, Robert L. *Tombstone: Arizona Silver Camp*. Las Vegas: Nevada Publications, 1979.

———. "Historic Mining Resources Conference." *CRM Bulletin* 13/4 (1990): 16–18.

Starry, Roberta Martin. *Gold Gamble*. China Lake, Cal.: Maturango Museum of Indian Wells Valley, 1974.

Sullivan, Walter. *Landprints on the Magnificent American Landscape*. New York: Times Books, 1984.

Sweeney, Thomas W. "Montanans Rally to Save Virginia City." *Preservation News* (July 1990): 8.

Thayer, Robert L., Jr. "Pragmatism in Paradise—Technology and the American Landscape." *Landscape* 30/3 (1990): 1–11.

Todd, Arthur Cecil. *The Cornish Miner in America: The Contribution to the Mining History of the United States by Emigrant Cornish Miners—The Men Called Cousin Jacks*. Glendale, Cal.: A. H. Clark, 1967.

Torma, Carolyn. "Gold Milling in the Black Hills: A Photographic Essay." *South Dakota History* 15/4 (Winter 1985): 290–311.

Tribe, Ivan. *Little Cities of Black Diamonds: Urban Development in the Hocking Coal Region, 1870–1900*. Athens, Ohio: Athens County Historical Society and Museum, 1988.

———. *Sprinkled with Coal Dust: Life and Work in the Hocking Coal Region, 1870–1900*. Athens, Ohio: Athens County Historical Society and Museum, 1989.

Upton, Dell. *America's Architectural Roots: Ethnic Groups That Built America*. Washington, D.C.: National Trust for Historic Preservation, 1986.

Vale, Thomas R., and Geraldine R. Vale. *Western Images, Western Landscapes: Travels along U.S. 89*. Tucson: University of Arizona Press, 1989.

Vierck, Steven Lee. "Regional Impacts of Substantial Reduction in Basic

Employment: Economic/Demographic Impacts of the 1974–75 Mine Closures on Bisbee, Arizona." M.A. thesis, University of Arizona, 1983.

Vine, Bob. *Anaconda Memories: 1883–1983*. Butte, Mont.: Artcraft Printers, 1983.

Vogel, Robert M. "Quadrangular Treasure: The Cartographic Route to Industrial Archaeology." *IA—Journal of the Society for Industrial Archeology* 6/1 (1980): 25–54.

Waldbauer, Richard C. *Grubstaking the Palouse: Gold Mining in the Hoodoo Mountains of North Idaho, 1860–1950*. Published jointly by the Washington State University Press, Pullman, Washington; Latah County Historical Society, Moscow, Idaho; and the Whitman County Historical Society, Colfax, Washington, 1986.

Walis-Tayler, A. J. *Aerial or Wire Rope-Ways: Their Construction and Management*. London: Grosby Lockwood & Son, 1911.

Walker, David A. *Iron Frontier: The Discovery and Early Development of Minnesota's Three Ranges*. St. Paul: Minnesota Historical Society Press, 1979.

Watts, May Theilgaard. *Reading the Landscape*. New York: Macmillan, 1957.

Webb, John W. "An Urban Geography of the Minnesota Iron Ranges." Ph.D. dissertation, University of Minnesota, April 1958.

Weight, Harold, and Lucie Weight. *Rhyolite: The Ghost City of Golden Dreams*. Twentynine Palms, Cal.: Calico Press, 1953.

Wells, Merle. *Gold Camps & Silver Cities: Nineteenth Century Mining in Central and Southern Idaho*. Bulletin 22. Moscow: Idaho Department of Lands, Bureau of Mines and Geology, 1983.

White, Joseph H. *Houses for Mining Towns*. Washington, D.C.: U.S. Department of the Interior, Bureau of Mines, 1914.

Williams, Ralph D. *The Honorable Peter White: A Biographical Sketch of the Lake Superior Iron Country*. Cleveland: Penton Publishing, 1907.

Wolff, David A. "Pyritic Smelting at Deadwood: A Temporary Solution to Refractory Ores." *South Dakota History* 15/4 (Winter 1985): 312–339.

Wyman, Mark. *Hard Rock Epic: Western Miners and the Industrial Revolution, 1860–1890*. Berkeley: University of California Press, 1979.

Young, Otis E., Jr. *Western Mining: An Informal Account of Precious-Metals Prospecting, Placering, Lode Mining, and Milling on the American Frontier from Spanish Times to 1893*. Norman: University of Oklahoma Press, 1970.

Zeier, Charles D. "Historic Charcoal Production near Eureka, Nevada: An Archaeological Perspective." *Historical Archaeology* 21/1 (1987): 81–101.

Zindel, Udo. "Landscape Evolution in the Clifton-Morenci Mining District, Arizona, 1872–1986." M.A. thesis, Arizona State University, Department of Geography, 1987.

INDEX

Illustrations are indicated by **boldfaced** numbers.

street railways, 93, 95
Sunday Creek Coal Co., Ohio, 39
symbolism, 203–209

Tacey Cromwell, 115
taconite, 134
tailings, 24, **25**, 29, 53, 129, 130, 147,
    148, 213
T-cottage, **46**, 157
"technological landscape guilt"
    (TLG), 207
technostalgia, 167
Telluride, Colo., 180
Terlingua, Tex., 175
Thayer, Robert, Jr., 206–208
threats to mining landscapes,
    184–186
Tintic Mining District, Utah, 88–89
Tintown, Ariz., 10, 104, **105**
tipple, 50, **51**, **75**, 213
Tombstone, Ariz., 177–178, 198
Tonopah, Nev., **10**, 14–18, 68, 79,
    145, 154–156, **164**
topographic maps, 14–17, 21–30
topography, and social stratification,
    87–88
tourism, 166, 177–179, 195, **196–197**,
    198–199
Tower-Soudan mine, Minn., **19**, 199
trailers. *See* mobile homes
tramways, aerial, 56, **57**, 58

transformation, defined, 127
Tri-State Mining District, 24, 93, 158

underground mining, 17–20, 89
union halls, 42, 43
United States Geological Survey, re-
    ports, 59
United States Steel Co., 137
"Unsinkable Molly Brown," 171
Upton, Dell, 109

vegetation, 14, 29–30, 147–148
Virginia City, Mont., 80
Virginia City, Nev., 41, 70, 107, 155

Wallace, Idaho, 8
Walt Disney enterprises, 199, 201
warfare, compared to mining, 204
Warren, Ariz., 31, **32**
Warren Mining District, Ariz., **24**,
    92, 130–131, **132–133**, 146
water quality, 147
Webb, John, 137–140, 160
wilderness, 4, 5, 9, 143
Windber, Pa., **44**, 95, 118–121
Wittry, Warren, 194
women, 20, 112, 114–115
World Museum of Mining (Butte,
    Mont.), 191–193

Young, Otis, 130